T0354465

MEDIUMS NOT SO RARE

PSYCHIC GIFTS OF THE MEDIUMS

EDWARD ROGERS

BALBOA.
PRESS

A DIVISION OF HAY HOUSE

Balboa Press books may be ordered through booksellers or by contacting:

Balboa Press
A Division of Hay House
1663 Liberty Drive
Bloomington, IN 47403
www.balboapress.com
1 (877) 407-4847

Because of the dynamic nature of the Internet, any web addresses or links contained in this book may have changed since publication and may no longer be valid. The views expressed in this work are solely those of the author and do not necessarily reflect the views of the publisher, and the publisher hereby disclaims any responsibility for them.

The author of this book does not dispense medical advice or prescribe the use of any technique as a form of treatment for physical, emotional, or medical problems without the advice of a physician, either directly or indirectly. The intent of the author is only to offer information of a general nature to help you in your quest for emotional and spiritual well-being. In the event you use any of the information in this book for yourself, which is your constitutional right, the author and the publisher assume no responsibility for your actions.

Any people depicted in stock imagery provided by Thinkstock are models, and such images are being used for illustrative purposes only.
Certain stock imagery © Thinkstock.

Print information available on the last page.

ISBN: 978-1-5043-5234-5 (sc)
ISBN: 978-1-5043-5236-9 (hc)
ISBN: 978-1-5043-5235-2 (e)

Library of Congress Control Number: 2016904367

Balboa Press rev. date: 4/11/2016

For my loved ones—here and beyond

We are not human beings having a spiritual experience.
We are spiritual beings having a human experience.
—Pierre Teilhard de Chardin

— ACKNOWLEDGMENTS —

With deepest gratitude to:

My sister, Meribeth, who took so much time from her busy schedule to help edit *Mediums Not So Rare* and who also helped me find places to cut and add to my website so the book was not so long or expensive! She was a voice for my father to reach me from the spiritual plane.

My children, Becky, Dean, Kathryn, Danny, Noah, Maureen, and Lauren, who encouraged me and supported me through my trials and successes—even while they fought their own dragons.

My former wife, without whom I would not have been able to have found the depths and despair of life but which led me higher and higher on my path seeking enlightenment.

My father, Jack, mother, Frances, and grandmother, Hilda who came to me with guidance from beyond the grave!

My brother, Dale, who I feel with me most every day and who was on an enlightened path when he passed.

Rosemary Altea, who, though she doesn't know it, was my mentor, my inspiration, and my model. She remains foremost in my thoughts when I need inspiration. I have read and reread Rosemary's books and hope some of you will do so also. (Books available are: *The Eagle and The Rose, Proud Spirit, You Own the Power, A Journey Towards Healing, Soul Signs, and Angels In Training.*)

— CONTENTS —

Contents

— PROLOGUE —

The best way for me to tell you about this book is by telling you what it is not about. If you seek a specific recipe for how to be a medium, how to communicate with the dead, how to travel out of body, or any of probably thousands of wonderments, this book will only create more questions in your mind.

However, if what you seek is enlightenment about the many gifts of the mediums, knowing more about healing yourself or others, or learning about how a medium or astrologer thinks, then enter this book with no preconceived ideas. Let it take your mind where it needs to go and soar to the pinnacle of your higher self and deep into the depths to examine your soul. It is there I hope you will fill your mind with the never-ending quest for enlightenment and spiritual knowledge and create an inner need to educate yourself in the areas that appeal to you, moving toward the light with mind, heart, and soul.

Don't be afraid to let your mind wander and follow your intuition. If food for the questing soul is what strikes you as being what you crave, dig deeper. If some ideas are just beyond what you feel you can believe for the moment, put them on the back burner of your mind to simmer for a time while your mind evolves. Use all the sources you can find to further your knowledge on all things spiritual. Learn to meditate; you may just discover yourself and your higher purpose. Open your mind to all things spiritual because the things you shut out may be just what your life path is leading you to accept! At the least, ponder all that you learn about spirituality; it may create a meal that will nourish you in ways you never thought possible, and it could change your life completely.

My life was utterly transformed by one medium. I have taken a new path that feeds my heart, mind, and soul, and I have not looked back since. I wish you the same.

— USING THIS BOOK —

You might think this book comes close to having the longest introduction of any book in your home library! Before you get to the interviews with the mediums, I write about how my life situation turned into a new quest for me. I have always been searching for more truth through spiritual means. So, bear with me as I explain what motivated me to write this book.

I wrote *Mediums Not So Rare* during the span of a couple years as I researched mediums and experienced them firsthand—up close and personal. The chapter on Christine Day was too long to include with the book, but you may read it entirely on my website. That was one of the first situations I experienced since she was part of the culmination of the events of 12/12/12 and 12/21/12. Christine is still moving forward, aligning the crystalline structures of those who work with her in her workshops and giving information about the Pleiadians and Lemurians, the Galactic Council, and more.

Abigail Rose Newman was a psychic I had gone to see for a psychic reading at Camp Wonewoc, and she became a good friend. The same happened with Laurie Stinson; she suggested some other diverse people in this book, including John Wayne, Penny, and Ayala Chen. I found others through research or via friends who were tuned in to what was happening on the psychic circuit. I used my intuition to seek those who spoke the truth.

Many names in the book are changed as a matter of privacy to those involved.

I did not use many quotes because I think you, the reader, will be able to distinguish who is speaking in these interviews. Sometimes I will be asking questions to the mediums and other times I will insert my own feeling about what is being said.

— CHAPTER 1 —

INTO THE DEPTHS

My life had ended. What good could life be after my wife of thirty years decided that infidelity was a more fun job and that I was just too boring? I was not able to look at the world through my rose-colored glasses anymore because they couldn't cover up all the pain and hurt I was experiencing. She was ready to abandon her three youngest children to go on her fling until her lawyer convinced her that it would be much more lucrative to keep them. My home, which had no mortgage, became part of a settlement. I was not equipped to handle the $84,000 debt.

During the divorce negotiations, I told my lawyers about the hardship of finding a job at the higher end of middle age. The woman I had loved sat across the small table with her lawyer, a bitter, sharp-tongued, thin woman with a huge chip on her shoulder. Both of them jeered me, pretending to wipe tears and shouting, "Boo hoo."

I had been raised showing kindness toward others and not malice. I was humiliated, a crumpled heap of garbage. No matter what people say, it is not easy to find a job when you reach your upper fifties. Visions of losing my children and my house ran constantly through my head, and I lived in a state of morose gloom. I wondered if my life was worth living anymore.

People I had thought were my friends avoided me, and they

would turn away to avoid talking to me. Debts from the lawyer piled up, and I could not afford them since I was making a few hundred dollars a month at my part-time job. More money was added to the mortgage to cover that. I could not think of anything good about myself; I knew I wasn't worth anything.

Obviously it was my fault. I had become disenchanted with teaching many years earlier, quitting my longtime job and leading my family on a wild-goose chase. I smelled the roses everyone in the media had been promoting for years. First, farming had failed. Then, I lost my substantial teacher retirement to save the farm from foreclosure. I worked as a school special education aide, drove a milk truck, and built houses until I was injured with an unfixable torn knee and could no longer do that type of physical labor. All my new jobs after teaching paid less and did not lead us to security.

My wife easily found work—and independence—at a hospital. I stayed home with the children as a Mr. Mom, loving every minute with them and watching them grow up. I think I sensed way back then that she was moving apart from the family and me, pursuing her own goals. She had been raised to believe that money and status were more important than anything besides what people thought of you.

I'd like to take you back to an earlier time when my marriage started to unravel. Even then, arguments were common. I would tell the children one thing, and she would say another thing. Unfortunately, that caused me to blow up at them constantly. It was not the real me, but it was what I allowed myself to become. Whatever she took out on me—always with support of her parents—I took out on those I loved the most. I would often cry about the way I treated those dear children, but the more disagreeable she became with me, the less I could control my temper. I would yell at them so much.

With my rose-colored glasses, I could pretend things were going well. Since I loved the children with all my heart, I did good things with them too. I taught them about botany and wildlife. I taught them an appreciation of nature, and they learned that curiosity about life surrounding them was a great gift.

I encouraged their creativity through art and music. My ability to play piano by ear enabled me to pound out bucketsful of rambunctious, frolicking, wild old folk songs, making them dance and sing at the top of their lungs until they were in a state of exhaustion with sweaty faces and sticky hair showing their delight.

In the midst of all this busyness of survival, our taxes quadrupled, our fairyland farm no longer affordable. The farm was sold, and we moved to a rural area not too far away. The last three children came along, and I continued to be their caretaker. Frustrations and arguments with my wife seemed inevitable, and I retreated more and more into myself.

"Why don't you talk to me?" she said each day.

I was afraid to tell her the truth. No matter what I said, it would be misconstrued by her, inevitably causing another argument that I would not win. She would remember and bring up every wrong thing I had ever done—back to before we were married—whether it had been my fault or not.

In the first years after moving from the farm, I found some time for myself each day when the children took their naps. For some strange reason, I felt the urge to write about our experiences back at the farm, which also included our ghosts. During the eight years we lived in our "haunted" farmhouse, I kept a diary that I would log in before bed each night. Real ghosts? Yes.

When we moved into the house, little things would happen regularly: bumps and scratches, rattles and scrapings. I would tell the kids it was just mice or bats in the attic or birds on the roof. Quickly though, the sounds became more defined, including footsteps coming down the stairway to the kitchen as we ate our lunch. I would run to look up the stairs, but there was never anyone there.

The final straw was when the ghosts appeared to our visitors. They described the ghosts—even what they were wearing! There were few who didn't at least hear our spirit residents, and there were many who saw them. Our benevolent spirit guests seemed to care for us and all we did. I had not believed in ghosts before moving to the farm, but I became a 100 percent believer!

Words poured out of my fingers onto the keyboard, and I soon produced a book about our ghosts and a series of children's science fiction books. My love of poetry grew, and more words flowed from my pen. I entered a contest in La Crosse, Wisconsin, about an hour away, and was surprised to win their highest award. I was thrilled to be writing at that level while caring for my family. A woman I competed against liked my writing, and she published some of my books. The best-loved book by my reading audience—and me—was my true story about our encounters with the ghosts.

My interest in ghosts led me to the local library. I inquired about books about spirits and ghostly happenings. The librarian took me to the audiobooks and pulled out *The Eagle and the Rose* by Rosemary Altea. After one listening, I was hooked. I listened to it again and again. I did some research and devoured more of her books. Rosemary talked to spirits? Yes! I was skeptical, but after the encounters with ghosts in my own house, I believed more and more in spiritual connections.

About that time, I landed a job as a church secretary. I regained some of my self-esteem and confidence, and I started to give talks about our haunted house and its ghosts. My marriage wasn't going so well. The arguments were becoming bitterer, and I suspected she was mentally moving away from me.

One day at the church, the pastor called me into her office to see her phone bill. It seemed that her husband and my wife were calling each other on their cell phones—sometimes during the middle of the night. If you have ever seen a tower of cards collapse, that is what quickly happened to my life.

It didn't take long to realize that my wife had been methodically moving away from me—and our marriage—and was looking for reasons for self-justification. She had also been poisoning the minds of the children so they would view me as she saw me. She wanted them to see how bad I was. Each mistake or infraction she saw became fodder for the kids and proved her well-thought-out untruths.

My life was now like a house of cards that met a cyclone. My divorce proceedings were quickly followed by the divorce of my boss and her spouse, culminating in the divorce of my wife's health-care patient and his spouse. The spouse said her husband had been unfaithful with my wife. Three divorces and three shattered relationships were all that my agitated brain reminded me of daily.

It is hard to describe how those caustic events affected me. Each day, it was harder to get up and find motivation to go on. I'd lost my friends, my money, my possessions, and—worst of all—my self-worth. To those who would listen to my story, I would pour out my heart, but that only seemed to increase my slide into despair. I had buried my soul in a deep hole, never to emerge again. No words of encouragement from anyone could dissolve that feeling, and I wanted to disappear into my misery and anguish and be done with it all.

— CHAPTER 2 —
IN THE TWINKLING OF AN EYE

During that time of deep loathing and desolation, one dismal day ran into another. I happened to find a website for Rosemary Altea, the medium whose books I had read and reread. On the site, she said she would do readings over the phone for five hundred dollars. However, it warned that it was not easy to get a reading. I pictured people lined up and asking for their own readings, but the cost loomed large in my mind, like a billboard flashing.

I found it oddly funny that all the money I had in the world was five hundred dollars. I had put it aside to pay for my winter heating fuel, which can add up to thousands of dollars per winter in Wisconsin. Spending that amount would mean I was truly out of money and would have no way to provide fuel to keep my house from freezing. Did I want to take a chance on something that might provide spiritual guidance like Rosemary's books had said? I was still very skeptical about spiritual guidance. It could very well be throwing money to the wind. *How could someone charge five hundred dollars for a forty-five-minute conversation that might be completely made up and phony?*

My mind seemed to make itself up for me. I sent an e-mail to Rosemary and inquired about a reading. At that time, she was probably receiving hundreds of e-mails a day. My chances of even being noticed seemed almost nil. Two days later, I received an e-mail from her secretary: Rosemary would do a reading for me! I arranged it for September 13, 2006—three months after my first communication with her.

My sister had been reading the Rosemary Altea books, and she had been interested in psychic phenomena and mediumship since encountering ghosts in my house some years earlier. When I told Meribeth about my upcoming reading with Rosemary, she was excited. She was willing to travel across the state to experience the reading with me and offered to be my secretary by writing down all that was said.

I was still struggling with my intensely negative state of mind—sort of a personal black hole—and dealing with a lawyer who didn't care if I had money to pay my bills as he worked through the divorce. The thought of my impending reading with Rosemary kindled a positive spark in my life that had not been there for a long time.

As the day approached, I became doubtful and cynical. Was I wasting money that could have been put to better use by paying for a month of heating fuel? Meribeth and I agreed that it would be either a complete waste of time or it would be amazing. When the day arrived, I resolved to go through with it. Meribeth arrived on the morning of September 13, and we chatted while we set up chairs, a TV tray, and paper and pencil for notes. We positioned the phone in a good place to talk while it was on speakerphone. We sat in our chairs at precisely 10:00 a.m. I took a deep breath, gave one glance of confirmation at Meri, and dialed Rosemary in Vermont.

Her secretary picked up, and I was quickly connected to Rosemary. Her delightful English accent put me at ease.

She said, "Please don't give me any information at all. For all you know, I could be a charlatan. You may ask three questions of me during this session, and if there is time, possibly more. Are you ready to proceed?"

My throat closed up for a second as I thought about talking to someone who was known internationally, had been on television, and who talked to the dead. I cleared my throat and squeaked, "Yes."

From that point on, time stood still. Meri and I were swept into a whirlwind of new ideas, thoughts, perspectives, thinking, and enlightenment. Thus began my new life!

Here are the notes recorded by Meribeth:

Rosemary Altea Reading Notes:
September 13, 2006– Meribeth
(From Edward's house with Rosemary Altea on the phone in Vermont)

After introductions, Rosemary asked Edward what he wanted to know—if he had certain questions, etc. He was just going to start telling her about the divorce, and she called out, "Stop! Don't tell me a thing! I could be a charlatan!" After some discussion about speaking with loved ones passed and Edward asking about his own psychic abilities with precognition, she suddenly said there was a "roomful of people" present with her.

The first one to come through she described as a woman, short, plump, with white hair, and she was jumping up and down and waving furiously! We said it had to be our Grandma Champion, and then Rosemary said she was smiling and nodding, "Yes! She described having heart problems which led to her death.

Next to come through were two men. They both indicated they also died of heart problems, but one was sudden and unexpected while the other was a problem that had gone on for a while—he mentioned being in the hospital, and was chuckling that with the health problems he had, he didn't think he'd make it as long as he did! (Note: My father said, at least once a week that he couldn't believe he had lived so long.) The first, she described as being tall, which we knew would be our Grandpa Champion, and the other was our dad, who was at her other shoulder. Dad, she said, was anxious to get started since he had so much to say, and was afraid we wouldn't have enough time.

Rosemary asked if there was someone else in the room with Edward (since he didn't introduce me, Meribeth, as being there), and he said yes, and gave my name. She said: "Meribeth, you have short hair! Your dad says he likes it. He knows you think it's too short, but it looks good."

A couple of references here from Meri: "My Dad usually liked women's hair a certain way—wavy, a bit longer and liked my hair that way too ... always thought he wouldn't like my hair so short. Plus, just the week before, I had a haircut and thinning ... when I came home I told my husband Dennis I hardly had any hair left, it was so short, but at least it grows out fast. I also said this in our bedroom where I have Dad's photo on my dresser, and often 'talk' to him there. I was actually thinking that day that he wouldn't have liked my haircut!"

Then Rosemary was trying to interpret an image meant for Edward from Dad about construction at an office or something of that sort "at your work," he said ... we couldn't figure out what that meant, so she had to go to her spirit guide, Gray Eagle, to ask for assistance. We heard her say, "Oh, okay ...," then ask Edward: "Did you get a new desk?" Edward said: "Yes, at the office at the group home!" Then Edward explained that he had just rearranged the office, moving things around. Rosemary said that Dad was a bit impatient with the time it took to figure that out.

Talk turned to Rosemary seeing things about Edward's life: she saw 2 connected divorces, lying, cheating, and things being a mess. She told Edward he wasn't going to lose in this divorce, but he wouldn't get everything he wanted.

She said it wasn't the first time that B (Edward's divorcing spouse) hasn't been telling the truth.

Then Dad started saying things and I didn't get good enough notes to always differentiate between Rosemary and Dad as things were going so fast.

To answer Edward's question about what he should do, Dad said, "Do nothing yet. Just go through the motions. It's way too soon (to decide what to do). Use this rule for now: When in doubt—DON'T DO ANYTHING! WAIT instead! Be very careful—don't make decisions out of anger or emotion. It will do you a disservice to act out of emotion. Just SIT DOWN, BE QUIET, and DO WHAT I SAY. Apply REASON and NOT emotion."

Then he added, "You're allowing her to ruin the rest of your life. YOU'RE ALLOWING HER TO RUIN THE REST OF YOUR LIFE." Then I was told to make a sign for Edward to hang up in a spot where he can see it on a regular basis, stating: "People can only do to you what you allow them to do."

Next, Rosemary started seeing things about Edward's future. Edward needs to work on spiritual growth, and he has a connection to healing. He asked if he should develop his psychic abilities, explaining how he sees the future quite often, but she said: "Leave that part of it alone. You have healing hands. Your abilities are hit & miss. You can't do this (psychic work) if you're not always sure. Take that sensitivity and learn more about HEALING. You'll be really good at what you do. You're not listening to yourself and your intuition. GET A GRIP!

This is probably from Dad. "Let go—she's winning—or beating—you! But WHY would you even care? You have new opportunities to be creative. Think of what you'd have liked to do if you hadn't been in this situation ... creative writing ... become aware of spiritual growth. You can't do that with hate inside you. B did you a FAVOR to do what she did!"

Grandma Champion(our mother's mother):

"This is the best thing that could happen to you. You have a future! Yes, life isn't always fair and isn't always nice, but you have a chance for new life and a new future! She's done you a huge, huge favor ... but will you see it? That depends on your attitude!

Dad:

"You are your own worst enemy!

You have 2 choices: hold the anger and be bitter—hold on to things and be negative, or open your eyes! YOU are the brick wall—STUBBORN!

You have the rest of your life ahead of you—and it will be LONG if you lay off the cow! (This refers to my love of eating cheese and dairy products. d)

Don't eat so many hard cheeses—be careful of dairy—once a week or so is fine." Then Dad was saying something about modern medicine should be able to help Edward with future health problems, but he should pay attention to his health.

Rosemary mentioned this was now coming from HER guide AND OUR dad—that … "the second choice is negative—harboring hate, feeling sorry for yourself, looking inward, being a pain in the butt! In that scenario, NOTHING good happens.

The road gets narrower and narrower—nothing fulfilling, you're miserable, lonely, unhappy. You are ALREADY on that path. BE AFRAID! If you stay on this path, you will get everything you're afraid of. MISERY!"

"Yes, you can change it. You'll get scared starting a new path. You'll swing back down to the old one, and come back to the new."

Dad says: "Meribeth, you should KICK him when he heads down the old path). Do NOT offer SYMPATHY! KEEP ON HIM!"

Rosemary said: "I (she herself) will be let down if you let it go."

"You have a choice. A WIDE, clear, clean path; you have nothing holding you back. This is an opportunity."

Rosemary said that Grandma Champion is Edward's spirit guide, and Grandma said: "I'm the only one you need (for help through this)!" Then Dad and the others were laughing, and he said: "We are all here for you."

Rosemary asked Edward "Do you know the Bible passage where Christ said: 'Healer, heal thyself!'" She said that applies to Edward. Then she said: "Someone is in your future if you take the right path! She wants someone to bring love and support and light to her, and she's been through some of the same things as you."

"GET OFF THE PATH—CHANGE YOUR ATTITUDE! (This is Dad talking now, I believe.) Grow up—don't be stubborn for stubborn's sake, or you'll lose your happiness." Dad said he knows this (about being stubborn) and he will help you and nudge you EVERY TIME you get off the path. You have health, and the opportunities are endless to learn about yourself. Your attitude stinks!"

Then Rosemary likened Edward to a Phoenix, and said everything has to burn first before rising from the ashes. She said: "You are the Phoenix who can rise and fly if you look to the positive. Are you going to stay in the ashes? You have 2 choices—it's up to you!"

Then she started talking about B, saying that ..." when you live with someone a long time, that initial excitement disappears and is replaced by something else. She is looking for excitement. She will end up with someone. Be grateful it's not you! Her fire will go out. She'll see that it's the same with anyone after a period of time, and it will be dull for them."

Rosemary said she didn't see devastation—she sees opportunity. ALL THE FAMILY WAS SAYING: YOU ARE YOUR OWN WORST ENEMY! They love you so much! Dad said: "Don't be like me (stubborn)—be better than me."

Rosemary said Edward had 2 or 3 more legal things to go through.

Then Dad said: "Meri, help him. I want you to do it. But Edward has to listen to Dad (through Meri) and do it! It's just as easy to have a miserable future. You've been given a gift."

Grandma said: "You are BLESSED, not CURSED (There's no "Young curse" like we always had said!)! I'm excited for you! Keep writing—don't give up!"

Dad said: "I love you very, very much."

Edward asked about the younger kids—what he should do about them. Dad said: "Tell them what you were told. They will gather around you. They will help you. Don't be like me—TALK to them. They will learn from you. Show them by example. Give them hope!"

Dad said: "I have a hammer and chisel, and you are the Great Wall! DO IT! Be a good example for your children—IT WILL PAY OFF!"

Then Rosemary once more mentioned the two paths: One of misery, or a HUGE, WIDE path with a NEW RELATIONSHIP, LIFE, and HOPE. Dad said: "Don't get mad when we kick you!"

Then Rosemary, winding things down, asked if I (Meri) had anything I wanted to ask. I was too overwhelmed by the experience to think clearly at that moment, and it seemed inappropriate, so I just told her to tell everyone that we loved them all very much! She said no one could say it better to them than me and that they were hearing it from me.

I hung up and Meri and I sat in silence, just looking at each other in awe as what we had just experienced. We had been talking to our dad, gone eight years, our grandmother, gone for 27 years, and had witnessed their continued role in life and how the love of family does not die.

Meri's follow-up comments: This experience changed my life. The love in the room- the feeling of the presence of passed family members was palpable. It is something I'll never forget- a high point in my life, and I can feel it whenever I think of it. I drove home feeling weightless- even giddy; the validation of life after life, being in communication with our loved ones, and their intense "interventions" which later seemed obvious that they were the ones that had made it happen!

Rising from my chair, I put away my phone book, and as I opened the cabinet door, was struck with the thought, "I can forgive." But, it didn't stop there. Not only in that instant did I decide to forgive my spouse, but in the twinkling of an eye, and most importantly, I forgave myself! I forgave thoughts of my inferiority, failure, collapse of my relationship, disappointing my children and others, and most of all, blame; releasing myself from bonds that had shackled me for longer than I could remember. I would no longer put myself down for anyone. In that brief moment, I felt a truly physical weight be lifted from my shoulders. I was light, my head held up higher as if attached to a helium balloon, there was a spring in my step and a smile on my lips. From this time on, I knew there was no returning to the old ways. I was now on a journey leading me into a place completely unknown, but a place where the phoenix could rise from the ashes and live again.

You don't realize how much effect a positive attitude has on others until you have changed overnight. The pastor at the church where I worked would now comment almost daily about how happy I seemed, and how I held up my head as if I had no burdens. People on the street would smile back and when I entered a room, people would say, "Here comes happy!" or "How come you are so smiley?" It was a good feeling.

— CHAPTER 3 —
OUT OF AN ACORN

Life went on. My dad had been right when he said there would be three more dealings with the lawyer. The divorce was finalized in December, leaving the three youngest children to be divided equally between my ex and me. They packed their bags to go to dad's house for one week and repacked to go to their mother's house the next week. Holidays were divided equally too.

The children were forced by the court to see inept counselors who were more concerned with what was wrong with the parents than in dealing with the real issues of how the children's daily lives were being devastated and changed forever. I wondered if those counselors, appointed by the court, really cared at all about helping my children sort out their broken lives. All they seemed to care about was making sure they were done at the precise minute of their designated half hour, without regard to how needy the conversations with the children were at that time.

No matter how a person's life falls apart, it will eventually reach some type of equilibrium that seems to mellow out the sharp edges. Sure, I was no longer able to volunteer at the school because of my part-time jobs, but we settled into a routine where I would pick up the kids from school on Monday nights and enjoy them for a week before they had to return to their mother's newly built house. It took what seemed like forever for my heart not to be ripped out when they left. I would walk to their rooms, look at the empty beds, and weep bitterly for the ones I loved being taken away. It only took seeing a book I used to read them or an old toy to remind me of my loss on those empty, lonely weeks. I would drop to the floor wherever I was and cry.

Time changes perspectives though. After a while, I started to notice how much better I treated my kids when they came to stay. It was more like having special guests who I loved to take care of. My days of yelling and anger were past. It was a new age of under-standing, compassion, patience, and teaching them by example. In *Charlie and the Chocolate Factory,* the Oompa Loompas always blamed childhood troubles on the parents. It was a new me, and I was proud of myself.

The elder children who had left home would talk about how easy I was on the younger ones and how they could get away with anything. At first, it irritated me, but I had to admit they were right. I was a new person, and the old one had passed away—somewhere to be forgotten. I would say, "Aren't you glad I changed for them at least? Why are you concerned about if I treat the kids better than you were treated? I'm not who I was."

My alternate weeks alone afforded me more time to read. I vo-raciously consumed book after book about all things spiritual. One of Rosemary Altea's books about meditation and healing drew my attention and I read it a couple times. The book explained the need to focus in order to meditate as well as meditating in order to heal. I practiced in my empty house with a candle. At first, I made sure no one was watching—even though I knew I was alone. At first, it was out of the ordinary enough to make me feel uncomfortable. I tried to get the knack of meditating, but I had to give up after a few minutes because I would lose focus. It only took the dog bark-ing, the phone ringing, or a clock chiming to distract me from my concentration.

One day, my hands were filled with a pulsing energy that grew and grew until I could feel energy in the air. It felt like spinning tennis balls in the palms of my hands. No matter where I turned my hands, I could feel pressure on my palms. The feeling was similar to placing them in water. If I turned them toward each other, they would resist and push apart like holding two magnets with the same pole together. If I turned them toward myself, I could feel the same resistance. However, I could reach through it to reshape the energy that surrounded me. My hand chakras (spinning wheels of energy) were beginning to work. They would be my path to healing with my hands—just as Rosemary had told me in my reading. However, I didn't equate it with healing power yet. It was just a really cool thing that happened when I meditated.

For months, I kept reading about all things Spirit and meditated. I started being able to bring about the impulses of my hand chakras on demand—anytime I wanted them to work. The power in my hands was palpable, but I couldn't see a use for it.

When I went to bed, I stretched my hands into the air and let the pulsing happen. During the quiet time before falling asleep, I could see faces and figures of people. They looked like white shapes on a dark screen. Those faces would sometimes be far away and tiny, or they might be only inches away. At times, they zoomed up to me. Occasionally, I would see figures walking like they were on a sidewalk. Once in a while, they would turn toward me and suddenly be in my face, peering at me.

For some strange reason, perhaps being led by Spirit, I kept recalling that one of the people in my ghost book was a member of a spiritualist church that was linked to a camp. With a bit of online research, I discovered the Wonewoc Spiritualist Camp in Wonewoc, Wisconsin. Their website was bright yellow with sunflowers. A long list of mediums came up on a page, and spooky music and dark places swam in my head. One of them even gave personal readings.

The most frightening subject of all was séances. Having been raised with fears of aliens and spooks and monsters in the fifties, this conjured up images of sitting at a rickety table, holding hands with those around me, and having spirits sneak up behind to sniff my neck or worse! I knew curiosity killed the cat, but it was all too tempting for me. Why did I have to thrive on the excitement of being frightened?

Camp was open for the season, and services were at ten o'clock on Sundays. I wondered what kind of services they had: sacrificing animals, drinking blood, summoning darkness, and raising the dead? The forty-five-minute drive to Wonewoc was full of apprehension, and my trepidation grew as I got closer to the camp. Passing a small sign on an electric pole, I slammed on the brakes and careened across the road into what appeared to be an alley. It went nearly straight up a cliff and through a wood. A massive orange gate could be pulled closed so no one attempted to get up the tiny road in bad weather. My car groaned, and the engine ground down to ten miles per hour by the time I neared the top. The camp was right at the crest of the hill.

I drove between two stone pillars standing sentinel as if in warning that there was no turning back, crossed the small field, and parked among ten other cars by the small hotel I had seen on the website.

A young couple was walking into the camp, and I nervously got out and followed at a safe distance.

Immense oak trees towered above me as I followed a diminutive road, which was more like two dirt tracks, into the camp. The sun filtered through the trees, casting yellow and green across my path as birds twittered and chirped happily in the branches. To my left, a small house with a homemade sign indicated the office. A line of tiny white cabins with moss- and lichen-covered roofs ran around the perimeter of the camp like wagon trains circling for protection. In the center loomed a massive building with a "Dining Hall" sign on its side. That was where the young couple headed.

The scent of pine needles filled my nose while I sauntered through statuesque white pines and oak trees. Of all kinds of scenes, the one I loved best was nature at its finest. My mind had calmed down—either from being distracted by natural beauty or from being snatched by some kind of strange power—and I was ready to take on whatever was cast my way. I went inside, but my fear was that I might never be the same after I entered.

The screen door slammed behind me as I entered a large bare-walled chapel connected to a dining area full of long tables and chairs. The walls had no covering, and the studs and outside walls showed. In fact, looking above me, I could see right through the rafters to the roof. The floor was polished fir, very handsome, and a lectern was draped with a colorful cloth with sewn-on sunflowers. On either side of the lectern, five chairs faced the audience, where guests were already filling in the solid wood benches. I found an available one in the rear, quickly sat down, and looked around me at the people of all ages. Some appeared wealthy, and others looked dirt-poor. Soothing Native American music floated lightly through the air from a nearby boom box.

The peaceful Indian flute was interrupted by footsteps as a line of five women and one man walked to the front and sat down on either side of the lectern. A conspicuous blonde woman took her place in the center, commanding all eyes. My fears eased when the service turned out to be o similar to the Presbyterian services I had grown up with: readings, a sermon (though it wasn't called that), and music. And, oh what music it was! I am a trained classical musician and was amazed at the out-of-tune, bottom-note-dredging, and pseudo-melodic first hymn. It was a challenge to keep from laughing, and I was a bit embarrassed that I didn't sing out loudly and try to lead the group. There wasn't a comfort zone for me yet.

The striking blonde lady spoke after the singing was done. "I may have lots of talents, but singing isn't one of them!"

Amen, I thought, and I felt my body relax more.

Sam's sermon was a tale of how she grew up as a strong Lutheran who attended weekly services with her grandmother and family, but she would go home and have psychic readings and séances in the afternoon. Our service was brief, or at least, it seemed to pass quickly. At the end, it was message time. Each medium in the front would take a turn walking among the audience and would give messages as Spirit moved them, asking each person to say his or her name aloud so the medium could tune in to their vibrations.

A couple in front learned there would be a grandchild in the near future. A lady who looked full of woe and worry heard she should get out in her garden and dig in the dirt to renew her bonds with the Earth Mother. Everyone else in the audience eventually was given a message.

A young medium asked if she could step into my vibration. "May I come to you?" she asked.

It was hard to get my voice to work, but I blurted out, "Yes. My name is Edward."

She rubbed her hands together a few times, closed her eyes, and looked at me. It was much more difficult for me than talking to someone in Vermont over the phone.

"You have a great creative streak in you."

I nodded in affirmation.

"I see you writing. Does this have any meaning to you?"

"Yes."

"Spirit is directing you to do more along this line. Keep writing. Something big is in your future," she said and nodded. "I leave this with you." And she was done.

Short and sweet, I thought. *And completely painless.*

The audience attempted to sing a final painful hymn, and the service was over. It was time for some cookies and milk.

I sat down near the others to eat. A medium stood and lined up varied sizes of L-shaped wires on the table in front of her, and the audience quieted down as she started her demonstration on divining rods. Her talk riveted me, explaining how the rods find water and anything else you set your mind on: lost wedding bands, money, and even places on topographical maps. When she finished, we were invited to try them out. The copper rods were handsome;

someone with much skill had bent the wires, and we had been told to get command of them.

Picking up a rod in each hand, the horizontal wires twirled around in circles.

"Stop!" I ordered, and they stopped. It was weird, but also very satisfying, to know I had the mind power to make things actually happen.

"Show me *yes*," I said firmly.

The rods twirled faster and faster, and they both stopped, facing away from me.

"Show me *no*."

Without hesitation, the rods did their stuff correctly pointing toward each other.

I felt a grin rising. "Will I come back to the camp?"

The rods answered in the affirmative. I gave up the rods for others to try, but I was very impressed at being able to do something I had thought only psychics could do. I walked slowly to my car, contemplating my experiences of that day.

I was busy through the summertime with my many enjoyable, but low-paying jobs: secretary work at a little church, writing articles about interesting people for an electric cooperative magazine, mowing a many-acre lawn (mostly up and downhill) at a motorcycle factory, and giving music lessons. My little part-time jobs very often kept me from attending the services at Wonewoc Camp, but the few times I went, I had fulfilling experiences, especially the messages and the "class" after the service where I could hear about subjects I had never thought of as spiritual.

Before the summer ended, Meribeth and her husband met me at the camp on a bright, warm summer day. We would each have a reading with Sam, who I had found out ran the camp. We arrived early to walk the grounds and feel the peace that pervades the whole place, ending up near the main building. We pulled a picnic table into the shade to eat our lunches. We talked quietly about what we thought about how a reading would come through for each of us, but our talk was mostly banter to divert our anticipation.

Soon one o'clock arrived. Sam's cabin was right across from where we sat, and we all stood when she came out from the cabin. It was decided that I would go first, and I walked over the glitter scattered on the ground, making it look like a fairyland, and went in the cabin.

We sat at a tiny table by a window, and sunshine streamed on the floor where the fuzzy dogs, Scooter and Peanut, lay for warmth. Sam took a deep breath and recited a brief prayer for assistance from the highest entities to come through with the highest information, and she promised to use it for the highest good. Then she asked for the White Light of Protection to surround us throughout the reading.

I learned that Spirit will tell things to people that they need to hear—but not necessarily what they want to hear. She also said Spirit will never give them anything that is not important or interfere with free choice. Spirit will never tell you what to do. Spirit might say, "If you do this, this will happen" or "If you do that, that will happen," but Spirit never tells you what to do.

Sam described a short, white-haired lady who was very excited to come through. It was my Grandma Champion who had come through in my reading with Rosemary Altea. Grandma talked about all my busyness with jobs and keeping up with writing. Sam said she saw me teaching a class in a school, and I figured I would be substituting in the fall. She saw someone there for me romantically, but there wasn't any time frame.

Sam stopped and asked if I had any questions.

I asked if there were any messages for my children.

Sam started talking about my youngest child, my son, but I told her my youngest was a girl. She thought for a time, and I could tell she was concentrating to reach Spirit. "Is she boyish?" Sam asked. "A tomboy?"

I chuckled and said, "My daughter is very feminine—no tomboy there!"

Sam said seriously, "I have to tell you what Spirit tells me, and I keep getting the impression she is a boy."

The rest of the afternoon went quickly. Meri and Dennis had their readings with Sam, and I waited for them so we could walk to the cars together to discuss what we learned.

A few months later, I found out my daughter (the supposed tomboy) was diagnosed with Turner syndrome. She was missing an X chromosome. Boys have XY and girls have XX, but my daughter had only one X. I think Sam was sensing that her gender could have been either one—or at least couldn't be told since half was missing.

Spirit knows, I told myself.

I was sorry when the camp ended at the end of August. I would miss the Sunday messages and learning activities afterward. I was also growing accustomed to the people at the camp and would miss their company and the bucolic atmosphere that pervaded every square inch of it.

— CHAPTER 4 —
CLEARING MY PATH

The months passed quickly, and I went to the opening day of camp in June. Perhaps I would get a message or a reading. Instead, it only ended up just being a flag-raising event next to a garden. When I left that day, an attachment to the camp had been created. I made sure to attend the morning services on Sundays, and I stayed for coffee and special classes afterward.

People in the audience became familiar, and we exchanged pleasantries. Most of the regulars also commuted to the camp, but the unfamiliar faces I assumed rightly were visitors who had come to spend a day or two absorbing the peace of the place. They lived in somewhat rough, mouse-filled cabins and attended weekend classes or whatever else was offered during their stay.

I felt at ease in the Sunday services, but I could sense a nervous anticipation in those who were not regulars. Those of us who came each week received our messages from Spirit with the determination of incorporating the advice from the spirits as part of our lives, but the new waves of people would usually end up in uncontrollable tears—weeping from joy or remorse—but the spiritual advice was revealing and helpful for all of us.

By midsummer, I had relaxed enough to sit in front of the lecturer of the day who spoke after the services and was brave enough to ask questions that had been growing unresolved in my brain. It was like being in a science class where the teacher would have explosions and produce images of great beauty as I took in and hung onto each portion of information given to me by people who truly had a psychic gift.

One Sunday, a large group stayed to listen to a lecturer on the power of the mind. I had to laugh when she passed out spoons and told us we could bend them. With few words to tell us how to hold the spoon and how not to force it, she said, "Make sure you believe you can bend the spoon. Just keep an even pressure—not hard enough to kink it though—and think of that area between your hands as becoming liquid."

Within seconds, short screams of surprise and delight popped up in the audience as the perpetrators held up their spoons in various states of malformation. Some had hills or dips, and some were wrapped in circles!

I tried harder and harder to focus my concentration. Suddenly, the middle of my spoon handle became hot as fire and turned to liquid. The spoon bent slightly before becoming rigid once more.

I relaxed in my seat, exhausted from concentrating. While all this had been going on, a four-year-old boy had been yelling out every few seconds. I turned toward him, and my jaw nearly hit the table when I saw bent spoons all over the table in front of him. They were not just minor bends; the spoons were twisted and turned.

He must be strong and is bending them by force, I thought.

He picked up another spoon, and as soon as it was between his hands, the spoon's center looked like it had become mercury. He bent it around and around with ease. I was completely frustrated by my lack of complete success as I watched how easy it could be. The lecturer finally had to tell the boy that there were no more spoons for him. I hid my barely bent spoon in my pocket and went home full of amazement and knowledge that the mind is certainly more powerful than we give it credit for.

By the end of that summer, I had learned about the healing power of mazes and how to make them. We heard about potent qualities of various stones and rocks: citrine (the happy stone), amethyst (the spirituality stone), lapis lazuli (the stone of universal truth and friendship), and quartz crystal (a multipurpose healing stone). A few learning sessions had authors who had written of their own spiritual growth, usually with a background of abuses and/or hardships from the past.

One of my favorites was spiritual smoke readings done by Rolland "Rolly" Bach, a white-haired, distinguished, by-the-book type man from the East Coast. I never suspected he would be so in tune with spiritual concerns.

Rolly set up a lit candle, a stack of papers, and a bowl of water, which he said was "insurance" in case of fire. He told us to hold the paper and think of something we wanted answered—perhaps by a spirit guide or totem animal. He put the paper nearly in the tip of the flame while moving it gently around so it wouldn't start on fire. He only wanted to blacken it.

The people in front of me had sooty, black shapes appear, and they were all completely different. When it was my turn, I asked my dad to come through for me. I held my paper in the flame and rocked and moved it just enough not to catch fire. I could see the flame through the top of the paper.

In a short time, my paper was turning black and gray. I moved the sheet evenly toward the edges so the blackened area was not confined to a single spot. A shape started to form, and I withdrew my paper from the flame when it seemed that no more soot was gathering on it.

Robert looked it over, but I didn't need his interpretation as he had done for the people before me; it was definitely a heart.

There were oohs and ahs as everyone completed their smoke readings. I tried once more and asked (in my head) for my spirit guide to show itself to me. In past years, I would have been skeptical that something like that hadn't been doctored up in our own minds, telling ourselves that we could really see a shape.

When I finished my second shape, I handed it to Robert to read because he would have no idea what I had asked for.

His eyes opened wider, and he held up the paper for me to see. "This is a Native American, most likely a chief or medicine man judging from the feathers in his headdress," he announced.

I had no doubt that he was right. Those looking on could see the Indian, my guide, on the paper. Apparently we can have more than one guide since my grandma had said previously she was my guide.

As always, the camp ended the last week of August, and it was time for the all-medium service on the final night. The evening was sultry, and the chapel was packed with probably 130 people, all waving something to try to cool off. A few people were lucky enough to be by the fans.

After a brief service, each of the twelve mediums in front got up to give messages. They would usually *feel* their way into the crowd and suddenly focus on a certain person.

"May I come to you?" they would ask.

If accepted, and most did accept, the person would have to stand and say his or her name so the medium could enter the person's vibration.

My ears strained to hear over the fans, but it was a delight for me to listen to a few words coming through the medium, usually from a departed close relative, which could change the whole course of the person's life.

It was obvious that some people were skeptical and did not have any intention of believing what was happening. Some mediums were fairly new at their gifts and seemed to have trouble interpreting the images they were being given from the spirit world. Others were true veterans and delved right into giving a solid message.

I thought back about my worries about talking to a psychic medium for the first time, wondering if anything would be said about wrongs I had caused or done during my lifetime. But I discovered up until then that Spirit is generous with praise and wants to lead us in the direction of a positive path. Spirit isn't concerned with chastising us for the past. Spirit wants us to move forward—toward a more enlightened path.

By the time my turn came up, hours had passed. I was about ready to escape in search of a drink of water. My message was short: another communication telling me the importance of my writing and that I should continue to pursue it.

Door prizes were given away, and I received a poetry book before leaving.

As I exited, an elderly medium, who I later learned was the camp president, came up to me and said, "I'm not supposed to give messages outside of the service, but there is a spirit here saying that you will soon do something important."

That left my mind hanging while I made the long drive home, wondering just what I was supposed to do—and wishing Spirit would be a bit more direct!

— CHAPTER 5 —

A NEW JOB

Autumn and winter came, and my desire to know all things spir-itual intrigued me like a starving person might look on a feast of extravagant food.

In the spring, I got a call from Sam. She was in Louisiana and wanted to know if I would like to work part-time at the camp that summer. "We'd feed you for free, and you could have all the classes, séances, and advice you could ever want!"

Though I had six part-time jobs over that past year all pieced together in a complicated, woven clutter, what would one more job do to my schedule? "Yes!" I said. "I can work my main job as a secretary on fewer days, but put in more hours so I can free up days to be at camp."

It wasn't long before I reported for volunteer duty so I could learn about what I'd be doing. I met some of the people I would be sharing the camp with.

When I arrived on the first day, Sam was just coming up the dirt road toward me. "Go see Harry," she said. "He'll have a list of things to do, I'm sure."

I had talked with Harry the summer before about his love for trains, and I had even given him a miniature train set from my basement. I found him building a boat in his garage.

As I approached, the air sent a whiff of his fragrant cigar

accompanied by beautiful classical music from Wisconsin Public Radio and I knew we would get along fine. Inside the garage, he was staring at a flat piece of plywood that was shaped like the bottom of a boat.

I knew I was interrupting his thoughts, but I said, "What are you building?"

I received a brief discourse on the sailboat he would build during the summer as he chewed the end of his cigar. The Pathetique sonata played quietly over the radio.

Within five minutes, I was seated on an ancient riding mower topped off with bags to collect leaves as it mowed. With the large acreage of the camp and deep oak leaves over the entirety, I would not lack things to do!

My daughter lived with me every other week and spent her days at camp when I worked. It was a joy having Lauren there to keep me company as my helper while I worked. The summer was dry as a bone, and the flowers that hung limply in the window boxes of the cabins—as well as many gardens—needed constant watering. We'd fill the golf cart with buckets and drive to each garden and window box where I would hop off, toting a bucket of water for the thirsty plants as Lauren took the wheel, ushering me to each cabin.

We scraped prehistoric paint off cabins and painted them brightly white. We watered flowers, dumped chopped-up leaves for mulch around the bases of gigantic trees whose roots stuck out of the ground as if from fairy tale forests, watered flowers, cleared brush, watered flowers, picked up sticks after each strong wind, watered flowers, piled firewood, and watered flowers. Did I mention watering flowers?

Many days, our dog would come to camp with us. Enya rode between us in the golf cart like a queen in her carriage.

Lauren was asked to babysit for a resident medium's baby, and we both fell in love immediately. As I dug up stones or tore down the inside of a two-story cabin, Lauren would walk and walk around the circuitous camp road, pushing the baby in his stroller. It was a picture of two gentle souls. His half-inch special glasses stood out from his face in a mantis-like posture, causing his countenance to be one of being professorial—or even psychic like his mother.

It was fun to go to the camp on Sundays for the "spirited" service and be able to see the fruits of our labor while not having to tend to any work that day.

After one Sunday service, I happened to look at one of the camp brochures, paging through to find what classes would take place during the summer. I looked forward to them so much. There was *my* name! For presenting a class? I read it again. Yes. I would speak about my ghost book. *How could Sam do this to me?* She had joked about doing it, but I didn't really think she would go ahead with it!

Giving talks on my book was commonplace for me, and I enjoyed talking to audiences about my experience of living in a haunted house for eight years. How could I speak about ghosts to an audience half comprised of mediums? How would they even remotely be interested in my descriptions of spirits when they communicated with them all the time?

Sam talked to someone about self-publishing my book on Amazon. That piqued my interest because it would be the perfect way to try to resell my ghost book. I asked Sam about it.

Sam said, "You need to talk to my good friend about it. Laurie Stinson self-published on Amazon. Maybe she could help you out."

I knew I wouldn't have time to do any investigating for a while.

Being at Camp Wonewoc so much was a wonderful feeling. I gradually got to know all the mediums by talking with them at lunchtime and having conversations around the campfire. Since I spent many hours dealing with branches and sticks that constantly rained down upon the camp, I usually had a nice pile of wood ready for the fire. On weeks when I was alone at my house, I had no obligation to get home at any certain time. In fact, I could even stay in a cabin overnight for free if I wanted.

There were showers in the bathrooms, and Sam or Harry

would invite me for supper. I'd wash up and have supper with the mediums. I discovered how we can be quite wrong when we assume what we *think* is always correct. I found that my idea of puritanical, straitlaced, quiet mediums was totally off. Depending somewhat on the composition of the mediums at camp any certain week, most of the meals were filled with hooting, raucous, wild jokes (sometimes dirty) and pretty much showing me that mediums are as *normal* as any person can be. They have the same problems as everyone else, have the same unique and varied personalities, and can be counted on to want good lives and good times. Maybe we were all a bit on the side of "lunatic fringe," but it was definitely a fun summer for all!

One of the mediums I had grown very fond of was Gustav. He was from Green Bay, Wisconsin. Originally from New York, he was a super-intellectual who normally spoke with such complex terminologies and subtle meanings that I would have to look up words in the dictionary when I got home. We had a similar sense of humor and would either feign verbal fighting with each other or gang up on an unsuspecting medium who we would try to get worked up into revolting against us. It was all in good humor, of course!

Following supper, Harry would begin the ritual of lighting the fire. He seemed to have been elected to that post long ago, and it stuck. As dusk approached, mediums would walk across the camp from their cabins—just as the ghosts that they would see walking through the camp so often did. Folding chairs were placed around the fire, and it was first-come, first-served for the best ones. I preferred to sit on an old red peeling bench; others sat on stumps. It was a time for the mediums to let their hair down after a day of back-to-back readings for the many campers seeking answers to their problems, their pasts, their futures, or their lives. Others were just curious. Since I was fatigued from physical labor all day and the mediums were exhausted from the readings, the fire circle would often start out quietly. Only the crackling and popping of pine and oak broke the silence.

Before long, Harry and Sam would sit with their two little nervous dust mops. Peanuts and Scooter would chase sticks or sit on Harry's lap. With different mediums coming and going throughout the summer, there was an endless supply of jokes at the campfire, usually naughty ones.

Toni, the pastor of a spiritualist church in Madison, joined the fireside group during the week she gave readings. She had given a talk after that Sunday's service about how she had been drawn to spiritualism after being severely hurt in a motorcycle accident. From her talk, I knew that she was very in touch with Spirit. We enjoyed the warmth of the fire and the canopy of stars through the statuesque trees. I had tears running down my face from laughing so hard at the barrage of comments between Toni and Gustav.

I relied on Gustav's special extrasensory perception concerning any tasty desserts in the kitchen. He signaled with a tilt of his head that we should go sneak some ice cream. Off we went, leaving the fire behind and traipsing through the dark to the kitchen. Before we had loaded our bowls with our sweet booty, the rest of the mediums descended on us. They wanted to enjoy the bounty together. It was a relaxing, good time for all. The relationships were strong. When we had finished our indulgence, though I don't know if it could be called indulging if there was no guilt involved, I decided to drive home.

Toni followed me out. "I had to talk to you before you left," she said. "Your dad has been talking my ear off. He has been saying that your mother has been visiting him lately. Is she passed on?"

I was amazed, but I remained calm. "She's still here, but her health has been deteriorating."

Toni was quiet for a few seconds, seeming to be in deep thought, and then answered, "But she's not completely earthly anymore. It isn't going to be too long before she passes, but some of that might be up to her. She appears to be living in two worlds at once."

Her comment initially brought thoughts of denial of my mother passing. She had always been here, and I wanted her to stay. I didn't want to acknowledge talk about her passing, but I knew that Spirit spoke truth and that death must not be so bad. Otherwise, Spirit would not talk about it so matter-of-factly. I hoped that if this knowledge remained sealed in the vessel of my body, I might avoid losing my mom.

Friday nights were séance nights. Though I was a bit wary of attending one (mostly from hearsay from people who didn't have any idea about them other than maybe they were evil devil-worship events), my curiosity got the best of me. I visited Tanya in the office to sign up for one. It came in handy that workers were admitted for free. I was also invited to eat supper with the mediums, and that would mean fish fry from town!

Late on Friday afternoon, Sam told me to turn in my time sheet and sign up for the séance.

The secretary had a menu from a place downtown, and I picked the broiled cod. She plopped a numbered card in front of me and said, "Take this to the séance so you can get in. We count the number of people and divide the proceeds between the mediums."

I picked up a bag of clean clothes from my car and walked down the road to the shower. The water felt good on my tired body, and I was full of anticipation for the séance.

The mediums waited in the kitchen for Sam's husband to arrive with the meals. Soon we were all seated, fed, and happy.

After a brief cleanup, we sauntered across the road to the spirit lodge for the séance. Early arrivals were already waiting to go in, and I was surprised at the number who would fit into the tiny one-room building. We entered and picked spots in a circle of chairs that stretched completely around the room. We were told not to sit at one end because that was where the mediums would sit. When the final person sat down, the door was closed and locked so we wouldn't be interrupted.

Sam sat in the center chair, surrounded by the rest of the mediums. I was taken off guard when she started cracking jokes! She had us all laughing as one joke followed another. This led into a story about how mediums sometimes see things in symbols and don't always understand what they are supposed to say. She told about giving a message at another séance where she saw a girl dancing on the back of a cow. The lady to whom this was directed was amazed because her grandmother had been raised on a farm and was too poor to take dance lessons like she wanted. Instead, she would dance on the back of one of her cows.

Once we were settled down, Sam said a prayer for protection and for only the highest entities to come through in the messages. She also noted that we should sit without crossing limbs because that would stifle our energy for receiving messages. After a hush, the mediums drew into their thoughts.

One medium looked directly at the lady next to me and asked, "May I come to you?"

"Yes," the woman answered. "I'm Sally." We were supposed to say our names so the mediums could feel our energy.

Around and around the circle we went. The mediums passed along messages, usually from close family, but sometimes a spirit outside of someone's family would step in with a message.

A woman near me was asked if she had owned a dog that had passed.

"No," she said.

The medium said, "There is definitely a dog sitting at your side and being very loving toward you. It looks sort of like a German shepherd and has its paw on your leg. Does this sound like a dog you may have had? It says its name is Sparkie, and he says thank you."

The woman started crying, and tissues were handed to her. She tried to regain her composure. "I never owned that dog. It was the dog of a neighbor. One day, I heard tires screeching on the road. I ran out, and Sparkie had been hit. I ran to him, held his head, and petted him as he died."

This revelation was amazing to me. I could see that my idea of spirits only being that of humans was completely mistaken. That night, my Grandma Champion came to me via one of the mediums and told me that I needed to keep writing. I had to get started on a book that would be important to people. At that time, I had no idea what I was even supposed to write about. I wished she had been more specific, but such is the way of Spirit.

When the last guest had received a message, we all stood, held hands, and raised them.

Sam ushered our thoughts into being filled with light. We pictured balls of white light over our heads, and we let them grow and expand. All of our collective lights were brought together in a continued expansion over the state and the country, and they were sent into the world for peace and healing wherever they were needed.

Someone opened the door, and we filed out into the beautiful summer night. Many small groups of people discussed what they had heard and learned. Some of us migrated to the fire pit, and Harry's fire danced and kept the chilling dampness of the woods from moving in.

— CHAPTER 6 —

MESSAGES, MESSAGES

That summer was a scorcher, the hottest on record, and a drought since April made it seem like I was working in a desert. The enormous pines at the camp were dropping needles and branches, keeping me busy with the mower and cart. I picked them up and deposited them in the fire pit. It was so dry that even the embers in the pit stayed hot into the next day, sometimes igniting the brush I threw in.

Though June was a bit sparse for the mediums getting readings to do for the public, attendance picked up heavily during July and August. The camp was filled with many small groups of people who would bolster each other into being brave enough to have readings. Most would come and go in a day, but there were always visitors who wanted as much as they could take in. They would arrive on Fridays for readings in the afternoon, go downtown for supper, and return in time for the séances. On Saturday mornings, they walked through the woods to the bluff overlooking Wonewoc from high above the steeples or meditate on the round bench surrounding the peaceful, gigantic healing tree. Many Saturday afternoons featured courses, usually outside, for drinking in enrichment of your spiritual self.

On Saturday nights, a past-life regression took place in the spirit lodge. For three years, I had read about the past-life regression session at camp, but I had not been brave enough to attend (even though it would be free for me). In my strong religious days—so very long ago—the thought of considering that we lived more than one life would have been ludicrous. I would have thought that absurd idea came from drug-crazed hippies or die-hard Hindus.

Reading books by well-known mediums, as well as talking directly to many mediums, caused me to look differently at life. Eventually, I embraced the design of multiple lives. In fact, the more I knew about past lives, the harder it was to hold on to my old ideas of living one life, dying, and living forever on a cloud while playing a harp.

If my brain gripped the idea of past lives, why was I afraid of encountering past-life regression? For that matter, what the heck *was* past-life regression? An online dictionary defined it as a "return to an earlier stage of life or a supposed previous life, esp. through hypnosis or mental illness." The part about mental illness did not bother me as much as it might have in the past since so many people figured that anyone associated with spirits, mediumship, ghosts, and ghost-related things were totally off their rockers and worth staying away from. The camp had been in existence since 1874, but people of the town considered anyone associated with it to be devil worshipers. They even called the place Spook Hill.

So, what was I afraid of? Nothing—except maybe thinking that revealing my past lives would not work for me. Worse yet, what if something really *did* happen? I made up my mind. I was going to sign up for the next regression.

At a séance on the last Friday in June, I received more messages about writing. I wished I could stay in a cabin overnight until the regression the next evening, but with a dog and cat to take care of at home, it just wasn't possible. My excitement and anticipation grew and flowed out of me as the day progressed. I played my trombone in the morning to divert my attention from thinking about that unknown terror looming over my head—and approaching ominously nearer with each minute.

I finally hopped in my car and drove to camp. Having never

attended a past-life regression, I was surprised by how many people were waiting at the spirit lodge.

Sam opened the door, and we piled inside and sat in a circle. After a prayer for the highest entities to assist us, Sam had us relax in our chairs. We closed our eyes as she talked softly about following a white feather higher and higher into a blue mist. Whether we realized it or not, we were traveling: to distant thoughts and space and past time itself.

I had worried that I might fall asleep, but I could hear Sam's calm, clear voice speaking softly. It weaved among my contemplative thoughts as I proceeded through the mist of time and started to descend.

As we landed, Sam told us to look at our feet to see where they were going. I was surprised to see that I wore leather boots and was coming in for a "landing." Below me, approaching quickly was dry ground with patchy grasses. For some unknown reason, I knew it was 1874 and my name was Tom. As my feet hit the dirt softly, I looked around. Slowly, more and more things came into view: a log cabin and a rugged three-step stairway that led to an open door.

Sam continued talking and suggested that we look around.

I stood still. I recognized a shack that was a blacksmith shed with a chimney. In another direction, I saw a fence and a field of corn. I walked inside the one-room log house and saw a fireplace with small burning logs. To my right, there was a bed with a dark green blanket and a crude table with some bench-style chairs. A young woman appeared, and she was holding a little one. I recognized her as my wife, but in my present life, she is one of my daughters!

Sam's voice came through again, and she asked us to move ahead in time to see what it was like.

Suddenly, I was in a town that I knew was near the cabin. I was dressed up in a typical long dress coat of the 1800s pioneer towns with a bow tie and tall hat. I felt like I was the mayor of the town. I think it was the Fourth of July because there was some kind of celebration going on.

Sam spoke almost like a narrator, asking us to look ahead to see how we died.

I was suddenly walking on a dirt road on a hot day. I opened my neck button; perspiration ran down my face. It got harder and harder to walk, and each step felt like a weight was being added to my feet. I took three steps and fell on my face—dead.

We were suddenly whisked back through the blue mist and brought back to our seats. We slowly became fully conscious. I breathed a deep sigh as if I had been working hard at something and could finally rest.

"How long do you think we were regressing?" Sam asked.

Everyone looked around until a couple said, "Ten minutes. Fifteen minutes."

Another person said, "Twenty-five minutes."

"It was forty-seven minutes!" she answered.

For the next half hour, Sam had volunteers talk about their past lives. It was surprising that only one or two didn't remember going anywhere, but Sam told them they might have strange dreams or thoughts for a while that have to do with their past lives.

The first person to speak was a younger woman who broke into tears and seemed agitated. She described being a small girl being chased through a cave and murdered.

An older woman told of drudgery and sadness. She saw her legs and feet wrapped in skins and then found herself hanging fish on racks near a fiord. It was relentlessly cold, and she hated the tedious work.

I told my story, but I wondered if my active imagination could have sparked the tale. I was exhausted after my encounter with my past life and was grateful to return home to sleep.

The long, hot summer marched on. Sam started talking excitedly about a friend of the camp who would show up twice a summer. Alice grew up at the camp, attending with her parents, and was present at baptisms and births and deaths when the camp used the old chapel that had become decrepit from large branches which had crashed through the roof.

Sam said, "Alice is also very psychic. She will tell you that she isn't psychic a bit, but she is very strong in it!"

A small, gray-haired lady drove up to the hotel and started to unload enough belongings for a long stay.

I knew it had to be Alice. "Would you like some help?" I asked.

"No, I can manage," she answered matter-of-factly and hefted a large suitcase out of her van. I knew she was a totally no-nonsense and independent live wire. I was reminded of Betty White, the actress, when I saw Alice and hoped I would get a chance to talk to her.

My wish didn't take long to come true. I finished mowing on the Friday night after Alice had been at camp all week, took my shower, and walked the quiet road back to the office before the séance.

Alice was sitting on a bench when I arrived. We introduced ourselves, and Alice said, "I watch you mow each day, and your father is right there with you. He says he enjoys the peace here, and you both enjoy nature."

We sat in silence for a minute as I pondered how nice it was for my dad to be with me.

She looked directly at me and said, "You know, there is a large Indian medicine man standing by you. He is your guide."

I told Alice that I had heard the same thing during a reading from a medium from New Mexico. I was glad, but wished I was able to communicate with him.

After supper in the camp kitchen, we went to the séance.

I made sure to sit near Alice since I liked her and the positive energy she emitted.

Before the mediums started giving messages, Sam said, "Alice, would you like to give a few messages?"

Alice denied having any psychic power, but then she went right into a message. "You know, I've had a man with me *all* day. He's been following me around. He keeps waving his arms like someone directing a music group. Does anyone here understand this or relate to it?"

Silence.

She related a few more attributes and waited for a response from the audience.

More silence.

"He shows me music and more directing. Like this." Alice demonstrated how he looked while directing, and she became visibly frustrated that no one was relating to it.

I blurted out, "That's the way my dad used to direct when he did church choirs."

Alice stopped and glared at me. "Well, why didn't you *say* something if your dad was a director?"

"Well, he was a professor, and he only did the directing for a church," I answered mildly.

Alice grumbled under her breath, and I nearly broke up from stifled laughter. The situation was so comical to me.

Sam laughed and said that during many of her readings, the people listening did not recognize what was being said until they left. *Then,* it becomes obvious! Sam asked, "Alice, would you like to do another message?"

I couldn't resist my impulse to comment. I exclaimed, "Only if she doesn't yell at me again!"

The crowd erupted into uproarious laughter.

Not long after that, I saw Charlotte coming from a reading she had just finished. "Hey, Edward!" she shouted as I hastened up the road on the golf cart. "I brought my table with me today. Be ready for tonight!"

I knew what she meant. Charlotte had been talking about bringing a special table to camp so we could have a night of table tipping. The night had arrived!

I cleaned up quickly after work and had supper with the mediums and Harry in the noisy camp kitchen. The atmosphere was full of chaos and laughter, and everyone spoke one right after the other creating nonstop conversation. We all played the mind game on the small black chalkboard where the word for the day was displayed.

Our objective was to create other words from the letters of that word or words. The two words were *table tipping*, and the string of entries underneath it was getting long.

A medium was at the sink, and I shouted, "Abby! Can you add *pip* to the list for me?"

After an onset of boos, everyone chastised me for using a three-letter word. "Too short!"

I laughed.

The group suggested getting to the table tipping as soon as possible!

After dishes were done and dusk was setting in, the mediums descended on the spirit lodge.

I was in heightened anticipation because table tipping was something from the days of old—from times of medieval witchery and dark magic. We all sat in a circle, chatting and joking.

Sam stood up and said, "As you all know, Charlotte brought her three-legged table tonight. We thought it would be fun to try some table tipping, especially for those who haven't experienced it yet." She smiled at me. "So, let's get started! How about Charlotte, Edward, Abby, and me for the first try?"

We pulled our chairs around the narrow table in the center of the room.

Sam said, "Some of you make sure you are ready to grab our chairs if something happens."

My imagined scenarios worried me a bit.

"Place your fingers very lightly, just on the edge of the table," Sam instructed. "Leave the rest to Spirit."

We did that, and I waited to see if the table was going to fly or disappear or who knows what. Nothing happened.

Sam said, "We need some good positive energy here to get this going! Let's have some rounds of 'Row, Row, Row Your Boat!'"

We all started singing, and the song got rowdier and sillier.

Suddenly, the table started rocking back and forth.

It tipped toward Sam, stopping short of her lap, and she said, "Do I have Grandma here?" I feel your energy, Grandma."

Apparently, that was all that was needed. The table started rocking back and forth, becoming so violent that it was nearly jumping off the floor! As it rocked, it started circling. We jumped from our chairs as the people behind us snatched them out of the way. We followed the table around and around and back and forth as it moved from one end of the room to the other.

The four of us desperately tried to keep our fingers lightly on the edge! I was truly amazed!

We kept it up with different combinations of people "at the helm" and found that the table behaved quite differently for each group. At one point, someone asked if a spirit was trying to get the attention of one of the people in the room. The table started bucking and spinning. The participants wildly followed along as the table made its way to one of the mediums—and stopped abruptly. We were all sweating from the activity and laughing about the comical table.

As we decided to call it a night, one of the mediums said, "How do I know that one of you isn't putting a bit more pressure on the edge of the table? Then all you would have to do is relax and the table would return to where it was. Push again and relax again, and you could have it tipping and moving,"

Gustav was a deep thinker, and I had to consider what he said. I realized there was no way to prove any reason for the table tipping and dancing; it was a time of trust with whomever you shared the tabletop.

As the summer wound down, the messages from mediums found a groove for me. Weeks of messages at camp services and from medium friends said the same thing. "Write, write, write! This is going to be a big or important book for you."

It was frustrating because I could not think of anything to write about. Try as I might, not a single idea came into my head other than to ask Spirit for help, which I did.

I threw myself into rewriting my ghost book. I expanded and

rewrote to add maturity to my writing since many years had passed since I'd written it. It kept my mind focused on writing.

I finished just in time for my talk after a service at camp. A nice crowd of people were interested in hearing about my haunted house. I was baffled that mediums were interested too—even though they talked to "dead" people every day. Everyone liked my talk and slide show. I decided to self-publish my ghost book on Amazon as soon as Sam's friend told me how to go about it.

I e-mailed Laurie and discovered that friend had helped her publish *The Blessing of Abuse*. I wrote to the friend, but I never found out enough information about publishing. Instead, I kept searching.

Laurie offered to discuss it when she came to camp for the last service of the summer.

I woke up ahead of my alarm with a spark of an idea for what I should write about. I had asked myself what I was good at, and my mind drifted to my award-winning success doing interviews for a local magazine. Then it hit me! I loved all psychic phenomena. I had a blast with mediums. I enjoyed the spiritualist camp immensely. I loved learning about all things spiritual. My book would be interviews with mediums so that inquisitive people like me would know that spiritualism was nothing to be scared of. It was something to be embraced and discovered!

As summer came to an end, the camp looked polished and orderly—like a postcard—thanks to Harry and me. All that was left to do was closing the cabins and ending the final night with an all-medium service.

On the last day, extra volunteers flocked to get all the chores completed. Charlotte, Trinda, and Sandy started working on the cabins. Each cabin needed cleaning, bedding removed, beds tipped up, windows and doors locked for winter, and other things. One vital item was to make the cabins less habitable to the mice that ran rampant—and had a knack for crawling over visitors—during the night.

My daughter and I watered plants around the camp one last time. The golf cart we used was so quiet that no one could hear it approach as we came up to Cabin 15. The ladies were removing the bedding and sweeping as they talked about looking for mice.

I told Lauren to keep quiet and snuck up to the cabin. I picked up an ancient frayed broom. Nobody noticed me as I squatted by the doorway and slid the broom across the floor, hitting Trinda's ankle with the bristles. I was halfway out the door when Trinda shrieked, causing the others to do the same. They showed amazing speed and chased me down the road with their brooms. I laughed uproariously and wiped my tears yelling behind me about why they weren't flying on their brooms. Apparently being a medium didn't alert anyone to the fact that they were about to be frightened by a very large mouse!

The air conditioners from each cabin were placed on the floor for the winter, but with the promise of another scorching day, Lauren and I moved them to the chapel. We set them up in the windows for the evening service. When the temperature hit the nineties, we turned on all the air conditioners to cool the place at least a few degrees by nighttime.

Supper that evening was a quick one so everyone could prepare for the all-medium service. The preparations mostly consisted of trying to cool the building before going to the chapel at eight o'clock.

A steady stream of people started arriving at six thirty, filling the place with wall-to-wall bodies. It felt like someone had put us in a giant oven. Sweat poured from everyone's faces, and I wondered how the mediums were going to do their messages for more than a hundred people. Somehow, they did.

By the time of the last person's message, the heat and humidity were unbearable and everyone rushed outside to try to cool off.

Laurie and I talked for a few minutes about self-publishing before she had to leave for Minnesota. We connected enough in that short time to maintain future conversations via e-mail.

A few days after camp closed, I got an e-mail from Laurie. "Do you have a father or grandfather on the other side who was bald or balding? I have a male and female energy here, but the male you resemble is stepping forward."

I laughed and said, "I'm sure it is my dad. He has been coming through for me for the past six years!"

Laurie stopped to retrieve the message and said, "He tells me you are apprehensive about your next venture or project, but he wants you to know that *now* is the time!"

— CHAPTER 7 —

FINDING MY PATH

That one suggestion from my dad, "Now is the time!" was what I needed to get out of my rut. Each day I thoughtfully considered what I wanted in my new book, but it did not move along like I hoped. "I don't have a title yet," I wrote to a friend in an email one day. A title was what I needed to get things moving.

It came to me while I was eating a steak supper one night, the thought hitting me with a double meaning, 'Medium Rare'. I laughed to myself at the symbolism. People would think of eating steaks but the book would really be about mediums, and I chuckled again. My computer was handy so I let Laurie know what I decided. She was my tester, the person who as in ancient times would test food for being poison or not, only she could test my ideas for being on the right path because she had spirits to help her.

She liked the idea. But, one day as we chatted online, she stopped talking as she usually did when a spirit gave her a message, and she announced that my dad was there. He was suggesting that I revise the title just a little and make it, "Mediums Not So Rare." I immediately liked that idea because the book would no longer be construed as a cook book! Now I could begin my writing and knew just where I wanted to start.

Abby Newman would be my first interview. She was bubbly, very intuitive, and did spirit art that I had never seen anyone do before; I already knew her from her work at Camp Wonewoc, and she was handy! I sat, notebook in hand, with her outside on one of the fading warm days of the summer when the leaves on the trees were casting off their glossy green in exchange for a new coat of colors. It was time to get to work!

— CHAPTER 8 —
ABIGAIL ROSE NEWMAN

Bio: Abigail Newman* was born and lives in Wausau, Wisconsin in the USA. She produces work through a meditative spiritual state, using a natural rhythm through which her artistic forms and expressions grow organically with layers to give birth to her distinctive artistic forms. "I AM NOT tied to any one idea but rather let the image create itself. While my mind is clear of thought, and I am inside a meditative emptiness, I am channeled into a different realm.

"I work in layers using different media, whether painting, drawing or sketching. My artistic images build layer upon layer until I hear a whisper in my mind or get a feeling of what the image is. I can queue into it, adding the last touches to the finished image. Often times, someone else can see other things in the art piece that I didn't even realize I had drawn. I do not even look at the next piece

---

*Note: Abby was one of the psychics at Camp Wonewoc but had quite a different skew to her readings. Most of the time she was set up in front of her little two room cabin with a chair for the person receiving the reading and just an easel with a pad of paper accompanied by a box of multitudinous colors of chalk. To give her reading, Abby would just sit on the ground with her pad and talk to her client as her hands flew back and forth across the paper. What appeared first as grotesque shapes suddenly turned into faces; loved ones, spirit guides, visiting spirits or whomever was talking to her through her own spirit guide.

of charcoal or art tool that will be used next. I switch hands when I draw or rotate the canvas numerous times during the creative process because I believe in random chance. It is meant to be that way because all things are connected with reasons that cannot be explained.

"I believe healing takes place in the creative process. When I step back and see something at a different angle, I know the healing has happened. What is right in front of you takes time to understand. It is the joy that fills my heart when I can help another see what it is beyond a piece of paper."

"I believe that creativity is a direct link to the Divine". Abby Rose, www.abbyrosespirit.com.

"Yay!" Abby shouts as she finds out she is my first interview. "That's because I'm an Aries. I grew up in Wausau, Wisconsin, in the country, in swampland! Not on a farm, just in a log cabin."

Are you kidding me?

"I grew up in a log cabin!'"

You mean like Abraham Lincoln?

"You could see the logs. It was a smaller log cabin and the logs were round- it's really a log cabin, not like these fancy log cabins you see that are all ... you know ..." (with a big sweep of her arm)."

Well then, were your parents hippies?

"No, my mom is an artist. She's crazy and awesome! I'd say artsy, but you see a lot of the hippies were artists too. She worked too hard to be a hippy, she was always working. Anyway my mom separated from my dad when I was six, so I don't know him too much."

Was he in art too?

"No, he was a postal worker."

So you got all your artistic talent from your mom.

"Well, somebody was telling me ..." (but Abby starts laughing as I drop part of my ice cream cone on my papers). "You have an ice cream cone in your paper. Is that a sign?" she laughs. I lived in

Mosinee in the country until I was six and had one sister who is now a veterinarian. So she was the science mind and I was the art mind."

So were you in any art school?

"I used to be in the special art classes- always."

And when you finished high school you went where to school?

"Beauty school and I was a hairdresser for ten years. Which, you know, I think that taught me a lot, and I think that a lot of hairdressers are intuitive. And I was doing readings when I was a hairdresser very nonchalantly, and you don't really think about it. You know what I mean? It was like training ground in a sense but I did my first psychic reading in 8th grade for my boyfriend on the phone and I told him how much he liked salad, and he hid that from everyone," she chuckles. "(He said) 'How do you know that I like salads?'"

What made you come up with that (giving a reading)? When did this intuitive talent start developing?

"You know, I think I always had it. And, in fact, I got a reading from Charlotte (a psychic from Camp Wonewoc) yesterday. Charlotte talked to my grandfather on my father's side, and HE had the gift, but he was persecuted for it- for having this gift. And he got his gift from his mother, but his mother, which would be my great grandmother, never talked about it. This is what Charlotte was telling me at a reading for me. That's the first time I found out about it. My dad was also probably gifted but he turned it off right away because his father got persecuted for it."

How did it come on? I mean, did thoughts just come to you when you would meet people? Or, did you have to try hard?

"No. I remember being able to see auras. When I was a really little kid I could see auras- when I was three."

What does an aura look like?

"It's like when you look at something, it looked like it had a haze around it. Everything had a haze. And for some reason I thought it was like the circus. I don't know why. I remember looking in my kids room and thinking this was just like a circus. Everything had an aura around it. Weird huh?"

No.

"Yes. But, that's how I remember it, cause everything had these colors ... colors were different when I was like three. I remember the reds and the blues a lot and they were intense! And, everything had this little fog around it. And so, I can distinctly remember my room and energies around objects and everything!"

Inanimate objects?

"Yeah. There was an actual haze around objects, is what I remember the most in my playroom."

Did people have different colors?

"I don't remember that, but I remember my room. I have a distinct memory of my playroom and thinking it was like the circus with the fog around it."

Did you start seeing people's auras?

"No. I don't remember that, but if I do concentrate, I do see them. If you like look at somebody and let your vision go foggy, you can see them in the corners of your eyes. I'm working on it but usually I only see one layer of auras like lime green and white, but I'm working on that. I'm taking my Reiki masters next month so I'm hoping I can see more auras after that."

So in 8th grade you gave this first reading. Did things just start unfolding from there?

"You know, if I think about it, it was probably around then because I was reading Sylvia Brown books then, so I was thinking a lot about this. When I was 12, I asked for my spirit art guide for help, 'cause my mom didn't want to help critique me. So after reading Sylvia Brown I thought, 'Oh, I can ask for a spirit guide to help me, so I asked for my art guide and his name was Pat. I remember him telling me his name was Pat. He's been hanging out ever since then but I have a feeling he was there the whole time."

How did you communicate with Pat? Was this a dream?

"No, I was sitting in my room drawing. It was funny because I was drawing out of my Riverside Elementary (that's where I went to grade school), I was drawing faces from my yearbook and they (the drawings) didn't look anything like them. I wonder if I was drawing their spirit guides then. Then I asked my mom to critique them and she said 'I really don't want to do this'. She liked to teach in a different way, which I understand now- she just taught differently. But I wanted somebody to tell me exact lines and blah, blah, blah, and they didn't look like these people. So, I asked my art guide and it was like the next day that I was watching PBS and they had this show about how to do watercolors. And so I took my cheap watercolors and made this duck. It was amazing, though I'd never done watercolors before! That was the first time Pat was working through me when I did this duck. It was very impressive. I won awards for it and no one could believe I was that old when I did this painting. But, that was the first time Pat worked through me. I was 11 or 12. I didn't think it was me being psychic. You know you don't realize exactly the degree, but now I realize that it was Pat, because I know I couldn't have just picked up watercolors and done anything like that without any training. I had only watched one PBS show and they were talking about landscapes, not ducks."

Go back to your very first reading in 8th grade. What was the kind of reaction you got?

He (the boyfriend) just couldn't believe it, I was talking to him, 'cause I told him about the salads and how he was so picky about cleaning his room and he didn't tell anybody about that. 'Cause he was a boy, and I was telling him about being so nitpicky about cleaning his room- that he really enjoyed cleaning and eating salads! That's what I remember, I just started doing a reading on him because I was reading Sylvia Brown and I wanted to try being a psychic and intuitive. I had it (the ability) the whole time though. It was just like I started talking.

So when did more readings come along? Did people ask you, or did you just go up to them and ask, "Can I tell you something?"

Well, I was an alcoholic for a few years, but I would scare people at parties ... a lot! When I was drinking I would do the most read-ings, I think that happens to a lot of intuitives. If I was at a party, I'd just go around the room and have a crowd of people get readings, and if I'd go to a bar, I'd go around the circle of the bar and ran-domly pick people to do readings for them.

And what was their reaction?

Amazement! Fear, a lot of fear! I know one time I was at this party and I was talking to this guy about all this stuff, and the next day I ran into him in the mall and he was like, 'I don't know you or anything about you.' He was scared of me, and a lot of it was, oh my gosh. But a lot of it was excitement 'cause I'd be at parties and a bunch of people were waiting to get their readings. And so I thought I could only do it when I was drinking but then I was a hard core alcoholic for six years. So, I don't drink anymore.

But, when I was drinking they (spirits) would come right though me, you know what I'm saying, so I was actually them! And I just started this week that they are again and actually talking through me this week.

With a voice?

Yes!! Like I'm talking for these people, like it happened three or four times this week. They're like swearing and talking about stuff; bad words and throwing their hands all over the place! It just started this week, but I used to do it when I was drinking. But, I'm letting them work a little more through me now, I'm trusting a little bit more, 'cause usually I just work directly with my spirit guide, because when you're drinking, it's not good to be doing this kind of work. If you let them work through you (while you're drinking) it's lower energy that really draws out your energy. You want to keep your frequency high and you want to set boundaries. I didn't know what the heck I was doing at all. It was almost like, you know, you have to set boundaries and set protection because you don't want them to draw out your energy. I don't know exactly what it was, but they can sort of attach (to you) in a sense, the energy attaches or something, kind of like a parasite. You know, those years are pretty foggy, so it was just a process (to get done).

I've also always been highly empathic and when I was doing hair I was taking on other people's stuff, like I would take on their headaches, I'd take on their joint pains ... stuff like that. I had my gall bladder removed about two or three years back, and I feel like there's a correlation between sucking in people's stuff and not being able to release it.

Now when I do readings I can get hurts and pains so I know where they (people) hurt, but I can let it go, do you know what I'm saying? So certain places will hurt and I'll ask do you have pain here, so I can ask them if it hurts, but I can let it go away. Before, when I was doing healings on people and didn't realize it, just like doing shampoos and messing with stuff as a hairdresser doing their hair, I was actually taking on their stuff. And my gall bladder was so sick, when I got it taken out it was like three times its size. The woman who took it out said it usually takes them a half hour to take out but it took them an hour and 45 minutes and they said it's a good thing you came in. When you start to get into this gall bladder stuff and people are sucking up other people's stuff, I think there's a big correlation with that.

Then I took Reiki this last January so now it's like I don't take in other people's stuff. It's like added protection or something. Maybe I just needed the training but now everything kind of works through me and I feel more protected. But, you know, this last two years I've gone through this huge process; I didn't even know I had this gift (art readings) until two years ago, because I've always been talking to my guides and finally I got this image of the purple guy with 5 globes around him, almost like he's juggling. I got an email reading from a woman named SG and she told me I can draw spirit guides and family members and loved ones, so I said, 'Oh, let's barter!"

So I bartered and got her spirit guide but anybody can say that's their spirit guide, so I started drawing them for work and I was getting family members and said, "Wow! I do really have a gift!" I started working with it and this last year I've just been going through the process of learning it- you know, pinpointing it. SG started a website for psychics and I still have her market for me now (psychic art) and I love her! She advertises for psychics now. That's where I do my radio show, with them, and I was one of the first ones they hired, or rather, their first client who joined up. I've learned a lot about networking because of them- we kind of learned together.

Go back to speaking about your Reiki, because people aren't necessarily going to know what that is.

Reiki is working with energy. Anybody who is psychic, empathic or intuitive, I highly suggest learning Reiki. It balances out your chakras. We each have seven chakra points and each point relates to an energy field on your body. You want everything (on your body) to be balanced and healthy and pure; and what Reiki does is it teaches you to work through your crown chakra through your hands, that is, spirit and angels and God work through you and channel through your hands, so you can actually heal chakras with your hands. It's a lot of visualization and not necessarily you doing the work! It's a higher power working through you.

And what is a chakra, because people will wonder what that is.

A chakra is an energy point in your body. We each have seven like the colors of the rainbow starting at the root; the root chakra being red and is the end of your spine or tailbone and that's the beginning of your chakras. I'm sure there is more but this is what I know.

You have your sacral chakra that is orange, your solar plexus which is yellow, your heart chakra is green, the throat chakra is blue, your third eye (forehead) is purple, and you've got the crown which brings things in, and that's white and on the top of your head where the energy comes through.

So you are empathic. But, what else are you, because there are so many different types of psychic abilities that when people see the names (clairaudient, clairsentient, intuitive etc.) and it scares them, sometimes they think it is some kind of foreign religion trying to break in on Christianity and destroy the USA and all it believes in.

There's all this persecution about it being evil and it's not an evil thing at all.

So another gift is channeling. What do you do?

I channel so spirit works directly through me. I do physical mediumship because I'm actually channeling and drawing.

Is that what you're talking about with the voices coming through you?

That would be physical mediumship too, because they're working directly through you, like I do with my drawing. My spirit guide works directly through me, but I don't know what I'm doing (while channeling and drawing). Another physical mediumship would be like making things move or bending spoons, or things that happen physically through spirit, just like you would be able to physically see the character (in drawings) coming through me from my voice and my actions; it's physically happening as you watch me.

There's mental intuition which is more like you are talking with spirit, or you're seeing things and talking about spirit. Physical mediumship has some kind of materialization. Or, like table tipping; that's physical mediumship, or automatic writing which YOU can do, by the way! It's actually true that people can start fire, but you don't want to do that because they'll take you to the pentagon if they know you can. (Abby is laughing here.) Or, some people can definitely mess with electronics as something physical is happening like somebody can shut down electricity. Levitation is physical mediumship! That I'd like to see! But, you haven't done anything like that though, have you? I've never levitated, no, but that would be cool! I do dream about it. I do too, I dream about flying. Me too. All I have to do is believe and it works in my dreams. As soon as I stop believing, down I go. That is a powerful statement, because if you believe it, you can do it, but you really have to believe you can do it.

Clairaudience. Some people have that. Do you?

I definitely have clairaudience which is picking up on other people's thoughts. Say we're walking and you're thinking of a watermelon, then I mention watermelon; I picked up on your thoughts. Clairaudience can be like when you're thinking of somebody and then they call you, or you say the same exact words as someone else. You have clairaudience but don't realize it.

Lauren (my daughter) and I do that all the time. You're picking up on each other's thoughts. So if I'm driving down the road and see a pretty lady walking, most times the lady will turn and look right at me. Oh, and feel the energy. Well, I think that's something else, picking up on energy, but don't know what that is. But it happens and it's really weird. Well, your energy is very strong because you are an intuitive, so your energy is more potent.

Does everyone have energies that they could use but don't? Sort of like me, not feeling like I could get a message from my dad (in spirit), or anyone. You just have to start talking. You know, in my own family I have problems; I'm not like intuitive with myself, but say you're having a conversation with somebody and you just trust and say 'okay, I'm going to do a reading for you,' just start talking and you'll amaze yourself! That's all you've got to do, just start talking and trust! So, try it. Find a random person and say, "I'm going to do mediumship," or rather mediumship is actually talking with spirit, but you could say, "I'm going to do a psychic reading for you," and start talking, start talking! That's all you have to do! No matter what you get (that is, the message you are telling) just say it, that's all you've got to do. Ask your guides to help you.

And, I want to make sure you get this in your book, you HAVE to ask because they (the spirits) cannot mess with free will. So if you want something from your angels or want something from your spirit guides, you have to ask them because they won't mess with anything unless you ask. Ask them for help? Ask them for help, ask them for a parking spot, ask them to help your intuition, ask them to help you find a new car or a new job. But, be careful for what you wish for and how you state it!

At this point someone brought by one of Abby's paintings for me to see. Tell me about your picture you did here.

That one, I had told a friend about it when I was painting it back in May or June, and I had read something about the eclipse on May 20, and it was about the Egyptian goddess, Hathor. I forgot about it and was just at the phase of my painting so I was finishing it up, but that reminded me of it (the goddess) and I looked up who this woman was. Everything in the painting matches perfectly or represents perfectly stories and the information I got about this Egyptian goddess. So it's pretty incredible.

I want to ask you about customers. When you do a reading for somebody, what's it like? I know at Camp Wonewoc the person waits outside and then when you're ready you come out and get them. What goes on during this time? Are things going through your mind before you meet the customer?

(Abby laughs) I'll tell you that at Wonewoc, they (Spirit) give me names in the bathroom! I know that for sure because when I had my reading you came out of the bathroom saying, Frances, Frances! That was my mother's name (who had been having health problems). Yeah. There is something about the bathroom, but usually I just try to stay disconnected until I'm right there (at the reading). Things come, or they'll be funny cause they work in mysterious ways and usually it's just kind of like they're there and I start talking and drawing. Like you said though, in the bathroom I kept getting names of people for my next reading! You just never know.

When you start talking to a client, what do you say to them and what do they say back?

Usually I tell them what I do, which is readings while I do my psychic spirit art, so I tell them I draw while I give the reading and I don't know what I am doing, I just draw. It's kind of like when you're driving from point A to point B and you think, "Wow, I don't remember the scenery!" Then I say we'll do a prayer first, of course I pray, then pretty much whatever pops up, pops up! It's very spontaneous. Nothing is ever the same, I guess, it's different for everyone I suppose, but that's basically what I tell them. If they have any questions I tell them to ask me and I also tell them whatever I'm getting or picking up (psychically).

What are typical questions that people ask? What do they come to you for?

Finances, jobs, relationships, health of other people as well as for themselves but people ask about their family too; I would say that about covers everything.

Is there one (question) that is most asked?

Probably relationships or finances or career. It depends. They go in streaks and cycles.

Do answers always come through?

No. (Abby chuckles.)

So what happens if you don't get an answer?

Something usually shows up, but when you're doing this it's kind of like you're talking (for Spirit) and you talk fast, it works fast! It's like randomness of subjects that, at the end, pull everything together I suppose. Usually I'll get something, but sometimes they (Spirit) don't want to talk about that so I'll get something else to talk about and start going back (to the original subject) and usually I'll get some kind of feeling or vibe.

Do people try and trick you? Do they make up stories to tell you to see if you come up with an answer to their fake story?

I've never come across that, that I know, of course I'm psychic but I've never had an experience of that sort. No.

Or, are some of the people resistant? Do they ask, but are still not open to it (Spirit advice)?

Yes! And that sucks!

What happens when they are not open to it? Do you have trouble doing a reading?

Yes. When people put walls up, you have to break down their wall to start getting in there in a sense. Like, sometimes you don't get anything (anything coming in for the reading from Spirit), and so then you know you have to kind of change your focus so you can break through that. What I usually do is say, "You put walls up, (because) I think you are resisting" or I'll say, "Do you have a hard time (with this)?" Usually the reason is that they don't want to know, or they are scared, or they just don't believe it, or they're emotionally shut off. And so, one of those things you can do is start talking around it, then they start opening up a little. It's like talking somebody into an awesome haircut that they'll love.

Do you get a lot of emotion from people?

Yes. You know, I even think (when I am talking to somebody) that intuitives are kind of counselors. So you know when you go to the counselor and feel like 'oh, I can cry.' But, you normally wouldn't cry (in a typical situation). It's kind of like we are prepared that something emotional is going to happen so it comes easier (for us to accept) I think, and you know on top of that, I have a lot of angels surrounding me and on top of that, they (clients) are getting things validated and they are having people come through so they may be very emotional.

So besides the spirit that is really wanting to talk to them (the client), like some nearby relative, what do the angels do? Do they assist you in some kind of understanding?

They heal particularly and guide. My spirit guide works through me, that is, my spirit guide is the main person that works through me. But the angels are there for protection and I think they also work with emotional blockages and they heal. Guidance, protection and healing; that's why they are there.

What are they protecting you from?

They are protecting me from any negativity coming in from the other person or any negativity that may be surrounding them, or just any kind of negativity.

I remember you saying that with your gall bladder you had been taking on people's negative thoughts.

Yeah, negativity, and you can actually pull that in and that's not good! So if you don't know what you are doing, other people have this problem if they don't understand, they can be picking up on a lot of people especially if they are empaths or intuitive people, they are very sensitive like a deer with the ears (Abby demonstrates super alert deer ears) and they can pick up anything. Or, a bat that feels vibrations off of things and pick it up. So being intuitive or empathic, you're very sensitive to energy, period; physical and emotional energy and spiritual.

And when you are doing the reading, what do you see or hear? Do you just hear voices or do you actually picture a little movie going, or …

I get a movie going. They like to show me houses to validate, and they like to show me weird things, they'll show me anything from Mother Mary's statue to a chicken hot pad, to the way a room looks- I can see the whole room, or I see scenes from people's childhood. Where I'm trying to validate somebody, they'll give me a scene so I can kind of explain what's going on. Sometimes they'll give me pictures. I'll also quickly get collections of thoughts, guided thoughts that need to be heard. So, I pick up thoughts in the morning to tell about. I don't usually hear different voices, but lately the voices have been coming through me, working through me, which is pretty interesting!

And, what's that called?

I don't know, but that just started in the last week I was at (Camp) Wonewoc so I don't know too much about that. It was like I had their whole personality, their voice … my voice would change a bit. It was still me, but what happened the last three times was that I was saying stuff that I normally wouldn't say, or the way I would say it they were talking right through me. But, the other validation is I'm doing the spirit art, so I'm constantly getting people's loved ones on there too.

Like last week. I was doing my drawing while the person (Spirit) was actually talking through me. Just crazy! That was pretty cool!

Do you think you are developing more as you go?

Yes! That Camp Wonewoc is awesome. Yes, I'm always developing and they'll work with you (the spirits). I have a new chemist (in spirit); I had asked my spirit guide for a new chemist and they mess up your head so you can get some of this psychic stuff going. And I think they were testing me! The last week I was there they were testing me to see what would work or wouldn't work. It takes awhile for you to catch on to what you are tuned to when you are developing and that's where your logic comes in, kind of like metaphysical logic where you're looking at something (reading psychically) and think, 'that was different,' and you notice a pattern and I'm starting to understand that gift more. It's like I was a two year old doing this for people; it's a process.

So you're getting better at it and more things come to you easier?

Oh yeah! Oh yeah, because I've only been doing this for two years, that is, a year and four months. I mean I've always done readings but I've only been doing this professionally for like three or four months.

Why do you think that being at Wonewoc is better; why does it inspire you?

Things hold energy. It's (Camp Wonewoc) like a sacred place and I think there are so many psychics that have been there, and what psychics do is amplify what is going on in people's lives. It's like an amplification of their world, like you're seeing it on a big screen in a sense, rather than looking at one little word. Psychics are also getting rid of blocks, or getting them (people) through things, and they're also doing a lot of healing. And energy sticks to things. That camp's been around for almost 140 years, so it's going to hold onto a lot of healing energy, a lot of intuitive energy; a lot of whatever was put in there. And also, I think that ground is sacred. Even before it was a spiritual camp, it was sacred ground. I truly believe that, and that's why they chose it (for a camp).

Sacred, meaning probably Native American?

That's what I figure, but I can't prove that, it's just what I feel.

I'm going to shift here. What do you consider is your occupation?

A psychic medium; artist/psychic medium.

So you have no other extracurricular jobs to get along with?

I do Reiki and my psychic art and readings, that's what I do.

How do people get in touch, or find you?

I network a lot and doing things live, like Camp Wonewoc, is exceptionally helpful! I have my website, which is, abbyrosespirit. com, and I always do a network constantly on Facebook which is an incredible business tool. I do a radio show (Blogtalk) and I do recordings live for people on computer. I've only been doing this a year and four months, but I think when you get out there and once you start getting people to know who you are in the area, let's say Wisconsin, I think I'll be doing a lot of psychic parties now. So, I'll be going places and doing parties for people, and do psychic fairs and that kind of stuff.

What's a psychic party?

A psychic party is when I get a group of eight to twenty people and I do readings at somebody's home.

So it's sort of like a séance, except by one person?

It's just me doing the art, and it's like a party! It's fun!

You do art for everybody or just for some?

It depends on what people are comfortable with. I'd rather it be on a one-on-one basis, because if there are messages, I don't want them to be interfered by … or rather, I don't want them (the person getting the reading) to feel weird around other people. But, you know, I could have 20 people in a room and if I pray and focus on that one person, it wouldn't matter (how many are observing).

Now are your parties just using your art, or do you have parties that you just do readings for people?

I haven't been doing this long and just started parties, so my art and readings are what I'm most comfortable with, but I could just do straight up readings.

That sounds really neat and I wonder how much you'd charge to do something like that.

It depends on the distance, like if I'm going to Illinois, I'm going to have to have at least 15 people and that will be $50 apiece. If it's closer by, (it's easier) that pays for gas. So, for closer by, I'll do $40 and a minimum of 8 people, or if it's four hours away, you have to have 10-15 people. But they book pretty fast! They're bookin'! I have some booked already. Yay!

Did you mention a psychic fair?

Yes. You go to these psychic fairs, like they have (in the Midwest and many other states).

How about when you do a reading from a distance (phone or email) if I'd want it done for my daughter?

I do a video of me doing the reading and artwork. Then after I'm done with the video, I send a picture of your guide right away (by email) so you can see it in front of you, then I send the recording of your video, and the art gets sent directly to you in the mail.

So, all I have to do is go to your site.

That's it, and then you just order it or set up a time. We could set up a time right now if you wanted to do this, or just email me.

Have you ever done a past life regression?

Yes, I did that while I was at camp (Wonewoc). I've never done it with people (others) but it is amazing! Have you done one? Yes. What did you think of it? I liked it! Well, I went back to 1877 and landed with my feet in what was like a farmyard. I could describe the cabin and how many steps went up to it, what it looked like inside, and there was a little blacksmith shop on the side of it. As I turned, there were fields, and later on, I was a mayor or judge or something ... I'd like to see that. (I was) dressed up in a bow tie with long ends hanging down and it was really cool! Yes, that's awesome! What was yours like?

I was a Native American. You start at your feet and my feet were in the water. (Abby shows herself dropping something.) I had two of them come through. But the one with my feet in the water, I looked down at my hands and had a rock in my hand, which I do all the time, and I looked over to the right and saw all these dead Native Americans, some in the water. I saw the blood coming down the stream in the water. So then I went into a teepee or something with a hole in the top and there was somebody else there who must have been my husband or lover, or whatever, but he was dead. And then I don't know what happened, but I went through the top of the teepee, so they must have been plains Indians. Then I went up and all of a sudden I was in another world. And, we had really long hands like my hands were this long (she shows me), and we had these black stones that we were putting in these orange cup things, like rows and rows and rows and rows of these orange cup things. Then I saw a platform with what looked like a huge plasma TV, but it was all like green colors and swirls (as she makes humming sound), and I was waving to them when I walked to the screen; a weird movie theatre type screen thing.

That's really neat! So you obviously believe in past lives?

Yes, I do. After that week, I went through a pretty hard time and I think it is important for people to go through these past life things because if they are carrying over karma energy from that past life, they can release it in this life. If you think about it, you can kind of see why you might feel certain ways about certain things because these past life regressions can be extremely therapeutic and helpful. Even if someone doesn't believe it, I think people need to go back to get over stuff so that they can move on in this life.

I don't think you were there (at a past life regression) when one of the mediums had her experience. What happened to her? She was a sacrifice and it was really horrible to her and she looked really upset for awhile! Another in my group was being chased by some man in a cave as a little girl. He went after her in this cave and that was really tough on her too because she was killed. That is awful! But it was really interesting!

Do you think all psychics believe in past life?

No. Look at one of our popular psychics at camp. He doesn't even believe he is working through spirit. You know, everyone has their own opinion, they have their own view, everybody is completely unique. And whether you are psychic or not, everyone has their own view on how the world functions and works. Whatever you believe is your reality. And not all psychics believe in angels, and not all believe in God! Everyone is just individual, period!

It seems to me that anyone who is intuitive should be able to experience angels and things commonly.

It's what you want to believe. Maybe someone else's word for an angel is a fairy. Or what I see as angel, they might see as orbs of energy or healing vibes or whatever. There is so much that we don't know and I think that other dimension is so much more than we have here that you can't necessarily put one word on any one thing. Or, if you did put one word on one thing, it would mean a lot more than just what we would see as one thing.

I experienced a lot of psychics coming and going from camp with me working there, and I met a lot of people and saw a lot of ideas and it seems to me like a lot of psychics are not enlightened. And, I think it just struck me as that's why they don't go farther than they (presently) are- because they are stuck.

I could see that. We all need to grow and I think a lot of times and as we're always growing, I believe we get into a certain level of being when we are no longer in this time and presence. Maybe we become another dimensional thing. I think we all grow until we get into these different levels. Sam (the camp coordinator) sees them as different levels, and I believe that we all have spiritual levels and I think eventually, you keep going and going and going to different levels, and these levels bring you into different realities. And when you stop growing or stop trying, a lot of times the ego gets involved and growth stops. Or, they are healing and can only take so much (change), or they don't believe in themselves enough (or believe that they can). I mean, you can't catch a ball unless you believe you can do it.

That makes me think of another thing. Did you go through table tipping when you were at camp?

Yes, and it was awesome!! Some psychics don't believe in that (that table tipping can be done). People have to go by their own reality, their own direction and their own path. And, sometimes fear stops people quite often. If you fear something, you have to get over that fear, and a lot of people get stuck because of that fear. It's universal. No matter what you are doing, fear will stop progress. And, until you can go through that fear and fill it with light, you're not going to move ahead in that certain circumstance or certain lessons. I think we find out place in the world through struggle, (that was a Star Trek quote). If you're handed something with a silver spoon, you never truly appreciate it, and if you never truly appreciate it, you can never feel the full spectrum of it. So, if you fear something, the struggle is what makes you appreciate it more, and by appreciating it more, it has more depth, it has more power to change you. I agree, and I'd even say that with 95% of the people on earth, problems could be resolved if they weren't afraid. Yes!

How can a person tell that they have some psychic ability?

Everybody has!

But what would be an indicator that they are receiving messages that they can perceive in their minds and know what's being told them?

When they go through enough ego work, (Abby stops and laughs). I think a lot of it is ego. When I say ego, I don't mean something like, 'he has a big ego.' Knowing the difference between what your thoughts are and (spirit). That's where logic comes in, because you need to know the difference between what is you and what you are picking up from another level. You know we're all taught culturally, we're all taught in a literal sense, we're all taught history and I think a lot of it has to do with questioning what is true and figuring out or deciphering what is ego and what is spirit. So, there is a lot of logic there because you have to kind of dig to see the patterns of what one of those categories it lies in.

The other thing is trusting and letting go. If you let go of your ego, and it can be hard at times, even for every psychic, you can let go of your ego and know you have to have faith and believe it and it will just flow. It won't be a thought like (when) you are thinking, it will be given through you and to you. We all have it. It's logical but you have to figure out what the patterns are in your own brain, and it's also faith and it's letting go.

I'm open to anything, but then it must be my ego that keeps me from receiving?

It's your belief in yourself, is what I'm picking up. It's not even your ego, (pause) but maybe it is since you aren't believing in yourself. So it's either ego or spirit. But you already have it and you can already do it. You just have to do it; you just have to believe that you can! You can! You can! You can! Ask the angels to give you more faith. You just have to ask; they're right there! The stronger you believe in them, the stronger your ability will become. I believe that.

Then why do some people have such an easy time at it, like from the time they are 3 years old?

I think they grew in their past life. You know how I was saying there were steps and levels, well; I think they are already at that level. They got rid of enough karmic crap that they were set free in the life prior.

Do you use tarot cards at all?

I used oracle cards and didn't like the tarot. With the oracles cards, they were a good cornerstone for me to start talking (to people through spirit). Sometimes you just need 'something' and when you're learning, the oracle cards are a great tool.

How do you learn about those?

Just pick up a deck of oracle cards and use them as event markers or emotional markers. Just get some oracle cards!

(Abby has been whittling a stick through the whole conversation.) Are you making a wand, by the way?

I got this new carving tool- sweet, huh? I'm having fun with these. Someday I want a tool shed with cool tools like this. (Abby makes wands to sell online which concentrate the energy a person has. They usually have crystals or special rocks attached.)

Have you ever had experience with astral travel, an out of body experience?

I'm working on it but, yes, I have. Not to the level that I can talk about and be knowledgeable.

Do you know a way to work on that?

I have been working on it. First of all I'm asking my chemist (spirit guide) to help me and I'm meditating. I have to get to a (particular) level of meditation. I've had experiences when I felt myself separate, but it was in a short period of time and I was back. It's almost like I have to let go of some more fear.

Do you think a lot of people travel in their dreams?

Oh, yes, for sure! I've had the same dream as my kid! I have my cat come with me in my dreams all the time and I'm always looking for my cat, but she sleeps right next to me. We've (Abby and her child) even had the same dream about a jungle gym. People do it all the time. People heal other people in their dreams. I've done that before. I had dreams about Camp Wonewoc before I got there, that there would be a spiritual community and we all had these tiny little homes that you didn't have to pay taxes on. It was these cool little homes, and I thought that I was going to build this community, but when I got to Wonewoc, it was what I had dreamed of! I was already visiting it.

I've had a lot of premonition dreams where, when it finally happens, the people are saying exactly what I remember in my dream. It's the same situation, surroundings, and conversation and the dream finally makes sense to me.

Yeah, then you are traveling into the future. A lot! And, daughter Lauren does too. That's cool; you are having processing dreams, that is, you're a processing dreamer.

Do you do anything with divining rods? No, not yet. Mazes or pendulums? I haven't gotten into that yet. I'm working on my healing wands. I do Reiki and do these healing wands. The wands are very powerful. If you know anything about Reiki, anything with a point, you can transfer energy through. You can actually feel it. With a wand, I'm doing a lot of blessings and putting good energies into them and I'm using copper, which is an excellent conductor of energy. I use gemstones which are an awesome energy too. You can put energy into anything, just like with Reiki. You can put energy into your car; you can give Reiki to your car. Whatever your intention is, if you sit there and put enough intention into it, someone is going to feel it. Even if you don't have any big ability, you can put energy into anything. And, with the wands, a lot of angel energy into this and a lot of intentions of healing into them. Whenever you put intentions into something and think about it and put time into it, it can be healing. Like my art; if I'm meditating on my art, what I'd like to get to is a level when someone looks at it (my paintings), and they can just feel the angelic presence because of the channeling and the healing meditations and the energy put into it.

How do you use the wand, for example if you are doing some healing at Wonewoc Camp?

I take the wand, and always say first, (and I know Reiki, so that helps), but anyone can do this, and I pray in the highest of light and love, angels, thank you for working through me and with me during this healing for whatever. I thank the wand, I thank the person involved, I thank myself, I thank anybody that I want to receive healing from; the angel Rafael, ascended masters, archangel Michael, Buddha. So you're praying and thank everyone and put that intention in there, then you point the wand, and depending on the wood, do the healing; woods all kind of work differently because they all have their own energy too, as well as the different crystals. Some of them I feel right away, some I get sort of a heartbeat and people can feel the pulsing from the point. Some of them are just like lasers, they're like zzzzzzzzz (Abby makes a buzzing sound). They all have a little bit different energy, but there are elements, other elements, I'm adding to them. The energy actually travels through the gems and different things (like metals), and conducts that energy healing wherever you need it; emotionally, spiritually or physically, depending on your intentions. Whatever you want to do, it works. What we imagine and what we feel have incredible magical powers and immense manifesting can be done with intentions, thought and belief.

Do you usually hold it with both hands?

It depends, sometimes, not always. The biggest thing is putting your intention in your heart and your thought into it. Or, knowing and letting go and letting the angels work through you. Being a blank canvas is a place for them to work through. Everyone does it differently. The main thing is just prayer, intention and thought, or not thinking- just asking.

Do you point it at the person?

Say they are having a neck problem, you'd put it right by the neck, or you can also use it to clear your aura; it will break up any negative blocks in your aura. Say I want to charge this crystal; I can point it at that and it will charge, but I also put in my intention too before I place it down and do a little prayer. This probably would be excellent doing distant healing too, but it's giving you something to physically see, that is, whatever makes you believe it more, amplifies it.

These (wands), though, are nice because they have energies within them, they have the stick, they have the copper, and they have the crystals, which gives them more power. I could just use this (plain) stick and heal with it because my intention's there.

And what kind of crystal is at the end of it?

This one has quartz. It's the first one I made, and here I have different kinds of quartz and I have a citrine there, but they all have different qualities so you'll feel the variations in the wand if you are sensitive to it.

What woods do you use? Right now I'm working on cedar, willow, and oak. Is one better than the other? They're all different energies. I wouldn't say one is better than another, it depends on what you're working with or what you want to do with it. I really like oak. Oak is very powerful; they say oak is probably the most powerful one. The oak seems to be more focused, where the willow is more emotional and cedar is more purifying. You should make one! And, you should take Reiki. I did it online and it's not that expensive. It took about 3 nights to do Reiki 1, and about 5 to do Reiki 2. At this point Abby had to leave, so we called it quits for now.

Abby's Psychic Art from Readings

*This spirit came through at my reading- my dad!
Here is my dad's old picture I found later!*

This is my daughter's spirit guide who came through at her reading.

CHAPTER 9

JOHN WAYNE

John's story:

I went to school to become an engineer in Baltimore and worked in the DeWalt Division, where they make the pretty yellow tools, and I had something to do with most of them. For the last few years there I worked on products for Europe and Asia so I was fortunate I got to travel there quite a lot. I had a manager who said, 'you will be there for a week or two on business, so take a few days on the company'. That was always nice. I quit there in '97 when I moved to Colorado, which is where I live now. I had been coming out here on business and met lots of people. In '96, I started my shamanic studies so would come out every couple months for that. In '97, Spirit said this is where I belong.

I got to Colorado by way of Oregon. My second wife, Joyce, and I started dating around 1990 and we were both interested in spiritual stuff. The year before is when I started my meditation. I had gotten interested because my first wife and I were having trouble. A a friend told me about a psychic reading he had and I was always curious or interested in but never had a reading or got into it at all. So, I made an appointment with this psychic they recommended, Nancy, from Baltimore. I went down to see her one day, and of course, I'm an engineer so I'm just going tell her my name and sit back and let her figure it out and see what she tells me. Well, she just blew me away! For an hour she talked about what happened in the past, what was going on then, and some future stuff that did happen. That kind of hooked me and I thought how do you do this. There's always got to be a logical explanation. I still believe that, 'cause it's logical to me, though it may not be logical to other people.

But that's how it started. I began taking meditation classes with Nancy Fox, some beginning metaphysical studies, and from there, it led me to the Baltimore School of Spiritual Science. Nancy was a graduate of the Washington school, and I understand there is also one in Philadelphia. I started going to that school and so did my eventual second wife, Joyce. I went there for six years and became an ordained Spiritual Science minister through them. Along the way I did other things; spent time at the Monroe Institute in Virginia, did programs and seminars and other things that were very beneficial. I don't know if it still is around but there was a group called Context Associates out of Seattle that had a series of workshops called the Excellent Series.

For a while they had an office north of Baltimore and I went to their program and a friend had convinced human resources to pay for anyone to go through that program. Beside the spiritual school, that program was the most beneficial thing I ever did for myself. In the first part there was a five day course, Pursuit of Excellence, where you look at yourself and your relationship to everything else in your life. It was six to midnight during the week and all day Saturday and Sunday. When they first told me, I thought good Lord, this was going to be a kind of chore putting all that time into this. But, it went so quick and was so amazing, it was just great.

The second part of it they called The Wall where they take you away on a retreat for five days and you look at the relationship in your life that is working least well, with the premise that if you improve that, your whole life will improve, and they're right of course. And, again, that was THE most beneficial thing I ever did for myself. In the third part, called The Advancement of Excellence, you go for a weekend and then once a week for five weeks to integrate what you learned from the first two seminars into your life.

Well, back to my second wife, Joyce. We wanted to move to somewhere in the country and we were both involved in spiritual stuff so wherever we went to, we wanted to teach meditation and beginning spiritual studies. So it was in 1991, (I'll say by accident, though we all know there are no accidents), we ended up in Sedona, Arizona, as part of a vacation and we wound up spending a few days there. I didn't know anything about Sedona then, of course it has the energy centers around town; vortex areas. Up to this point, Joyce and I would talk about where we would move to and I mentioned Wisconsin, partly because I had been there and it's pretty; the lakes and the trees and all that stuff. Well, on our second day in Sedona we decided to hike around one of those vortex energy centers so we went out to the one near the airport.

Now, it was kind of funny, I had directions on how to locate this area so we were walking around looking for this spot, thinking it was 6" in diameter and we were going to find this spot, and we realized that it was not a little spot, but the whole area where we were was the vortex area. We came on a big rock outcropping where someone had built a medicine wheel out of stone so Joyce said why don't we sit here and meditate, and while we're meditating we will get some kind of indication we're in the right area.

We were sitting there back to back; I was facing Cathedral Rock about 5 miles away. Of course we had our eyes closed, but before that I could see there was a thunderstorm around Cathedral Rock and while we were meditating we would even feel a drop of rain or two from that storm. I'll say the meditation wasn't anything spectacular, but when we were done and I opened my eyes, we had wanted a sign and there were four complete rainbows in the sky like an artist had taken a brush and made four complete arches. I told Joyce, you wanted a sign and there it is.

Another thing that happened a couple days later; we were walking around another of the energy centers on the southeast part of town and had gotten back to the rental car for a bite to eat and some water. I had a pair of shorts on that didn't have any pockets so I ended laying the keys inside the trunk. When we were done we decided to go hike around some more and I shut the trunk. I walked a half hour down the road to a gatehouse of a gated community and the guy there chuckled because once a week he had to call a locksmith. It took the locksmith about 45 minutes to get in there. I spent the 45 minutes with this man from Wisconsin, listening to him tell why I did not want to live there! For me, that was a message from Spirit that I shouldn't be focusing on Wisconsin. So when we got back from our trip I said 'okay guys (Spirit), where do you want us to go?'

Almost immediately we started getting all kinds of messages about Oregon. For instance, our offices where we worked were in the same area, so we were driving home (together) and decided to take back roads rather than the interstate and talking about where we might move to when some little car pulled out of a driveway getting my attention, and of course, it was from Oregon, and you never see an Oregon car in that area. One time, probably a year later, I got a call from a headhunter who started the conversation, 'hey I wondered if you would be interested in a job down in the Carolinas'. I told him I might in a couple of years but it would probably be west or north, rather than south. The first thing he says is how come a couple years. I said I'm going to this spiritual school for a couple years and then I'll be ready to move. I started telling him about it and he said he wished there was something here (his home) but there was nothing. So I asked, where are you, and he said I'm in Oregon.

So, a month later the same guy calls and starts the same conversation about a job in the Carolinas and I said I already talked to you about this. The guy said no you haven't. I keep records of who I talk to and I never talked to you before, so I start to remind him of the conversation and he remembered but said it was really weird that he had no record of ever talking to me. So it was another indication of Oregon.

We got married in 1992, finished school as ordained ministers in 1994; both quit our jobs, sold my house, got a big motor home and headed off to Oregon. I didn't know where in Oregon I was going and I didn't have a job lined up. We went to Alaska for two months first before we drove back down to Oregon where we went down to the Medford/Ashland area for a couple nights. It happened to be a Saturday night and was 10:30PM so it was dark. Joyce looked over at me and said what are we supposed to be doing? I said I wasn't getting any messages on what to do. As soon as the words were out of my mouth there was a knock on the door. I opened the door and there was a guy standing there who looked like Santa Claus except he wasn't fat, he was trim. He said hi, how are you doing. I just wanted to see how things are going for you. There's a neat little town on the other side of the mountains you ought to check out, called Bend. I think you'll really like it over there. Well, I just wanted to say hi. I got to run. I'll see ya. I looked at Joyce and said we're going to Bend! You couldn't ask for a clearer message.

So the next day as we were driving into Bend, we looked at each other and said it feels so good to be here. We found a beautiful spot for the motor home as we were going to live out of it until we got our life going. On Wednesday, Joyce saw an ad for a metaphysical church group in the paper. They were having meetings in a senior center on Sunday mornings so that Sunday we went to the meeting. When we first went to the meeting I stood there for an hour and cried; the energy in the room was amazing! By the way, they were looking for a minister and people to teach meditation and beginning spiritual studies. It was pretty clear why we were there. After being there for a few months, Joyce wanted to be back in Maryland and I was torn, I didn't know what to do. It was pretty clear what Spirit sent us there to do, but she was my wife and she didn't want to stay. We wound up going back to Maryland, and once back, things really fell apart between the two of us. As soon as Black and Decker found I was in town, they called me up to come to work and counted the six months I was gone as a long vacation. We split in

'96 and in '97 I quit work again to go to Colorado. So, when things started to get worse, Spirit spoke to me and said Colorado is where you belong.

It was Memorial Day weekend; I drove my pickup truck out here loaded up with my belongings, most of which were gone when we moved to Oregon. It was an older truck that only had a cassette player and did not play CDs so I had a little boom box on the seat so if I wanted to listen to my CDs I could do that. As I got into Colorado I turned on the boom box and started to open one of my CDs, but Spirit said 'no, no, don't listen to that one! Listen to this other one!' I put in the one I wanted to listen to and it wouldn't play and ejected all by itself. So I switched CDs and the lines of the first song were something like, 'Doesn't it feel good to be home again.' Then I said I got the message and asked now can I listen to the one I wanted to? I switched and it went fine; they just wanted me to get the message.

When Joyce and I were having trouble in '96, we were going to come out to Colorado on vacation and part of that vacation was when I started my Shamanic studies here in Colorado with a group of people. A week before the vacation she told me she wasn't going to come so I came out by myself. I would call her once a day and say get on a plane and come out here. She told me not to come home. While I was here, one of the people in the Shaman group mentioned Caroline Myss and I knew who she was. I heard that she and the doctor she worked with had seminars on a farm in Missouri. I called the farm and spoke to somebody about being part of one of their seminars. The person said they had seminars about 4 times a year but limit them to 25 people at a time, and by the way, there are 418 people on the waiting list. I figured I'd never get there. But, there would be a seminar in February aboard a cruise ship so I said you can sign me up. The person said we'll try to pair you up in a cabin so the trip is less expensive.

About a week before the cruise, they hadn't found somebody for me to share a cabin with so the cruise was going to cost me about $600 more. So, talking to Spirit I said come on guys, why can't you find me someone to share a cabin with? Spirit said you aren't supposed to have a shared cabin because you are going to meet somebody on the cruise. That was kind of the last thing I had on my mind after leaving my wife three months before. I got to the ship and out of the roughly 2,000 passengers, there were 206 people who were there for the Caroline Myss seminar, and of those were only three guys!

At the dinner they seated us with other people in the seminar. I showed up at my table for eight and left one seat to my right empty. I was sitting a few minutes when a woman from Australia sat across from me and immediately Spirit is saying 'This is the one! This is your next relationship; the person you are supposed to meet'. I always want a hundred confirmations of everything, so we were docked off a shore and we arranged to get on a smaller boat. I was one of the first people to get off the big ship onto this boat. I noticed there were steps that went to an upper deck, so I walked up there where it was out in the open. The first two benches were full so I went to the third and slid all the way down and sat. People were sitting close, and yet my bench was empty. Well, guess who comes up the back steps looking for a place to sit! She sat next to me and the rest of the bench filled up. So I said (to Spirit) I get it! Susan and I really did hit it off so we spent most of the time together on the rest of the cruise and even spent a few days together back in Miami.

As it turned out, she and her ex husband developed some kind of healing modality that works with the brain. When I was talking to Spirit on the plane back to Baltimore, Spirit was very clear they wanted us both to move to Colorado which we did in January of '98. We're no longer a couple, but she is still here in Boulder practicing her healing methods. She's even written a book or two and has been on Oprah Winfrey. Insurance companies would even pay for her energy work. She was able to get things straightened out in the brain as well as kids who were ADD were straightened out. Spirit wanted us both to be here and here we are!

The Lakota Tribe accepted him to learn their pipe ceremony, a position of honor that not many non- Native Americans achieve. The man teaching him the ceremony said John should buy a pipe, but John said Spirit told him that one would be dug up from the ground for him. At a cookout with friends from the Colorado Center for Spiritual Growth, John was relating this story when one of the members who lived in the mountains started to laugh, saying, "Oh, so that's why I dug it up!" He had been given a pipe a few years earlier but the energies were too intense for him so he wrapped it up and buried it behind his house. The man said he was prompted to dig it up but didn't know why, "but, now I know. It's because it is your pipe!"

He now works as a shaman and a real estate agent and keeps active with spiritual matters giving talks and journeying for people as a shaman. Lately John has been working with people with brain abnormalities.

How did you meet Laurie Stinson out there? (See Chapter XV on Laurie*)

It was not that long ago I was showing property and I was supposed to be 'on the floor' covering phones at the office, but of course, when you are showing property you can't be in two places at once. I was on my way back to the office and she called and from day one Spirit said 'you two can be beneficial to each other,' not as a couple, but helping each other out.

Did you have stuff happen to you as a kid; weird dreams and visions?

No, I don't remember anything like that but I did have an imaginary friend as a kid though not for very long. There was a period of time my brother and I shared a bunk bed and I was on top, but as I got older and bigger my parents switched us so he was on the top. I was about 11 or 12 years old. That summer I started being visited by what I termed 'my little green buddy'; my alien

---

* Note: Laurie's chapter will relate to John's as they were both in Boulder.

friend, or whatever you want to call him. I don't remember much about the visits. All I remember was I could hear him coming for me and I'd be scared to death hiding under the covers. The next thing I'd know was I'd wake up and it was the next morning. That happened throughout that summer. I got thinking that since my brother and I had switched places in the bunk, maybe it was him they used to visit.

The summer of '88, my first wife, Carol, moved out and I bought her half of the house, and I was living in the country in northern Maryland. There happened to be a Sunday night when I got up to go to the bathroom, about 3:00AM. I walked in the bathroom and looked out the window and there was a spaceship in my back yard. My first reaction was to open the window and holler, I'll be right out! But before I could get the window open, they were in my bedroom saying 'come on John, let's go!'

I followed them and got within 20 feet of the spaceship but don't remember anything else. The next morning, a Monday, I had taken a shower and was drying my hair and brushing it and found four scabs in a rectangular pattern of about 1" by 2" on the back of my head. Each scab was the size of a baby fingernail. And I didn't think anything of it. I went to work that day and stopped on the way home to get a haircut and the gal that cut my hair mentioned it, but I still didn't think much about it. This is when I had started my meditation classes with Nancy Fox, so on Thursday it was class and I went to her house. I walked in the house and gave her a hug hello and sat on the couch. She just looked at me and said, 'you got visited this week, didn't you?'

I said, yup, and she said, they put something in your head, didn't they? I said, yup. She's a psychic, so she knew that. She said they put something in my head to make me a better receiver; they fine-tuned me I guess. I didn't notice changes immediately but now I hear voices, I see things and stuff where none of that used to happen. For probably two or three months after that, they used to come for me every night! As soon as I got in bed, or even when I walked in the bedroom they'd be there. It was the same thing, I'd get within 20 feet of the spaceship and I'd wake up in the morning.

What did they look like?

They were about 4 1/2 or 5 feet tall, with the traditional eyes and head you see a lot of traditional pictures of, and were kind of blue violet in color. I think they were just part; we all have a soul group or soul committee that we get together with before we incarnate in this lifetime to go over the kind of issues we are going to work on and I think I'm just part of that group. I'm here because I'm the lively one of the bunch. After that two or three months, I haven't seen them since.

In March of '98 I made my last trip to Mexico with people I studied with here that was just for fun. We stayed in some town in the Yucatan and had a week of meditation, yoga and swimming and lots of fun. I was in a room by myself, and one night they came for me there; 'come on John, let's go' I walked out to the beach, we walked down the beach turned to go into the jungle, and there was the spaceship. That was the last time I am conscious of them being around.

I've been reading about Pleiadians. Do you think that's who they are?

I think that's what they are and that's what I am and where I'm from. I remember on a (Shamanic) journey one time I asked Spirit to take me to the planet I am from and they took me to a Pleiadian planet. It was all red in color and with crystalline type structures. I got to stand there a few minutes and just look before they brought me back here.

Wow! This is like adventures beyond science fiction. The truth is harder sometimes to believe than fiction.

I've developed the idea that science is never going to find the missing link because there is not one. I think God, or Spirit, or whatever you want to call it got tired of waiting for evolution because it was taking too long for man to evolve from whatever he started from so we were brought here from other planets. There's four different races on this planet, so we came from four different planets.

Tell me about being a shaman. What does that involve?

As I said, it was when my first wife and I were having trouble that I went to that psychic reading with Nancy Fox. Well, after things went haywire with my second wife, I went back to Nancy for another reading to see what she might have to tell me. It was then that she told me that a shamanic journey may be a way for you to get messages for yourself; by the way my classes start this next week and I'm limiting it to five people and there's room for one more. So I thought okay, I'm supposed to be in this class.

Now, for me, all my meditations were never that spectacular. I'd go to meditation group and usually it was a bunch of women and if there was a meditation we would share what happened and sometimes they talked about places they went, beings they saw and they'd say, "John, what happened to you?" and I'd say I saw a flash of blue light. That's all I ever did.

But, when I went to that first shamanic journey class, and journeyed for the first time, I got out of my body and I was seeing guides and it was just wonderful. I knew this is what I want to do; this is what I'm supposed to do. And I know I'd done this in previous lifetimes, I'd spent multiple lifetimes as a Native American and I was a shaman. So, journeying, a shamanic journey, (and you might meet some shamans that don't do this at all- they do regular energy work, Reiki and that stuff), but what I do and what most shamans do; I'm able to lay down and leave my body.

Shamans journey or travel to a drum beat, so you can have somebody else beating a drum like the rhythm of a heartbeat, but I have a CD and I play that. It just makes it easy for us, and it gives my body something to focus on and help me pop out of it. That's the only way I can explain that. So I'm able to lay down and leave my body, and once I leave my body I have guides who meet me. When Nancy taught me to journey, and I'll say typically she calls it Celtic Shamanism, so my guide that redirects with me was a black knight from medieval times. And once I started working with the group out here in Colorado, that was Toltec shamanism, and my guide in this Toltec shamanism is a large female wolf named Sheba and the knight's name is Belcher. Shamanism as we know it today is the oldest form of spiritual practice that exists and dates back over 50,000 years.

All tribes, primitive cultures, or whatever had shamans. The chief was the medicine man and the shaman was like the spiritual liaison between the group and spirit. Shamans worldwide pretty much do the same thing (with little difference). When I journey, there is a porthole I use to go to other worlds and shamans are told to go to the lower world, the upper world or stay in this world, and the porthole is there to help us with that. So when I first learned to journey in Celtic Shamanism, the porthole I used was a tree in England. Once I was out of my body and I would go to this tree, then could go down the roots depending on where I was going or the purpose of the journey was. But, we (shamans) depending on where you live, do the same thing.

A shaman in Africa might have a giraffe, or rhinoceros, or elephant as a guide. A shaman in Northern Europe might have a guide that is a black knight, and I know somebody who has Lady Guinevere as a guide on journeys. King Arthur existed, but not on this physical plane. A shaman in North America might have a mountain lion, a crow, a turtle, or something in their area. Now if you ask shamans what they do, the number one answer would probably be a soul retrieval. Everything is energy. Your soul, being energy can fragment due to a traumatic experience, so whether it's from this lifetime or a previous lifetime, a part of your soul can sometimes be stuck in the time and place of that traumatic experience. Shamans travel back to retrieve those pieces of soul and bring them back (to the owner) to make them whole again.

Shamans carry crystals on these journeys so when I'm out of my body, even though there is a physical crystal in my physical body, there is a spiritual component to it that I carry with me.

Crystals store energy. When I encounter pieces of people that have fragmented off, I'm able to store them in that crystal. When I come back into my body then I'm able to integrate that energy back into the person's physical body using the heart and crown chakra.

When you look at part of a person, do you see just energy or some form?

I encounter that part of a person and the person themselves. To me in the journey it looks like it is the whole person. I can talk with them and get information on what caused that fragmentation, and then bring it back. I have a rattle I use to open up the person's aura, then I blow those energies from the crystal to the heart and crown chakras and close their aura up again.

I'll give you an example of one I did when I moved to Colorado. A friend of mine called me up and said, 'John, can you do a soul retrieval for my mom?' I said alright, what's going on? I found out that Mary was Iranian, living in Boulder at the time, had been sent to live here in the USA when she was three years old to be raised by relatives. For whatever reason, her parents could not leave Iran so Mary was raised here. Since the age of three, she had never seen her parents. Her mother visited in the 1990s and at that time, she was about 70 years old and didn't speak English. So Mary said her mother 'had a really big pain in her chest and we've had her to two hospitals and three different doctors and they all say there's something wrong with her. So we know there's something wrong and we want you to make a journey for her.' Mary explained to her mom what was going to happen. When I journey, people ask can I watch. I say sure, but I lay down when I leave my body and all they will see is just my body laying on the floor looking like it is asleep.

Mary explained to her mom and her mom was willing to try anything. We lay down in Mary's family room and I set up some candles by an alter where I can play my tape. So I pop out of my body, I meet my guide, and the first thing we do is go to this really large lake. Now, whether it's a dream, a meditation, or shamanic journey, the symbolism is the same. Water symbolizes emotion.

This lake was a very large lake, so I knew she was a very emotional person, and it was also dead calm so I knew if the water was quiet, everything emotionally was okay. Then my guide said, 'now we're going to walk up the river that feeds this lake and as we do, we're going back in time.' So we walked up this path along the side of the river that I could tell was between five and six meters and there was a waterfall. With water being emotion, a waterfall meant something upsetting that happened. And there was Mary's mother at the base of the waterfall. She didn't speak English, but in journey, we could understand each other. The only thing she would say was she was afraid and didn't know what was going to happen and didn't know what to do; that's all she kept repeating.

I was able to absorb that part of her into the crystal and my guide said, 'now we're going to go way upstream to where she is 17 years old. When I see her, she's in a multicolored dress and there is a party going on, so I knew when she was 17, everything was okay. My guide then said, 'now we're going to step back and look at what happened between these two time periods.' The waterfall was when she was 65, and the time now, she was 17. As we move back down the river, there wasn't a calm spot. It was all waterfalls, whitewater and rapids and since water was emotion, her whole life from 17 to the last waterfall was just one big emotional wreck.

Well, years ago when I first walked the journey, I met these people I call the dog men that live within the earth, called the lower world. The dog men do healing on people and places. So, on this journey as my guide and I are watching the river, the dog men show up and start to walk up and down the river picking up pieces of her heart. Now, the dog men have a shaman as well, and his name is Kakuma. They handed all those pieces of her heart to him, and remember this is all symbolic. I watched him sew all those pieces together to make a whole heart, then he gave it to me to give back to her. So that is the two pieces; the heart and the waterfall that I brought back to her. I came back to my body and do what I have to do to get those energies back into her body and I start to tell her what happened in the journey.

It was five and a half years earlier that her husband died and that was the waterfall I could tell was between five and six years. She was 17 years old when they got married and had their first child and that was the happy time. He was a very controlling person and she could not do anything in her whole life except breathe without his permission. That's why when he died; she didn't know what was going to happen because she never had any control in her life. There was a lot of conversation about that and I learned a lot about her parents through the conversation so that aided in the healing. It was a couple days later that Mary called me up and said all the pain in her mother's chest was gone! That's an example of a soul retrieval that also had healing effects and that can quite often happen.

I worked on a guy years ago that had abdominal problems and my journey took me to retrieve a piece of him that (I don't remember, four lifetimes ago) when he was stabbed in the gut and killed. The subsequent lifetimes after that (you've got six other bodies besides your physical body) as you incarnate into physical form, you cut through these other worlds, you cut through these planes or other vibration levels, whatever you want to call that, and you attract this subtle substance to you in each one of those planes. Now when your central makeup has that traumatic experience of, in this case, of stabbing, those other bodies are your aura. So when he came to those other planes and attracted the subtle substance to him that made up his aura, it was all charged emotionally with that stabbing. In this lifetime, everything manifests in physical form, and though it took 40 years with that being in his aura, it manifested into this physical ailment of abdominal problems, so once that piece was retrieved and brought back to him and explained to him, his problems went away.

If somebody isn't having problems that they know of, do they ever ask for retrieval to see if they had anything in their past that they need help with?

Yeah. I've encountered a few people that did not have some kind of fragmentation. Sometimes things can be so subtle. For instance, a child whose father does nothing any day but go to work, can wind up with a fragmentation and an issue around abandonment, even though the father never abandoned the child, that's the way the child perceives it; dad is going off to work every day and leaving me alone. So when I talk about traumatic experiences, it may not look that way to an adult, but does look that way for a child.

A lot of times a soul retrieval can bring back a piece of soul that is fragmented that, even at the time, doesn't seem like that big of a deal. But, once it's brought back and explained to the person, they can see how it's affecting their life. Not long ago I did a soul retrieval for a younger gal and there was a piece I brought back from when she was four or five years old when she was playing on a playground and all her friends ran off and left her; they didn't want her to be part of the group. The way that manifested in later life is that she now self-sabotages any relationships and friendships because she's expecting that to happen. So, rather than have it happen to her, she sets up some scenario that drives the other person away because she doesn't want it to happen to her. That's something that is pretty subtle, not a big traumatic thing.

So my fear of airplanes and claustrophobia could be from something in my past?

A past lifetime probably. Your body is a computer just like the one you buy in the store, preloaded with programs from past lifetimes. In this lifetime, other things are programmed in; your parents, grandparents, people who raised you, and things that happened when you were younger. An example of something from the past life; we're born with a major archetype pattern. There are eight of those, though I don't remember what they are anymore.

Years ago I went to a Practitioner of Healing worker and when you get there they identify the major archetype pattern you are going with and kind of explain how it's affecting your life now. If you ask them to, with the help of angelic forces, they will change or remove that. When I went to that person, he explained to me that my major archetype pattern was the soldier/slave. What a soldier/

slave does or doesn't do is they don't do anything until they're told to; they can't do anything until they're told to. So, just hearing that, the lightbulb went off. My light was Black & Decker (John's former employer) up to that point where I had a boss that wouldn't let me do anything unless he told me exactly what to do. I knew what to do and tried to do it on my own and he would say, 'no, I want everything to come through me'.

Well, after having that reading, within six weeks, I was transferred to a different boss that gave me free range to do anything and everything I wanted to do. It was just amazing! Now, another frustrating part of the story, once I moved to Colorado, (I work as a real estate agent now), I got my real estate broker's license. When I first got it, I hired on as a buyer's agent for a big guy in Boulder, who had about eight buyer's agents working under him. We were supposed to give all our listing leads to him and he was supposed to give us buyer leads, but that wasn't working out. So, after a few months, I started working on my own.

That night I had a dream. In the dream I was at my funeral and I watched as a woman walked up to the casket and put a little piece of army helmet on that casket. So, to me, deciding not to work for the big guy, and working totally on my own was the last bit of the soldier that was dead. She put that little tiny piece of helmet right on the casket, I knew it was my funeral, she was probably saying, 'the soldier's dead'.

What do you do for people that you charge for?

I have a fee but generally reduce it if the person has come to me before, depending on what needs to be done. Sometimes real estate agents call me because they need me to do a clearing on a house. I do a soul retrieval and that's the only one I do where a person has to be with me because I have to be able to put that energy back into the person's physical body. I journey for healing or reclamation too, and I get calls from time to time from all around the country.

However, I had it happen one time, my friend Jane, who used to live here, asked me to do a journey for her sister. My conscious mind went to work; she is in Maryland and I'm here, how am I supposed to do the soul retrieval? And Spirit said you just do it and it will work! So I grabbed my crystal and lay down to journey, but spirit said go wash your crystal off first. That's how you clean a crystal; you can set it out in the rain or whatever. It had already been cleaned, but they wanted me to rinse it off. I went to the bathroom to rinse it off, and they (Spirit) knocked it out of my hand and a little piece of the crystal slivered off. So I thought to myself, okay, this is how it's going to work, I have to take that little piece that broke off for her soul retrieval. (After the retrieval) I mailed that little piece to Jane with instructions of what to do with it when she guides (her sister). She was able to put the soul piece back into her sister's crown chakra, she was a very spiritual woman and used my instructions to finish it up. That was the only time I didn't lay by the person.

Do you delve into past lives?

It depends on the intention. If it takes me there, that's fine, but I wouldn't use it on a past life regression or anything like that. Quite often the journey will take me to a past life to retrieve part of somebody. Maybe back four or five lifetimes, there is a piece of the person that is bad or something happened to them, then I bring it back. It really doesn't matter a whole lot whether the past life was within that time, because my guides will take me wherever I need to go to do that retrieval.

One time, I was doing a retrieval for a woman here in Boulder, so I went on the journey and popped out of my body and meet my two guides, Sheba and Belcher and I say okay, guys, who's going with me, and they both said, 'not me'! If that ever happens again I'll be a little more leery, but then I didn't think anything of it and went on the journey by myself. I encountered a piece of this woman when she was eight years old and being molested by her mother's boyfriend. It was almost like a scene out of Poltergeist. This male energy did not want to let the piece of this little girl go, it was windy and there were branches and tree limbs blowing around and it got kind of scary. I tried to convince this eight year old girl to come back with me instead of this man who was molesting her, but toward the end of the journey Sheba the wolf did show up. When Sheba showed up, it helped the little girl trust me and came running right across that street with all the branches and things blowing around from this wind. I then came back in my body and just to prove that things manifest from spirit into physical form, when I looked at my body, it was covered with bruises from where those branches hit me on the journey.

Were the branches blowing symbolic of the turmoil that was going on?

Probably, yes. In the journey it's like it is all real but is symbolic, just like the water represents emotion; it was symbolic of all the turmoil that there was still an actual majority of physical damage at home being done by that. I guess it's possible that something could have happened that might have stopped me from being able to get back into my body at that time it's not impossible; in which case, you could say I would die if I couldn't come back to my physical body and I would have stayed there forever. If you've ever read about anyone who has had out of body experiences, or near death experiences, it's all the same thing. Your etheric body, the body next to your physical one, forms a silver thread that ties your consciousness back to your physical body and people who have had the near death experience see that silver thread. If that thread gets broken, I understand you're going to die, that is, your highest self won't be able to get back into your physical body. I've never talked to anybody who has had it happen (who is now deceased), but that is my understanding.

My son-in-law travels out of body and looks back to see a silver thread but it is attached at the navel.

I don't think it matters where it is attached, only that it is attached somewhere. He should find a group or teacher that he could study with.

The only thing I've really been told, though I've never encountered it, is to avoid anything with a stinger. I'm not really sure why, maybe in the journey it could puncture your aura and could give you some damage, but I've never encountered anything like that. Another thing I've been told is that when you journey for someone else, you may encounter one of their guides or a totem animal. When you encounter them, you want to ask that guide or totem the same question three times; 'are you a guide for this person? Or, are you an animal for this person? Or, are you who I should be talking to for this person?' You have to ask them three times and get an affirmative answer three times.

One time I encountered an owl and I asked the owl, 'are you a guide for this person?' The first two times it said it was. The third time it said, 'no, you must talk to this golden eagle.' So I don't know why it works that way, but there's something magical about asking three times and getting the same answer three times.

What would you say your gifts are? As I talk to different mediums, they seem to have very varied (specific) gifts.

I guess my gift or talent is being able to journey. Everything I do, whether it's a soul retrieval, whether it's a journey out of body- say, specifically for healing, I do what I call, 'exorcisms', where if there are entities or things attached to people, I'm able to remove those. I clear energy and negativity from buildings or homes and that kind of stuff, but no matter what I do, it's all from a journey state. So I guess the one talent I have is to be able to journey. Once my intention is set for my journey, I just go and watch and see what- ever happens. Very little do I at that point have to direct anything further. I just experience what goes on and bring back information, watch Kakuma or other beings, or the angel, Michael, do what they do. Sometimes they ask me to participate and help them bring back certain things.

Since I've moved to Colorado, spirit has had me deal a lot with dark energy; clearing dark energies. I worked on the Jon Benet house, I worked on Columbine High School after those shootings, I worked on the World Trade Center after that happened, I helped those involved in the Virginia Tech shootings, and in awhile I'll be working on the theatre shootings here just to help those beings move on because a lot of people, when they die, don't know what to expect. They haven't been taught, or what did their religion teach them maybe that they were going to hell. So, a lot of times when people die and don't know what to expect and because this was the only world they saw when they were living, it's the only world they see when they die and are out of their body. Just because you can't see an angel next to you when you are in your physical body, doesn't mean that when you are out of body you will see it either. You kind of have to be prepared and know what to expect.

So a lot of what I do in these circumstances when I'm working on a house or building is I'm able to go in and talk to the beings that were there and help them see the other realm. And once they see the help that's there for them, they usually don't want to hang around. They want to go!

Is it easier for them to see angels when out of body compared to when they were in physical form?

Yeah. Even if they don't see anything when out of body, when I show up in journey, just the fact that they can see and talk to me … you know, everything is energy, and I always say in these journeys I act as a transformer; transformers step energy up and down. So when I show up in a journey and they can see me, the energy levels raise up enough that they can see beings there to help them, and they don't want to hang around, they want to go.

Are they embraced by the others (spirits) that have been around them?

Yes, definitely. We're all going to have somebody there for us when we die, or pass over, or whatever you want to call that. Years ago, when I first got into meditation, I realized that my guide, (if you want to call it a guide); the person who was there for me in spirit was my dad's father, Gus. Once I started studying and learning, I attracted other guides to me who would help me do whatever it was I wanted to do for the next step in my life and moved on. When my mom passed away when I moved here in '97, I always knew her parents would be there for her. And the night she passed away, I journeyed for the full purpose of seeing my mom, which I did, but I encountered her parents first and I talked to them. We all have help in that realm, but a lot of people don't know what to expect when they die; have never been taught what to expect, so they don't know to look for that (spirits).

What did her parents talk about?

It was kind of like 'hi, how you doing?' shoot the breeze kind of stuff. And, it was funny that my mom, (who spent the last 12-15 years of her life in a recliner in the living room, she had diabetes and couldn't walk especially the last year), well, when I was young, she was the boss of the house. She ran the household and the family and when she barked out her orders, people jumped. So, as she got older and was sitting in that chair, she still barked out her orders, but we listened less and less. And it was interesting to see my dad have to take over her roll of being leader of the house after all the years when my mom was boss. So, she died and that night I journeyed, and I met my grandparents and they were all happy and smiles and how are you, but they kept chuckling every time I was talking to them. 'What's so funny?' Well, they finally stepped aside and there was my mom in a chair barking out orders to everybody around and nobody was paying any attention to her. I have seen her since, and she is no longer that person in the chair. Years later she looked like she did when she was 30 years old. And since then, she has moved on as there are lessons to learn there as well as here, so she'll be learning those lessons there before she comes back here again.

That's good to hear because my mom is living in a chair right now and it's so sad to see her that way when she's been such an energetic person all her life.

Why would someone go to a shaman rather than going to sit with a medium where they can hear things about themselves?

The medium, or psychic, is going to give you some insight into what's going on in your life and the direction you should take. A shaman is going to retrieve pieces of a fragmented soul. When I first moved out here, I got involved in a group called the Colorado Center for Spiritual Growth but I ended up being the president for three years. A couple years after that I got a call from somebody; it was this guy and his son who started having these episodes where he would go into some kind of fit and go into a rage and he destroyed a bathroom in their house. He was only six years old. The father said, 'we didn't have much religious upbringing or spiritual understanding, but we've been to two different psychics to get some understanding of what's going on and both of them said I need a shaman to do what needs to be done.' This is the first exorcism I ever did.

I was on an hour drive (to his house) and talking to my spirits saying, 'okay, guys, help me out here, I've never done one of these before and I don't know what I'm doing.' So, I got down to the house and did one of my journeys; I'm actually lying down in the little boy's bedroom. I pop out of my body and encounter the little boy, and there is something being stuck or attached to him that looked like a monkey. That is, it looked like a monkey but had no arms or legs and his tail was entwined around this little boy's spinal column. Other beings showed up to help me remove it from the boy, and what I was told was when the little boy was two years old, he had an operation. At the time, a guardian spirit assigned Red to protect the little boy during the operation. (When you are cut open, you are really susceptible to a lot of stuff coming in and attaching itself to you). Red was assigned to protect the little boy, but since Red was put there by some other being, it could not leave on its own. For years it had kind of stuck there with this little boy.

What seems to happen when there is a being that is stuck, whether it's in a house or to a person, they start to act a little bit nasty and end up attracting the kind of help they need to help them. So, by acting a bit nasty, this little boy was having an episode where he destroyed a bathroom and he would tell his parents he was going to kill them and his sister and this kind of stuff. Anyway, I encountered Red and learned this information and other beings showed up to remove him. Ethereally it left a big hole in the boy's aura so I used a golden light to fill the voids in so it could heal itself. So, with Red removed, the little boy was fine. A psychic wouldn't be able to do that. Only a shaman once we're out of our body can see those things, talk to those things and attract the other help that's needed.

Okay. So psychics can tell but the shaman acts upon it.

Yep. Basically the two psychics they had gone to couldn't really give them a lot of information as to what was going on but all they told the father was that you need a shaman to get those things done. I will tell you these stories; when I first got into all this stuff back in Maryland, not far from where I lived, a friend named Jane Howard, had just written a book at the time called, Commune with the Angels: A Heavenly Handbook. She did angelic energy and channeling sessions. So, I went to her for one of her sessions, and I'm kind of new to all this stuff. I was lying on her massage table; she's waving her hands around, and telling me what the angels are saying. At one point in the session, it got kind of quiet, and she said 'wow'. I said wow what and she said the Archangel Michael just showed up. At the time I didn't know who he was. He said he's taking his sword and placing it along your spinal column and he's doing something to align your energy to his. (Again, I was still laying there, thinking okay.) We got done with the session and as I was leaving her house, she said that sometime in the next three days, your body will give you an indication that this alignment will have taken place. (This was Wednesday afternoon.) So, Friday, at Black & Decker, I got to my desk and as soon as I sat down my body started to do something that is pretty much indescribable. It was vibrating, you couldn't see it, but I could feel my whole body vibrating, I could feel every drop of blood going through every vein, artery and capillary in my whole body. I could feel my blood system through my whole body. I just sat there for 15 minutes experiencing that, but I knew not to be afraid of it because this was what she had been talking about. I guess it was confirmation that this alignment had taken place.

Now, usually after lunchtime there would be five to seven people standing around my desk talking and of course, that day there was nobody. That was about in 1988 or 89, when that happened. On one of my last business trips with Black & Decker, before I moved to Colorado in 1997, that spring, after my couple weeks of business, a few of us went to Rome for a few days, doing all the touristy stuff. One day I wanted to go see the Sistine Chapel. The four of us got there and there was a big long line, about a block long, so the other guys said they weren't waiting and left. I figured I don't know when I'll ever get back here so I'm going to wait. I got in line and it wasn't five minutes later they opened the doors and the line disappeared; it goes through a big part of the museum, then you get to see the Sistine Chapel, then you go through the rest of the museum and back out on the street. So, after they opened the door everyone moves off to the side and it's not a crowd like you'd think. It was an all day affair at the museum and was about 5:00 when I walked outside again onto the boulevard in front of me. I looked at my watch and wondered, do I want to get something to eat, do I want to go back to the hotel, or do I want to find the guys I came with.

While I was standing there with nobody else around, this little Italian grandmother who looked like she was 100 years old and about four foot nothing, walked up to me all dressed in black and purple, and probably mumbled something in Italian, but it sounded to me like, 'this belongs to you'. So I went to take it and look at her to tell her I think she's got the wrong person, and she had disappeared. She was not there! I unwrapped this thing, and it was a figurine of the Archangel Michael slaying a demon with his sword. That was kind of an indication that this Archangel Michael was there!

In February of 1998 (after moving here in 1997), I went to the movies with a group of friends here; the movie, Fallen, with Denzel Washington. It's a neat movie, where he is a cop and investigates the murder of another cop a few years earlier. At one point, he's at this other cops cabin in the Midwest woods. He throws this book down on a desk and opens it up. As soon as he did that, as I sat there thinking, that's Manly P. Hull's, Secret Teachings. As soon as I had that thought, a spirit shows up in the movie and starts a conversation with him basically saying you need to go to your storage locker and get your copy of the book. He questioned what for and was told there are a couple chapters you need to read up on. (Then John wonders ...) What chapters are they? Just go get the book; you'll know which ones to read. Why do I need to do this? Because it's a house I want you to work on. Well, what house is that? It's the Ramsey house. What do I do when I get there? You just go and you'll know what to do.

Do you know what I mean by the Ramsey house, Jon Benet Ramsey, the little girl (in Boulder) who was murdered? Well, this happened in February (to me at the movie) and it was March when a group of shamans were going down to New Mexico, and I was going to wait until I got home from that trip to do work on the Ramsey house. Spirit said, no, no, no, you do it before you go. I'm a real estate agent, and the house was for sale at the time; and when I do journeys for houses, I don't physically have to be in the house, but I was curious to see what the house looked like, so I physically went down there and let myself in; there was nobody living there at the time. I lay down in the living room and put on my tapes I play when I pop out of my body and I go outside the house and I'm looking at it. It's like something out of a Hollywood movie, dark and dingy with weird sounds, and I'm thinking I still don't know what I'm supposed to do here.

Well, this is a journey of when the dog men show up. They all surround the house and they are beating drums but I still don't know what I'm supposed to be doing. All of a sudden, this presence walked up behind me, this intense light that shines all around me, and I knew the Archangel Michael was standing right behind me. The next thing I know is that his arm comes around and he handed me his sword and that just blew me away! My next thought was, "Why can't you (Michael) do this?" And yet, some energy levels can't interact with others. It's like, in our physical body we may not be able to see an angel that's in the room, because there are some levels that are higher up than others so they can't interact with each other. But, as a shaman in these journeys, I can act as a transformer. I can interact on both levels where Archangel Michael couldn't interact directly.

So, I've got his sword in my hand and I walk up the sidewalk and it was like a Hollywood movie; the darkness just moved away! I took the sword and pierced the front door with it. I don't know what told me to do that, I just knew to do it, but then it was like the roof blew off and for five minutes it was kind of like the energy was released to the heavens which meant it cleared or transmuted or whatever. I walked around the outside of the house with this sword and didn't see any more of these dark energies. I gave the sword back and went back into my body and returned home figuring I was all done.

But, two days later Spirit said no, no, no, you're not finished. You need to journey again to that house. So the second journey I didn't go there, I just lay down, popped out of my body and went down to the house. When I got there, all that dark energy and stuff was still gone, but there was the little girl, JonBenet still in the house, and there was a light cord of energy that ran from her to every room in the house. As a child, that's the only thing you know is your home, and she was very connected. So, another angel showed up and handed me this flaming torch and I walked into the house and burned through those cords of energy. When I burned through the last one, three angels showed up and took her away, and, in the journey, set the house on fire. All this was transmutation or cleansing so in that space, the house was cleansed out. I gave that being the torch back and I was back in my body and was gone. The house was clean, the little girl was gone. You can't get a psychic to do that. Psychics use a different tool, they do different things.

That's exciting. But, you never got any feeling of what had happened?

I was given information and it was confirmed by other psychics I know. That death was an accident, the death was not intentional. Her parents were involved with a group of pedophiles, high powered and influential people which is why they've been able to cover it up so well. They were having a party, they knew who was with their daughter that night, but the death itself was an accident even though it was pretty bizarre. I've talked to psychics in town and they all say the same kind of thing. That's why Patsy (the mom) wrote that note, and why they've been so successful, they didn't want anyone to know of course that there were other people involved at the party. Since then they've remodeled the house, it's been added on to, and doesn't look anything like it used to, except on the outside and they've changed the address to keep people away.

When you see angels, do they have wings?

No, wings are just the light. They have such an intense light about them that it can kind of look like wings. Why would an angelic being need wings?

Logic told me that, but people swear they saw an angel with wings, and I thought that if there was such light and energy being given off by them, it would look like that.

I have a friend here in Boulder, who as a teenager, lost a sister and for so many weeks and months was so distraught. She told me that one night, in the middle of the night, she went to church (and this was back when churches were open), didn't turn on any lights and felt her way to a pew to sit down. She sat there asking why couldn't it have been her instead of her sister. All of a sudden an angel appeared in the church and lit the church up and she said this angel was probably 15 feet tall! To her, it looked like it had wings. The angel told her that it couldn't have been her (who was taken), and said other things that made her feel better and get over her grief. I think a lot of times it's possible that people may not see wings, but to a child, who may expect it to have wings, it may just appear that way or they wouldn't know what it was.

Jesus has appeared to me and some friends asked what did he look like? He looked like what we would expect him to look like the pictures we've seen. If he'd shown up looking like Ronald McDonald, I wouldn't have known who it was. An angel, especially to a child, may appear with wings just so the child knows it is an angel. If it was a being that just showed up, the person would probably be scared. I think a lot of times what you expect is what happens, Caucasian Jesus or Middle Eastern Jesus. I'll tell you a story.

When I was working at Black & Decker I told people I was taking classes to learn how to meditate. As it turned out, two of the guys I worked with were born again Christians who decided to save me from this devil worship. Maybe that was a good thing. I would talk to Spirit and say I don't want to do anything that is wrong, so if this is wrong, you just let me know. So, just the opposite was proven over time, and over time, Spirit would answer any question I had, whatever it was, they would answer except when it came to Jesus they wouldn't answer any questions. I kind of realized they wanted me to develop my own thoughts and my own beliefs. So, probably 10 or 11 years ago I was living just south of Boulder, it happened on a Saturday night I was sitting in my living room in a chair and I started thinking about Jesus. I kind of went down this checklist of 'this is what I believe'; this happened, this didn't happen; this is why this happened, and went down this whole list of things.

As soon as I was done, he appeared in my living room just as solid as you and I are, and he confirmed my whole list and pretty much said I was correct in my head. He kind of told me to keep up the good work and he disappeared. That was pretty cool!

Where are you going from here? Do you see yourself growing in other ways in the future?

I don't really know. I ask spirit all the time that if there is a next step, to let me know what it is. I'm probably happy doing this work for the rest of my life because it has great benefit to it. Years ago, not long after I moved here, a friend of mine who was a Baptist minister and I would get together once in a while and have some nice conversation, well, one time when we were at lunch, it was just a couple weeks after the Columbine shooting, I said to him that I'd like to do some shaman work, clearing work, on the school. After lunch, we went back to his office which is where I left my cell phone. I checked my messages and had one from Jane, the Jefferson Co. High School Administrator who was having lunch with a friend of mine, Faye, who is a shaman I had been studying with. She told Jane 'I want to get someone to do some clearing work or energy work on the school and Faye said 'get my friend, John'. And that's how I came to do Columbine High School.

Bill, the minister, was a member of the Rotary Club and a couple of times asked me to join one of their Wednesday breakfast meetings, so I finally said yeah, I'll go with you to your next meeting. Before that, I had been talking to Spirit and said you know one thing I could do with this talent, or whatever you call it, is I could help find missing children. I went to the next meeting and didn't realize they had speakers at these meetings. That meeting the speaker was David Rogers, who was the head of the missing children's taskforce in Colorado.

I told him a little bit about what I do and he started sending me cases, kids that were missing, that I could journey for to get information. Depending on the child I would see different information. I'd see a picture of a house; I'd see an address, or a car or a truck. So I started doing this for him so they could find some of these missing kids. I had some limited success but for whatever reason, it stopped working. I don't know why or maybe it didn't stop working, maybe the information just didn't pan out for one reason or another and he stopped sending me cases to work on. But, I still would like to do something like that.

I talked to Laurie (see Chapter XV), who I taught and she has been journeying a little bit, and I said with America's Most Wanted, might be a way to make some extra money if we could get some information on how to catch some of these fugitives (and they have a reward), we could help out by helping catch these people.

I've actually done that for a couple different cases and I don't know what happened, but I've given tips to police on a couple different ones but so far I don't think anything panned out on them, but I'm going to start doing that more and more too.

Do you sense any shift coming for December 21, 2012?

I don't think there will be any great things happen. As far as Earth changes go, I think they have been going on for some time. Let's face it, earthquakes, hurricanes and tornadoes have gotten worse in the last several years and I think that stuff may continue. As far as the Mayan calendar goes, you know we've got calendars that end every December 31st and January 1st still shows up. It will be interesting to see what happens, but I don't think it will be the major catastrophic events that were predicted years ago. The Mayan calendar, or prophesy, says there will be two outcomes to December 21st. One is all major catastrophic stuff and the other is not so bad and I think we're going to experience the one that is not so bad.

I think what might change is changes of attitude. People may become more informed and educated and it may change the way some governments operate, including our own. Those kind of changes with systems and management of governments; I don't think it's the major physical changes to the earth.

There's a series of books called the Kryon Series (Lee Carroll), a Kryon is a channeled being. The first book that came out in the 80s, talks about how there will be some changes to the earth even in the 1990s. In 1998-99 there was a major shift in the earth's magnetic pole moving several degrees from its rotational axis, so much so that a lot of airports in northern Europe had to be numbered; for many months homing pigeons couldn't find their way home because of this magnetic change that happened. Kryon says that the way beings can judge the consciousness of the many on the planet is the distance, or how far the magnetic pole is away from the rotational axis.

There was a woman, Laurie Toye, who, many years ago, was

visited at night by beings of light and they showed her a map of the United States and what it was going to look like after all these major changes. It's called the I Am America map. The first map showed major changes like the Gulf of Mexico was up to Omaha, Nebraska. California dropped away and Washington and Oregon weren't there; they were under water. The east coast wasn't there. The Great Lakes drained into the Gulf of Mexico; lots of changes. Over time, months later, they (the light beings) would appear to her and show her maps of lesser and lesser severity, so the last map she was given didn't show any changes at all. So, I think it's an indication like the shift when the magnetic axis changes from the rotational axis that our consciousness has improved and maybe humanity doesn't have to suffer the major change that was planned maybe a hundred years ago. I don't think that's going to happen.

Thank you for your time with me! I'd like to get down to Colorado to try out your traveling for me.

(John speaks of future traveling.) I've never had one this dramatic myself, but I have heard that soul retrievals could be so dramatic depending on the energy that's brought back, people's eye color can instantly change. I would imagine it was a huge piece that has gone back (has been retrieved). Certainly in my circumstances there is physical healing that takes place; quite often a relationship with another person changes right away. Sometimes when it is an issue of the molestation of a young child like years ago when one person does the work (retrieval), all of a sudden in two weeks the other person is calling up to apologize and it's amazing that can happen.

— CHAPTER 10 —

CHRISTINE DAY

Bio: CHRISTINE DAY is a leading spiritual teacher, healer, and channel who has been working throughout the USA and internationally for over 17 years. Following a traumatic childhood in her native Australia, Christine was diagnosed with advanced Systemic Lupus at the age of 31 and given a short time to live. Shortly afterward, she experienced a profound spiritual awakening with the Pleiadians; the energy of which moved her to a place of complete self-healing. Since then Christine has been working with the Pleiadian initiations of people throughout the United States and internationally.

***

Who are the Pleiadians?
THE PLEIADIAN STORY by Christine Day

IN 1994 I HAD MY FIRST CONSCIOUS CONNECTION TO AND communication with the Pleiadians. It sounds extraordinary, I know, but this is exactly how it happened.

I was out walking in nature. I turned a corner into a meadow and found myself staring at a huge space ship about 20 meters away from me. Coming out of the ship was a group of ten Pleiadians. As they moved towards me they were greeting me telepathically. I was immediately filled with an overwhelming sense of their love for me; a love that instantly awoke within me a deep remembrance of my Pleiadian heritage. It brought me to the memory of what I had pre-agreed to do on this earth plane in this lifetime.

With startling clarity, I instantly remembered my mission here: I was to act as a Pleiadian ambassador here on this earth plane. My role was to be a bridge between the Pleiadians and humans; to create a deeper understanding and awareness of the existence of the Pleiadians, so that we, as human beings, would have an opportunity to open up and receive the support that they can bring us. This support is essential for all of us at this time of great change on this earth plane.

But my most important role was to bring an understanding to the Pleiadians of how we need to process as human beings. This understanding was necessary for the Pleiadians, and would allow them to create a series of light initiations that could work for us, while bypassing the human ego. The Pleiadians activate these light energies in the form of light initiations so that we can birth ourselves within these energies and fully utilize and work with them for our awakening process.

The Pleiadians are here on our earth plane to aid in the dimensional birthing of our planet and to assist those of us that are willing to awaken to full knowledge and understanding of ourselves. They hold what they call 'energetic platforms,' which open up powerful opportunities for us to re-align back into our natural spiritual natures, which is to say, our higher self.

You may be asking yourself why the Pleiadians are helping us? What's in it for them?

Understand that the entire Universe has its attention on planet earth at this time. The reason for this is that we are dimensionally transforming as a planet, and soon we will all be energetically re-aligned back into 'the family of light'. We will be taking our place and rejoining the 'whole', the Oneness, the God essence, whatever term resonates with you. The Pleiadians play a supporting role in this, as do many other alien energies. They want us to be part of the collective consciousness so that everyone, including them, can be complete.

The Pleiadians call this time 'The New Dawning,' and they say that we are 'The New Dawning.' There is a mutual birthing taking place within our planet and within the cells of our body, and it is moving us from a 3rd dimensional consciousness to a 4th/5th dimensional consciousness. They convey news of the dimensional shifts that are taking place on our planet, along with messages of Truth and understanding. They say that many of us hold a lot of fear around these changing times, and that their goal is to reduce our fear by bringing in the Truth of our next steps along with an understanding of our process so that we can more easily navigate our way through this transition.

The Pleiadians are here to support us on a personal level as well; however, they will always honor our free will as human beings, and thus will never enter our energetic space without our permission.

One of the most powerful messages the Pleiadians bring is the reminder that we are human beings birthing ourselves back into our spiritual natures. They say that we are "perfectly imperfect," and that it is in our very imperfection that we carry a vulnerability that is very important. So they remind us to always hold our human aspect with love, compassion and patience. They say it is important to understand that we are here to continue to have a human experience while birthing our spiritual natures.

The Pleiadians say that both we and our planet are going through a birthing of a new consciousness; our hearts are being transformed in readiness to anchor new levels of our own light. They also speak about the new energies of 2011. These energies demand that we begin to live differently; that we become accountable to ourselves with regard to the way we navigate the earth plane. They remind us of the importance of living in integrity and right action, which means honoring ourselves and being prepared to live our Truth, no matter what! They counsel us to stand tall and to call in the Universal energies for the support we need on a daily basis. We are not alone. It is time to join the Universal family of light, of which all of us are members. It is time to take our place, to open up and to receive all that is rightfully ours. All it takes is just one step from you, and a willingness to ask for support on a daily basis, and to receive that energy through your heart.

Each one of us has been called forth at this time because we are ready for this transformation. There has been a pre-agreement made for many of us to reconnect at this time. We all are energetically aligned with everyone else. You may not be aware of it on a 3rd dimensional level, but your spiritual light knows the importance of the connections being made here now on this earth plane. Together, you will birth individual aspects of your light, but collectively you will form a powerful synergy of light that is going to affect the entire planet as you work consciously with each other. It is not important that you remember this pre-agreement, what is important is that you are here, that you have come.

The Pleiadians honor and bless you for all that you are in this moment. They salute your courage in living your path at this time.

***

I had heard about Christine from my friend, Laurie (Chapter XV), and visited Christine's website to glean some information about her before I requested an interview. The Pleiadians come from a solar system in the star system called The Pleiades. They are said to be other dimensional and a race older than ancient! Some say they came to Earth to help with Earth's evolution and have only loving thoughts for us as well as our betterment. Some humans are able to channel messages from the Pleiadians and below, is a message channeled by Christine Day in 2012.

***

Message from the Pleiadians

Dear Ones, we greet you with love and appreciation for all that you are in this moment. This "Language of Light" work has been brought forth at this time to enable those of you who feel called to do so to take giant steps toward your own enlightenment process. We have crafted energies that will support you in being able to move back into a place of re-alignment to the Self, and remembrance of your place within the Universal Consciousness.

The time has come for many of you to reconnect to this aspect of your Self, so that you can navigate your place within the Collective. As you make your way back towards Self, you undergo a transformation that enables you to hold an "energetic platform"— an energetic mirror, as it were—for others to meet that aspect of themselves. In this manner, you enable many other humans to follow in your footsteps. This is part of your mission here, it is what you came here to do, and now is the time for this unfoldment.

We have many tools that will enable you to awaken to your Self. This Course is specifically designed to facilitate and accelerate this process. Our mission is simply to assist you when you call upon us, to adjust your energies, to aid you throughout your integration processes, and to support you in aligning back to your original design.

Our role is to provide you with the tools, and to open up specific energetic dimensional spaces that afford you the opportunity to move forward and awaken on different levels. We hold a loving space in which to birth yourself.

Know that the energetic grids we have set in this program contain an in-built support system that enables the spiritual realms— the Angels, Light Beings, Masters, and other light energies to come forth when called upon. The dimensional energies we set enable the spiritual realms to work with you in a unique way, supporting you in the most appropriate and beneficial manner, according to your individual needs as they arise.

We rejoice in your birthing and remembrance of yourself as spiritual beings, and we hold each one of you in your humanness as you take this next step; a journey that is designed not only to move you back into conscious remembrance, but also to provide you with a direct experience of your Spiritual essence. We honor you in your humanness and hold you with love as you embark on this important journey back towards Self.

Blessings,

The Pleiadians

***

Christine was just too busy with writing, seminars, lectures and media slots to be able to interview so I thought I'd try the next best thing; I'd get into her next seminar to observe firsthand. There was an email address I had to write to in order to apply and I waited and waited for an answer as to if I had gotten into the early fall 2012 seminar. It was especially important to get into this before the pre-dicted changes of Earth came about on 12/12 and 12/21. Finally too impatient to wait longer, I contacted Christine directly. She said she thought her seminar was already full with the 300 limit but would check once more and let me know. I heard back shortly afterward that, yes, it was full, but Spirit had told her I was doing something very important and she should make an exception of letting me in for free as an observer/participant. I was delighted.

I arranged a place to stay with Laurie's friend, Nancy, who lived north of Minneapolis where I would travel at the end of the day following the first seminar. The hotel across from Mall of America was fairly easy to find and I arrived just in time for the seminar. I wondered what kind of people would be here: the curious, the skeptic, the believer, or what. Members milled around in a lobby waiting for our room to be set up and most of them seemed quiet and reserved with an undercurrent of anticipation. There was a hustle and bustle as someone arrived into the crowd and people were fawning over a well dressed lady, giving her much honor with hugs and verbal complements. I stayed in the background, not wanting to be noticed, but suddenly there Christine Day was at my side. She gave me a hug, which many mediums will do to gain a feeling of you, and told me I have a big heart, she was glad I had come and that it must have been important for me to be there since Spirit told her so. That was it. The doors opened and we all quietly entered an enormous hall.

With so many world tensions these past years, many people have looked toward some kind of saving grace that would come to aide them. Talk of the ending of the Mayan calendar appeared to many as that moment. I took the three day seminar with Christine two months before 12/12/12, which would be an initiation, her first given, to life changes on earth within each one of us. Her seminar would push the 300+ of us into integrating a new crystalline structure to our cells, bringing us closer to those in other dimensions and the spirit world. We anchored ourselves to an invisible grid where we sat (crisscrossing of energetic lines) connected to the crop circles and pyramids and megalith sites. This would be our base. The seminar was broken up into segments that we experienced; that is, we would learn a lesson from Christine and either take a break to recharge, or go into the crystal vortex.

I think my jaw dropped as I surveyed the football field sized double room with half being filled with chairs, and the other half empty except for the center being filled with a sort of crop circle formation of quartz crystals ranging from finger size to a center megalith of tremendous girth and height that must have weighed more than I weighed. The picture below is not nearly as big as our vortex but gives an idea of how it was arranged. When we added our own crystals to it, the sight was amazing. A long row of chairs pushed tightly together separated the two areas but for a small opening which I assumed would be our doorway into the other side. Up front was a large platform with a soft easy chair and lamp, looking like it was a scene from a random living room. Christine climbed the stairs up to the platform, looked us all over, and spoke.

Our Crystal Vortex

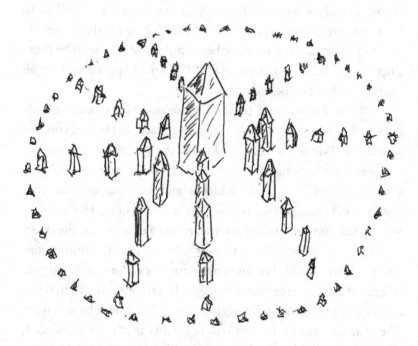

Seminar– Christine's Introduction:

I acknowledge each one of you and all that you are and the beauty of your being. You may not be aware of who you are at this point, but I get the advantage of seeing that energetically and really appreciating you. It touches my heart deeply and I feel tremendous love flowing through, and it's not just love flowing from me to you; I can feel the essence of you flowing toward me and it's very, very special. I'm sure this week you're going to connect with each other and I feel that important alliances need to be made between some of you here. I know that that is another part of a workshop or seminar. I can feel the importance of that at this time.

Many of us reconnect; it's like a reunion as far as I'm concerned. And this reunion needs celebration because we are at a place in our evolvement right now where so much is happening. There are so many important energetic alliances that are to take place right now, not only between us as human beings, but between us and the collective consciousness: the energies of the Pleiadians, the angels, the light beings, the Masters, the Lemurians, the Galactic Council. It is a new dawning era for sure and a time when we start moving outward to these energetic alliances; the alliances we have made pre-agreements to be with. We have made these pre-agreements and now is the time to become active; for us to be reaching out and opening up to work through these energetic alliances, and to fulfill our mission, to fulfill our destiny, and to support our reuniting with ourselves and other energies from this planet, Earth, and from the universe. That touches me so deeply. The work that we are doing this weekend, part of the objective is to reunite you with yourself; self empowerment through a lot of these initiation processes through the energies of the crop circles that will be with us. Part of their role right now within our earth plane to assist us to awaken. They hold the energetic blueprints for us so that we can start aligning and remembering ourselves on a whole new dimensional level.

The Pleiadians bring initiations to bring you into a state to help you align and own your ability to create, and (they) activate that creative element in you. So we're going to be working very strongly with that creative energy and you, claiming your own creation as you create. And when you do that, your whole world, your whole alignment to yourself transforms to become another aspect of you. You actually realign back to something you have forgotten about. That is going to empower you to go out into the world and create; to be the creators of your own world, your own environment, which has always been to move back into those roles, and now is the time. And it just shows me by reviewing what we're going to be doing this week, it just tells me that the veils are lifting at an accelerated rate on our planet, and so each one of us moves into a new way of being. That's what these few days are about; you reuniting with yourself in a whole new way- for self healing, for self empowerment. And so, we will get to have an individual experience and a collective experience. That collective experience is important and the individual experience is important.

I know there are many sorts of people here in various levels of awakening. Some of you are here for the first time and you think, 'what am I doing here'? (chuckling in the audience) And maybe some of you who have been here before are saying, 'what am I doing here'? (more laughter) I could say that to myself but I'm very clear about my role and I take it with joy and gratitude. But even if you are thinking that, or if you've been dragged along by somebody, it doesn't matter because, guess what, you were always meant to be here. This place will take you on your own journey, at your own pace. There's no competition here. You can become as large as you need to be, you can be in your own unique process but you don't have to compare yourself to anybody else in this room.

This is about you having an experience of letting go and allowing yourself to just be; to return back to a space of being so that you can let go of all the struggle, the time, all the illusion of this 3rd dimension that's on the earth plane. But it's intense right now, everything is intense and it's going to get more intense! Now that's not to put fear into you, it's just the truth. And the fact is, it's about each one of us coming back to a place of realignment with ourselves so that we can stand differently in the world, so that you can be more a witness to the drama and not be a part of it. That's really where you want to be. And, when you can just be there and watch the drama, but not be a part of it, just breathe and feel you there, then your world can change. It's time for all our worlds to change significantly. What I love about this time is the veils are lifting and we have been given an incredible grace at this time to move very quickly into our awakening process. That's really the good news here.

It is just the time. It's not that great that we are here and doing this; it's that it is the time for us to be doing this. We've made pre-agreements to now move in this direction and open into this awakening. To allow ourselves to start opening up not only to other human beings, which is probably the hardest thing. It's much easier to open up to the angels and light beings and spiritual realms and natural forces because they are operating in 4th and 5th dimension without the ego. When we meet another human being we deal with a lot of the human 3rd dimensional ego. That is also changing because that 3rd dimensional element is beginning to melt away on the earth plane, and so very soon we are not going to be able to hang onto our stories: the struggles and the pain and the fears and guilt. It will just start to slip away and we'll soon, with ease, align the truth of that aspect of ourselves to the 4th dimension, which is that ability to know who we are and remember. That is what's coming for all of us. A tremendous number of us are already experiencing that remembering process.

Each one of you bring your own unique aspect to the room, which means the collective energy, an essence we can hold together and work as a group and individually. I'm honoring you taking your place. Everything is about conscious choice. We can no longer just wait for something to happen, so this weekend is for you to consciously know you chose to be here on this earth plane at this time as a pre-agreement. You consciously said yes to being here to fulfill your mission.

This weekend you will get to activate those pre-agreements and activate the reunion process with yourself so that you can accelerate on your path to fulfill these destiny energies. Drink plenty of water. What is going to be happening is that your cells are going to begin vibrating at a higher frequency as you embody more of your light; which means there is friction in your cells and an attitude in your body and you can dehydrate very easily with that. The water will help you integrate the new light that's coming into your body as you work and it will really help you utilize each initiation process.

Some of you have brought crystals. This is the first seminar where crystals have been allowed into the vortex. We are going to be doing a special telepathic process where you begin to work consciously with telepathic communion with the Lemurian and Pleiadian energies. You are allowed to bring a crystal into the vortex and let it sit there and be programmed with this communion energy. (If we didn't have a crystal, there were large and small ones for sale in the lobby.) If you have more than one crystal, then they can go on the back table and they will absorb the initiation anywhere in the room. You will leave the crystals in the vortex until Sunday and you will use them when you go in. There are six candles around the crystal vortex and your crystals will go around the outside of the candles. Make sure you always put your crystal back in the same position and you won't need your crystal until this afternoon.

Now I want to get onto talking about our objectives for this weekend and later we'll go deeper into the processes and energy. If you don't understand what I'm saying, put your hand up and I'll answer your question. I want you to understand, because in the clarity of what I'm saying, you're going to be able to let go and move into your process and have your full experience. But, if in your mind you're thinking, I'm not sure about that, it's enough to stop your experience. (A hand goes up.)

How do you feel about using a crystal ball versus a normal crystal? The crystal ball will hold the energy but some crystal balls that have not been created consciously; the core energy of the ball can be damaged. I'd like to check it. If it's been done consciously, it can still hold the program. (Hand) I have a case for my crystal. Is it okay to bring that in with me? No. It has to be just by itself. (Hand) Would my chakra necklace work? The necklace is fine to wear because it will take in a lot of nice initiation energy, but you want a crystal that is standing by itself: not on a necklace. The crystal itself can be Lemurian or another type of crystal but it does have to be crystalline and not an agate.

(Hand) Can you tell me the significance of the Galactic Council being here at this time? The Galactic Council, in all the 20 years I have been working with groups, has only appeared last week and today. They have not been involved in any sort of seminar work with groups for me, but I can only speak for me because I don't know what anyone else is doing in the world. What is the Galactic Council and what role do they play? Part of their role, is they are a collective consciousness that interacts with life as a force of love in the universe, not too much through rules, but with principles and levels of principles within the universal consciousness.

Its job in part, is to impact levels of principles to each group of energies. When I talk about groups of energies, human beings are one group. Then there's another group of energies: the Sirians, other alien groups, there's also life force groups like the natural forces- the mineral kingdom, the animal kingdom (and so on). So, they work with all consciousness and different levels of life-force groups. But, only through a collective group of love, of imparting principles of teaching: principles within the universe, that's been their role. They are a guiding force within these principles.

Now the words themselves are highly inadequate because our language does not accurately speak any truth within the universe. But, they are the words closest to their role. What they are going to be doing here; on Sunday when we have done all our preparation, we have realigned and are in a much more expanded state of awareness, they are going to create a vessel to come over the crystal vortex, like a cover over the whole area and we will all be in that. They are going to open up a dimensional vessel that we are going to enter and align into and awaken through. It's going to be a very powerful and empowering process, and we will be ready for that by Sunday. We are going to get ready for that; we have a lot of work to do, not just for that one process, because what you're going to be doing here is activating your telepathic abilities. We are going to be working a lot within the telepathic center of the brain and we're going to activate the crystalline structure that was housed and anchored in your body on 11/11. Every human being received that crystalline structure. You are going to learn step by step how to open and access your telepathic center to create an 'on' bridge. Because, your telepathic center has a bridge that you can turn on or off. Depending who you want to align your energies to, you can actually turn it on and align to a specific alliance group. Then you will be working with the Lemurians and the Pleiadians through telepathic communication.

So, today, we will be activating the crystalline structure in readiness for that alignment tomorrow with the Lemurians and Pleiadians. You will also, through your telepathic center, begin to align to the crop circles. Now, the crop circles themselves, have just started to activate their full role of being here on the earth plane. They have been on the earth plane a long time, created by the Pleiadians, and now they're coming into their full role of activation on the planet in readiness of the earth changes. They are aligning around the earth with all the megalith sites and that's like Stonehenge, the pyramids, or any stone sacred structure; the cross symbols are realigning to these megalith sites and realigning the megalith sites into their purest form as when they first came onto this earth plane. They will all be realigned and recalibrated back into that pure structure. So ley lines have been created between the crop circles and the megalith sites. There is a sacred webbing forming now around our earth plane. This is one of the roles of the crop circles. Through these ley lines and sacred webbing, there is a whole new network of gridlines and energetic vortexes opening up on our earth plane for the full anchoring of the 4th/5th dimensional energies that are coming. And, they have started to come; opening up a whole new energetic surface.

As well as that, another role of crop circles is that the crop circles hold the blueprint energy for every human being on this plane. What is the blueprint? Your energetic blueprint is something that you made and agreed to before you came onto this earth plane to support you in fulfilling your mission at this time. And at this time, the crop circles are now ready to release and activate the blueprint energy through you for you to remember and realign back to your original aligned energy.

So, you've got the crystalline structure in your body that, when it's activated, it's going to be able to hold your alignment so that you can embody more of your divine self in this physical form. At the moment, your energy can't carry the divine light; there is too much electrical energy that would burn you up. So you house yourself outside but with the activation of the crystalline structure we're going to be doing today, your body's electrical energy is going to change; you're going to be able to house a huge amount of your own light in the cells of your body.

The crystalline structure also is designed to work in alignment with the crop circles so that the crop circles can align to you electrically through your crystalline structure and transmit and activate the blueprint energy through you so you can start moving quickly in your awakening process. This is part of the grand plan that we have come to fulfill here, each one of us. So we have the crop circles transmitting the blueprint energy and we're going to be working with our telepathic center, going into the crop circles and activating the blueprint then receiving it into the body. The crystalline structure will not only align to the crop circles, but it's going to align to every cell in your body, creating a regeneration of the cells.

There is going to be a self healing process that is going to happen naturally. You are just coming back into a natural realignment to yourself; there's nothing new here! And, there's nothing scary about it because it's you working with your mind, no one else's. The Pleiadians, the Lemurians will be here to hold energetic room for you, to birth it; you birthing your light. So this crystalline structure is designed to really create a self healing in the cells of our body. The cells are going to transform with the activation of your crystalline structure. With that, we are designed to live a lot longer this lifetime, every one of us; to move and spend a lot longer on the earth plane than any other group of human beings had in the past because of the crystalline structure. And it's the crystalline structure that gives you back an aspect of being able to realign back to your natural abilities as creator. And, that's another level of what we're going to be activating this weekend. You're going to learn to create an energetic alignment through your energetic field.

As you open up to create those fields, the creative principle within you; you, as the creator, are going to be activated through your crystalline structure. Yes, you will be working toward the energetic alignments that are going to support you during 12/12/12, but it's also going to activate your creative ability to create what it is you need for yourself at this time. And, we have forgotten that we are creators, natural creators. All of this is you coming back to a natural state of alignment with yourself.

We are going to be working with what we call, code forms. We use sacred sounds and we use four codes. These code forms are specially designed like a picture. What you are going to be learning how to do is to touch your consciousness to the picture and the telepathic aspect of your brain is going to absorb that thought, that code form, in. That code form, when it naturally absorbs into your telepathic center, will turn your bridge on. And through that code form, you'll be able to start working back into that natural ability of telepathic communion with any energetic alliance that you choose because you're the one in control; it's your telepathic center. You get to turn it on and off and direct it to any energetic alliance you feel comfortable opening up to.

We are also going to be working with sets of tools that you'll be able to work with in 12/12/12, and they are to integrate the illumination ways that will be coming onto the planet at that time. You'll be taking away a packet from me on the last day with the step by step processes and directions with these tools so you can utilize them. I'm sure there will be some surprises. One other thing we are doing on Sunday is you will be initiated into the crop circles and as a group, we are going to enter the sacred webbing with all the megalith sites and all the crop circles on the planet; joining that sacred webbing through our abilities. I know that will be a very powerful and transformational process for each one of us.

I'm wondering why you chose the Twin Cities in Minnesota for doing this. I'm guided to. I set the programs where the Pleiadians want me to be. Minnesota has a very powerful set of energetic vortexes here. We have power centers in America; we have Shasta, we have Sedona, but there's a certain level of vortex here that is different than anywhere else in the country and this is where they want the energy anchored; it's here it will have the most impact on the country itself and on the planet.

I just want to read you a message from the Pleiadians:

> Beloved ones, (here Christine choked up and said, 'I get emotional because they are going to say that it comes with a very pure love and it hits my heart') We greet you and welcome you here. We honor you taking your place within this space in taking your next step. This is a special event; one that will bring you to a new awareness in the alignment aspect itself. This is a birthing event and we witness you and support you in your process. Together you, us, the Pleiadians, the spiritual realms, the Lemurians and the Galactic Council will move forward into an adventure together.
>
> That's so important because they all see this as an adventure with you and you see it as an adventure with them. And we come together in a state of love, and to me, that's everything.
>
> You have come here to change, and changes will happen. You are ready to receive the realignment and tools to birth yourself. The time is now for you to take big steps forward. The energies are set for you to move quickly now into this awakening of yourself. You have come here to receive

healing and awakening; both happen simultaneously. Some things, most things your eagle mind
will not understand because we will not be operating in the 3rd dimensional plane. All processes will
take you beyond eagle mind and allow you to soar
with your multidimensional aspect.

There is nothing new here; just a remembering
and reunion with aspect of self. A reemergence
of your divine aspect will happen. You are being
asked at this time to open up and live through
your heart center. It's through the heart that you
will begin to understand your true path and be
able to understand this new perspective of living
by being. It's through the heart that you will come
into a realization of truth of who you are in your
life essence, and most importantly, what are the
next conscious steps that you need to take toward
yourself in your evolution at this time. Self love
birthed through the heart.

When we talk about love, we talk about au-
thenticity and integrity of action with yourself.
Remember that you are human and that you
are not perfect, so there will be mistakes made.
Forgive yourself as you take your steps forward
and begin this new alliance with yourself. Open
to forgiveness and love of self. Let go and open to
this great opportunity that is before you. Have fun
and play with your ability to create. You have all
come here to prepare yourselves for your next step
on 12/12/12. Part of this next step is to align to the
new energies that are birthing on the earth plane
now, and open to your own divine light that you
are ready to receive now.

-The Pleiadians

(Questions) Is there a way for someone to prepare for 12/12/12 if they can't be here? Yes. Look at the broadcasts that are for free on the website. There are six of them that have some processes that will really support them in that preparation.

Will we be able to share the information with our dear ones that couldn't be here? What you're going to find is that they won't receive the initiations here so it would be very difficult for them to do those processes, because you're going to be initiated here to be able to work with those processes. The energies are intense. Without the preparation of the vortex and the birthing you're going to do, you would have a problem doing those processes.

You said everyone received the activation on 11/11? Yes, the crystalline structure actually entered every human being on this planet on 11/11/11. And there those who would not have chosen that? All pre-agreed to be on this earth plane to receive that crystalline structure at that time; wherever they are on the planet now, whatever they remember or don't remember, there was a pre-agreement given because everyone on the earth plane said yes to being here at this change. Now, the crystalline structure anchored, but it didn't get activated, and it hasn't been activated yet on many many levels. You have to anchor the crystalline structure or activate it through conscious choice. There's going to come a time on the planet when even those who are not spiritually awake, but they're good people and they're on the planet; when the change happens on this earth plane, when we go purely to a $4^{th}/5^{th}$ dimensional structure, and the 3rd dimensional illusion actually drops away, the crystalline structure in everybody will activate at that time, and that will support every human being that's here.

There are people here on this earth plane who are into violence, control, killing ... those people will not be staying on this earth plane. We are all going to take a step on this planet. Every one of us on this earth plane, regardless of who we are, are going to take our next steps. Some of us will stay on the planet taking our next step and those who cannot align to the $4^{th}/5^{th}$ dimensional energy, who are not ready for that awakening, will step off the planet. There's always a next step. As there is no such thing as death, the Pleiadians say we're just taking a step here and a step there and they're very matter of fact about that.

But, what I meant by good people; there are a lot of people who are not spiritually awake, but they're people who are meant to be on the plane and the planet and are staying here during the changes. You don't have to be spiritual to be here on the planet; we're not going to have this mass exodus of those who are not spiritual. The people who are ready to take that step, and who are not into control of power or violence, will stay.

People like us end up being the 'way showers'. We made pre-agreements to wake up before a lot of others and we will hold energetic spaces and support these other people who are coming behind us. We will forge their pathway and they will come into their awakening and we will be the support for them.

Is this what's happening on 12/12/12? 12/12/12 will be another turning point on the earth plane. There will be waves of illumination that will be coming onto the planet at that time, this is different from 11/11/11 where everyone received the crystalline structure and in that moment, guess what, the 3rd dimension shifted off for a short time and it's never come right back in its hold, so no one can quite get into the drama like they used to. We may try, but we can't be as dramatic as we used to be because of that. But on 12/12/12, the illumination waves are not for the masses. They are for a group of people who are specifically on the path to receive a level of illumination and transformation through conscious choice. And so 12/12/12 involves conscious choice and we will be talking about that. It's about consciously choosing to step forward and to receive because that is the era. On 12/12/12 those illumination waves are very specifically for the awakened group on the planet. And 21/12/12 (December 21, 2012), is another level of illumination. We need to integrate the 12/12/12 illumination waves to fully utilize the waves of 21/12/12. There is a step by step process there.

What you'll be receiving here is going to support you incredibly to be able to create a space for yourself through your energetic field by creating a series of energetic alignments that you are going to learn how to do here. You'll do them the night before or the day before, and set them up, and it's going to enable you to fully utilize the awakening energies of these illuminating waves on a very profound level. It's going to support you in being able to stand and take a new place within yourself, with yourself. It's going to allow you to bring in a level of self healing energy that will transform your souls to another level of awakening and energetic realignment to aspect of self. So there is a whole process and we are going to birth this process together this weekend.

Is this light work connected with the ascension? I'm not sure what you mean by ascension. Awakening and moving into the higher levels. It's totally ascension! It leads right into that process. I'm also going to say this one more time; you can't leave your humanness behind. The human part of yourself is so important in your enlightenment process. You cannot become enlightened without honoring your humanness and understanding your imperfections as a human being. We did come here on this earth plane to have a human experience and that is not going to go (away). The fact is, we have to learn to turn back toward our human selves and build a new relationship with ourselves as human beings.

It's now trying to move into a new aspect of loving yourself; embracing yourself and loving yourself for all your imperfections, for all your vulnerabilities, it's part of your enlightenment process. We are meant in this lifetime to change the dynamic, change the relationship with our humanness, to self-love from a 3rd dimensional standpoint of separation and self-condemnation, to a $4^{th}/5^{th}$ dimensional experience; of self-love of accepting ourselves in our humanness with our vulnerabilities and our imperfections; to honor ourselves with a journey that we've had up to this moment of time and to honor all suffering, everything that we have gone through, all the things we have created in order to learn, to have all our experiences, all the decisions we've made that have brought us to a series of experiences in order to learn. We need to come to this place within ourselves and we don't have to do it perfectly. Get that! We don't have to do it perfectly!

One moment in time of holding yourself with love and compassion for everything you've been through, that one moment in separation, silence, and in that one moment where separation ends, when you hold yourself with that love and that compassion for everything you've been through, shakes every cell in your body. One moment: self-love. And, it's accumulative. So this is about you beginning a process, one moment a week will do, of holding yourself with compassion over something that you did or didn't do; the journey that you had and all that you are in this life, all that you are, the magnificence of yourself. And that may be too much for your ego mind, and that's okay. But, do understand, this is part of your enlightenment process to begin to turn back toward yourself. One moment; if you can commit to one moment a week, and that moves you out of separation just for that moment.

And then one day, guess what? It's like a tight ball inside of you, a ball of twine. Every time you touch yourself with compassionate love, that ball of twine loosens. And then one day, guess what? It's so loose it can't roll up anymore. Everything falls away. You don't have to complete everything. Just start with a list about everything you have against yourself, a huge list probably: you know, didn't do this, said that, shouldn't have done this, should have done that, wasn't there for that person, guilt, shame, condemnation; make your list. Start with one thing on the list. And just be with that, and breathe and feel how you did your very best in each moment, and that was enough. It's enough for the universe; it's just not enough for the ego mind and how we punish ourselves and hold things against us. So, this has to happen as you do the other. You can't just think, I'm going to be enlightened here and then the next day the rage stuff comes up. Know that we all have our idiosyncrasies, we all have them. We have to learn just smile at ourselves and say look,

look at myself again. I did this again. blah. And hold yourself. It's okay, I know I must have been afraid to do this again. Something made me afraid.

Give yourself a break. We have given ourselves so much of a hard time in our lives, we've been through so much, and now is the time to let go. What I love about the work we're going to do here is, it has a lot of letting go energy in it. It's an energy that the Pleiadians transmit out to assist you as a human being to let go more easily. There's an energetic womb in this room and it's holding each one of us and it has a letting go energy in it also. So, letting go opens up your alignment; through letting go, you align.

Let's take a break right now with letting go. (At this point, we all 'let go' with audible sighs after breathing deeply.) Let go together. I'm really supporting each one of you in working with this human aspect of yourselves and being willing to give yourself a chance just to let go of the judgments. One moment, one moment in time; that's all. And then you move forward as your enlightenment process accelerates because know when you hold things against yourself you are in separation. To become enlightened, you have to end separation. When you end it inside, guess what? All of a sudden you just love everybody too. You start loving everybody else because everyone is a mirror to you. If you're judging this, then you're judging all of that.

An automatic repercussion of this self-loving, this change of relationship with yourself, is that the whole world changes. You set yourself free; you liberate yourself, and it is time for liberation. We deserve that. Spirit sees us in our pure beauty; each one of us being a jewel, a brilliant light. And the human part is the part we came here to have an experience with. In this lifetime we were meant to come here in our humanness, love ourselves and consciously awaken to our own spiritual self and anchor it into the body at this time. That is what we're all meant to do here now.

What I love is that the crystalline structure makes it all possible. I was wondering how that's going to work. But with the crystalline structure it's like AHH! We can hold ourselves together, we can hold the line. So, that will be some of the activations we do first is to get some of these crystalline structures active so that you can realign back. Let's take one more breath and we will start activating the grid and opening up the crystalline structure.

Seminar Part I:

(Christine filled in with some questions and information as the crowd filtered back in from our break.)

Through conscious choice you've placed your crystals (in the vortex) and the activation has begun in certain areas. Understand the crystalline structure right now is in the telepathic center of the brain, it's in the thyroid, which opens up the divine factor, it's in the heart center and it's in the spine. The crystalline structure in the spine has a very different dimensional structure that any of the other crystalline structures. What I'm being told is that the work we are doing here is going to activate your crystalline structure to a certain level. With the illumination on 12/12/12, part of that will be the activation on a dimensional level of your crystalline structure, and 21/12/12 will bringing another level. There are many levels to be activated through our crystalline structure for our awakening and they come as we're ready but we have to be consciously open to that.

First of all I want to activate a gridline in this room. Now the grid energy that's going to be activated, activates everyone's seat in the room. It's an energetic grid that aligns you to a 4th/5th dimensional energy in readiness for you to be able to integrate your initiations over the next three days. Every day we will be setting a new grid energy and it's already been activated. We did it about 7:30 this morning; it's lined up waiting for the activation now. And so I'm going to use a series of sounds to bring in and create the activation through the grid which means the place where you sit now is going to start opening up like a doorway. Know that the grid is multidimensional and each one of you have a unique place on the grid to anchor into. It's almost like your own personal holding place or womb that will open up.

This is going to really support your integration and allow you to birth and expand dimensionally and yet, stay very anchored in your body; grounded. Because in this awakening we no longer go out and come back to our body. It's about anchoring and birthing a light in the cells of our body. So, I'm going to open up the grid and I want you just to take a conscious breath in and out of the mouth. Here we all breathed in and expelled audibly. Remember, in and out the mouth says, yes, I'm willing to let go, and yes, I'm willing to receive my light. That is the conscious breath.

At this point as we continued our conscious breathing, Christine began speaking an imploring language which, to me, sounded much like a Native American tongue. She continued this while interjecting directions to us. Just take a breath and claim your place, like roots of a tree going down into the earth. Place your hand on your chest and breathe and I will activate the grid. Through conscious choice, you take your place. Tones now with quick stops to tell us to breathe, always repeating; breathe and let go and anchor yourself on the grid as it opens. Some in the crowd would suddenly yell out a vocal sigh much like the end of a large yawn. Bring your conscious awareness into your place and just let go through conscious choice. Let go, which allows a level of alignment to begin to open through you. Because you burn into your place consciously, there is a new level of alignment taking place; you make it possible to let go. More tongues and sounds. Claim your place on this grid. Claim your place on this earth plane and claim your place within the universe.

Some of the group started singing a tone and some shouted out guttural sounds as Christine continued. Keep letting go and letting the natural realignment to take place. The whole grid is opening and receiving you. Many of the people were making tones as Christine spoke over them and continued her own tones. Breathe and let go allowing everything just to flow away. Allow another dimensional place to expand within the grid. The sounds of humming and chanting and loud sighs reached the point of making me uncomfortable since I enjoy silence much more as a way to be able to think and connect. However, this ended up being a climax as all the jumbled sounds suddenly ebbed, though Christine continued tongues, tones, and words of encouragement. Take one more breath and allow the full opening of your place as you touch the opening with your conscious awareness. Allow your place to unfold with your conscious awareness and your breath.

You may feel like something needs to come out of the throat. Let it come. That is the divine energy opening up through the heart center and the throat is connected with the heart. Sounds of the crowd started rising once more with some people even yelling out or making sounds like barks or hoots. Now the sounds descended once more to a whisper. Good work everybody. Just take a soft breath and let go, allowing your full conscious awareness just to open up into however that place in the grid is presenting itself. It might feel as big as this room. It may feel like you are in a whole different space energetically. That's okay, just let go. It may feel very subtle. That's okay too. Just take your time and bring your conscious awareness into the space, however it's presenting itself. Feel the space with your consciousness. Just breathe and claim this space; your space here. More tongues were spoken. Understand that you're place on this grid will present itself wherever you sit in the room. You can change seats, you can move, tomorrow you may be in a different position, but know that your grid energy is aligned and anchored to you, your place. And it's like no one else's place on the grid. This is yours and you're being received there during this birthing process over the next three days. It will continue to unfold and evolve as you do. It's your integrating plan that supports you and anchors you and integrates you as your birth. There will always be an energy there to receive you within that space. And it will build, and become more on some level, however that presents itself.

Now our next step, now that you've anchored your place on the grid, we are actually going over to the crystal vortex. Maybe some of you have already looked over there; very powerful, multidimensional space. The crystals have been placed in a certain geometrical form by the Pleiadians to open up a birthing womb for you in this process. Sometimes during the process I may dial the crystals. The Pleiadians show me which crystals to move, and as the crystals move, another dimensional space is opened up for you to work with. We're going to start with the base dimensional space that's there, it's enough for you to begin with.

When you go in there, there are some rules. You can all take your crystals in there. You can leave them around the outside of the candles; the candles are in a circle and you leave your crystals on the rim. When you go in there, it's not a place for social conversation because it's a sacred place. It's a very powerful place where you are going to be doing a lot of your birthing and communication processes with the Lemurians, the Pleiadians, and the Galactic Council as we work. It's where you are going to be birthing some of the crystalline structure. There are two doorways into that space and one of the assistants will open the door and let you in. (The 'doors' were just two of the chairs moved to create an opening in the solid row of chairs across the room.) The thing is, if you feel overwhelmed in there, you can either sit on a chair, lie on the ground, stand, sit; you can be as close to the vortex as you like, as long as you're behind the candles. You cannot touch any of the crystals in the main vortex though; the only crystal you can touch is your own crystal. You can't take water in there, so you have to take a drink before you go in. And then when you come back, you come back to your place and re-anchor into your place in the grid and integrate whatever you activated in the vortex itself.

Our first step in the vortex is to energetically align to the vortex. Now, the Pleiadians read our energy through the right hand. It's through our right hands that they identify our divine energy and so we place our hand out to the vortex if you feel comfortable, but it allows the Pleiadians and Lemurians to read your energy so that they can support you in the process. That's all it means. You put your right hand up towards the vortex almost like saying hello, I'm here. You'll feel an energy as you bring your hand up to the vortex and bring your consciousness into that energy. You're going to feel energy, maybe love, maybe peace, maybe electrical energy coming into you. Sometimes you'll feel it coming right into the palm and there will be a moment when you know 'I'm done', they've already read me, and you put your hand down. That's our first step, to align to that energy. If you don't feel comfortable with the palm of your hand, just bring your conscious awareness in and feel the energy of the vortex itself. It is a multidimensional energy that is set up to birth you and realign you back to yourself. It's you aligning to your own dimensional light through the vortex.

We're going to use the vortex first to initiate or anchor through the palm, then we're going to activate the first level of crystalline energy. Now we're going to work with the thyroid and the new crystalline energy that's birthed in the thyroid itself is changing the role of the thyroid in our life. It actually activates what the Pleiadians call Our Divine Factor. So, as we activate the crystalline structure here, your divine factor is going to begin to activate. Your own uniqueness is going to activate through the cells of your body and your crystalline structure is going to birth and expand and respond to the activation of you through conscious choice, opening up to work through your crystalline structure in the thyroid. We're going to do that in the vortex because it's the very best place for you to do your first crystalline activation or if you have already started activating your crystalline structure, you're going to activate another dimensional level of your divine factor.

Whichever that is, it can feel intense, it can be emotional, you may feel peace, love, intensity, electrical energy; there can be many things. I'm going to get you to breathe and to open and we're going to take it step by step and slowly open up this crystalline structured within your thyroid. So you may feel like you want to sit on the floor, sit, lie; you can move around the vortex, we've made it big so we could all do what we need to do in there and that is, be ourselves. You cannot touch another person. If someone is emotional, you don't touch them because you're interfering with them letting go of something that's leaving their body. The assistants will be watching if you need help; just put your hand up. If there's something going on in the process and you're thinking, 'I'm not getting any of this, nothing's happening here', (then) you might be in your head trying to make it happen. You don't have to try to make anything happen, it just is. But if your ego mind wants to get active and go 'okay, we're trying to see, trying to visualize', you lose your experience because you're in the 3rd dimension in your ego mind.

It's different if you just see something. That's not trying to see something, you are seeing something. Seeing visually is one of the gifts many of us have and some of us are more sensory, we don't see anything, and that's okay. Nothing's more than another, it's just different. So be in your experience, just breathe and let go. The letting go is the best way to work with the process.

To get at the crystalline structure in your thyroid, you're going to touch here (an area near the heart) which we call the DAP, the divine access point. This is the area of the body where the life of the self comes most readily into your body. You're simply touching, you're not pushing, touching gently with these two fingers, and then bringing your conscious awareness to that place opens the doorway and you are going to move through that doorway into the crystalline structure and we'll work from there. Questions?

Do we use right hand or left hand? It doesn't make any difference. You said there would be no talking to someone else, but can we talk to Spirit? You can make sounds. Just don't have a conversation with someone. You can't take a jacket off and put it on the ground, it has to be on your body, you tie it to your waist. If you're going to wear shoes in there, you keep them on your feet. I'm curious as to what the different dimensions are. 5th dimension is unconditional love and oneness with the universe; no separation.

6th dimension moves more into the Godhead energy which is a very different energy, a dimensional space within the universal consciousness that is not just oneness, it's more specific.

We're going to talk about the vortex now. Your crystal is going to stay in there and hold the programming until Sunday. If you don't have it right now, bring it in later and I will program it. I just need to hold it. Christine, a conscious breath is going to be very important in working with the vortex, can you give a review of what a conscious breath is? Okay, the conscious breath is in and out the mouth; it's just 'HAAAAAAAAA' (vocally). It's not all the time, maybe once a minute, but that breath in and out, allows you to let go of all the old 3rd dimensional issues out of the body and allows you through conscious choice to start birthing and realigning to your light self and coming into the body. So, you want your mouth open. If you don't open wide only a little comes out. Whenever I say take a breath, take a conscious breath. If you use a nose breath, it suppresses everything and pushes everything down and keeps everything held tight in the body. With the vortex energy it (the breath) transforms, it doesn't get released, just transforms into the light that is in this whole room, so it doesn't go anywhere. When you talk about letting go, just what is let go? It's you letting go of struggle. You are the one choosing the letting go. No one else can do that for you.

The energy is here. We have the angels, the light beings, we have Mary, who is here a lot, we have Jesus and we have a lot of their energy. They are holding energetic spaces for us to birth ourselves. They don't interfere with you at all without your permission. I can come in and work with you simultaneously but I need your permission to do that. I will never enter your energetic field without that permission. It's the same with the spiritual realms here, the Pleiadians and Lemurians also. You need to open up now and see if you want to give your permission, so open up and see if you want anyone to come in energetically and support you during this birthing process of your crystalline structure. You may now enter the vortex, with your crystals, without your crystals, whatever feels right. Have a good journey everyone.

We walked silently through the chair 'doors' and took places all around the crystal vortex filling up the whole room but leaving space so we could lie down if we wanted. Through a meditative state we listened as Christine spoke her language and made tones. Placing our first two fingers of one hand on an area between our heart and throat, we drew ourselves into the vortex energy. Again, some of the people made tones and yips, yells, barks and other sounds as they tuned in, though I found it a bit annoying as I tried to relax and focus. But, I knew it takes all kinds and what was good for me was not necessarily good for all.

The words above were in my fast scrawl and read: Opening the Vortex. 1ˢᵗ time the Galactic Council is here with Pleiadians and

Lemurians together. My view: Finally I went through a gap and the hills fell away leaving a piercing white light radiating to me.

What I saw with the opening of the vortex. There were immense tall mountains that were more like screens than rock. As I moved through them, a bright sun appeared. I discovered later that one of our codes looked much like this! I did not take my recorder to the vortex.

Seminar Part VII: The Second Line of the Matrix

Christine spent some time talking about the vortex areas on earth and said that the Minneapolis area up through and around Lake Superior is a very powerful sacred spot that is anchoring tremendous energy onto the planet right now. She feels a strong Lemurian influence working around the lake itself. It is creating balance not only of the area but affecting the entire planet.

Someone asked, 'Since you have said how children are being born with the crystalline structure intact, what do you feel about special needs kids?' I feel strongly that they are here to carry a very unique frequency; they have come in to help with the anchoring at this time. They are transmitting energy out to the other dimensions and out to us on this planet. I have a daughter with down syndrome and this last year has been so bad. I think what you need to understand is that she's spending more time out than in and it's very hard for her to orientate herself because she's being almost aligned on the other dimensional sides, so that there is a reentry problem for her. I would look for someone working with energies to help her integrate when she comes back so it's not so intense for her into the 3rd dimension. She's really not of this world in lots of ways. She came to this life to transmit out her love for others.

Now it was time to go back to the vortex and work on moving into the second line of the matrix on our sheets which will prepare us to go into the crop circles. This was nearly identical to our first experience when we went into the first line. All of these were in preparation of working with the crop circles. When we came back to our seats, Christine asked for words to describe our experience, though to me it was something hard to describe. A person almost would need a different vocabulary to talk about what we were experiencing.

Seminar Part VIII: The Vortex and the Crop Circle

(The group was fairly quiet after this venture into the vortex with the crop circles. Christine asked for feedback when we were in our seats. One lady told of her parents in spirit being there holding hands and started crying. Christine said to let it out, it was good to cry. Another woman said that a Rhodes physicist had worked out the geometry of our crop circle and it was the basis for all creation.) Another asked, are we going to be only attuned to this particular crop circle or will we be able to get information and see things in other crop circles?

You are going to be given access to this one because this is the one you need for your awakening right now. You will be more aligned to everything though, with all the energy and anchoring and birthing going through you in these three days. You can look at another crop circle and sense it telepathically but not in the sense of this one which is carrying a tremendous birthing energy. Remember the crop circles are connected to all the megalith sites right now, creating a sacred web around the earth. Tomorrow we will take our place within that sacred webbing. You are ready now for the crop circle connection; you've begun with two lines of the matrix, which has created an electrical birthing through your heart. Your crystalline structure has begun to transform the cells in your heart so you can carry a much higher frequency of your own light through your heart.

It also means you can align to a very high dimensional level of light to another being or another energetic source so your alignments are going to be expanding. Using the code form on the crop circle sheet you are going to activate the telepathic bridge. You know how we used a symbol to activate the bridge? You've come a step now and won't use that one, you will use this code form. It will do two things. It will activate the bridge and at the same time, give you the key to go into the crop circle and begin to expand into the multidimensionality of the alignment of the crop circle itself. You just created an energetic union with it through your heart, but here you are going to enter the multidimensionality of the crop circle. And the very many intricate pieces and patterns within the facets of the crop circle hold tremendous knowledge and ancient wisdom. Let me read a little bit ...

"The crop circle carries the ancient knowledge for us on the planet at this time. They are playing a powerful part on our earth plane as they move into their full role. They are linking to all megalith sites on our earth plane bringing the megalith sites back to their original pure state. These connections are creating lay lines between all crop circles and megalith sites around our earth plane. This is creating a giant webbing that is assisting to anchor the new dimensional energy on our earth. The crop circles play another role in becoming a transmitter for us so that we can awaken. They transmit many codes for us with knowledge and understanding as we are ready to receive them. They are a part of the great plan; the sign by the collective consciousness to bring us into this new dawning time. They are here to assist you in alignments to your crystalline structure for your enlightenment process as well as transmitting to you through the matrix. They work closely with the Pleiadian and Lemurian energies and have been created by the Pleiadians for our awakening and our enlightenment."

Seminar Part IX: The Lemurians and Pleiadians

Questions? I hear you talk of Lemurians and Pleiadians but not Atlanteans. Is there a reason for that? Yes, there is a reason; because the Lemurians have pre-agreed to assist us as a human race to integrate our crystalline structure. The Lemurians were spiritual when they worked with the crystals. The Atlanteans were scientific. So, we are at a time of spiritual evolvement and that's why the Lemurians are aligning energetically with the Pleiadians to support us in the unfolding of our crystalline structure and the restructuring of ourselves. The Lemurians specialize in the crystals through a spiritual aspect. The Lemurian crystals are very different than the Atlantean crystals; they have a very different energetic. The Lemurians are here as that pre-agreement working with us as the Pleiadians are and they've only just come in to working with me in the last nine months. I had a very big awakening coming to me and from then on and since then they've been working on the crystalline structure with each one of us because that's their specialty.

The Lemurian energy is very different from the Pleiadians. It's very soft, and really this pure loving energy. The Pleiadians (energy) is pretty intense. It's been very beautiful working with them after I had a really powerful awakening. It opened me to another aspect of myself when I was kind of initiated with them some months ago and I'm very grateful for the presence of them here with us. The Pleiadians and Lemurians have formed an energetic alliance for this time on the earth plane while we go through this transformation; not that they were ever at odds with each other, but they haven't worked together in this way. It's very much for the new event of our dawning time here on the earth plane. We are very lucky to have both the elements of them here to assist us especially with the birthing of the crystalline structure and it seems like it's a rapid process. I think it is the crop circle energies that have birthed you very quickly; that's a lot of activation of the crystalline structure in the heart and I really haven't seen an accelerated awakening of the crystalline structure like the one this afternoon. You need the Lemurians. We are about to go into a process to work telepathically and connect to them in the vortex.

Any other questions on the Lemurians? In most of my work today I've been fighting the sounds and noise people make; rapid movement and all this twirling going on because even physically my body is very quiet. I'm not getting crabby about it, I'm excited, but I wonder if I'd feel such a connection; when you talk about the Lemurians I feel like I'm from a place that was very soft and quiet. I was going to say that I think you have a Lemurian connection. It's going to be interesting when we go into the vortex now to see what that feels like. Many of you here have Lemurian and Pleiadian connections. It doesn't mean you are Lemurian; it may mean you are, and it doesn't mean you are Pleiadian but may mean you are. It may mean you have pre-agreements to work with the Lemurians or Pleiadians in this lifetime during this whole new dawning time. Whether or not you have a Lemurian or Pleiadian aspect, or if you have no aspect, it does not mean you don't have a pre-agreement with them to do the work and unfold and bring the elements of the energy of your essence to the planet at this time. Each one of you are here absolutely through pre-agreement because I've never seen a workshop like this put together with all the crystalline activations.

And now we're moving into the telepathic opening for you to align and commune or communicate with the Lemurian or Pleiadian forces. What's going to happen is that we're going to be opening up into the vortex but there is going to be a column of light that is activated through the vortex; the Pleiadian and Lemurian energies are going to come in through that column of light in the center of the big crystal (this is the huge crystal in the middle of the vortex). You can choose your alignment, but it will choose you actually. You may experience both those energies or you may be only aligned to one particular energy, whether it be Pleiadian or Lemurian. This is about your pre-agreement you made with them and has little to do with me, and little to do with your human ego choice. You may already be sitting there and thinking you know who you are going to be connected to because you have a know-ingness of truth about your alignment connections. It's really about being in the experience. It could be telepathic communication or communion because both your centers are open; the bridge works through both centers, so it will be the way you need it to be when this first telepathic communication consciously opens. You will be asked to open your bridge through the column of light. That column of light gives you access to both Lemurian and Pleiadian energies.

Questions? Are the Lemurians still in physical form on Earth? Absolutely! They exist energetically but they are working underneath the earth and underneath some of the waterways like Lake Superior, a Lemurian anchored place. They are here. They are not in spirit form but they do vibrate at a very high rate so they are fluid in form. Like the Pleiadians, they are in their incarnation fulfilling their pre-agreement mission for the grand plan within the collective consciousness. The Pleiadians originated on the earth plane and originated at the time of Atlantis, where they were working under the oceans on crystals on a spiritual level and the Atlanteans on the earth were doing their work scientifically with the crystals. Their energies are still in place and they (the Pleiadians) are still working within the earth, I don't know their movements elsewhere, but I'm sure they have many. I don't know any more than that; I'm still really young in my connection to them. I do understand a lot of their essence, but I don't understand their history very well at this point and I don't read (psychically). I've never been given that information, I've been told not to read. What they give me is all I know. Probably some of you have read books and know more. I'm ignorant until they give me information they feel I need to know when it's relevant.

What about crystal skulls? Well, there is a master crystal skull; I know of one in existence on this earth plane that is holding the master energy and knowledge of the crystals and the ancient teachings that still apply today. There is nothing new here. We are all working with ancient teachings and this skull holds all the mysteries of the ancient teachings. I do know that it is operating on the earth plane, it's been moved through different groups on the earth plane for initiation and awakening, and it's supposed to be very, very powerful.

Who designed it in the first place? It was a Lemurian design; I get my feeling around it, but I could be wrong on that. Other people might have more information. (At this point we took our code forms to the vortex for more initiation and communication; mostly practicing our bridge connections so they became more familiar and easier.)

(One person asked about coming earth changes and Christine answered): Minnesota is the safest place in all of America during the entire earth changes and the earth changes go well beyond 12/12/12. I won't go into all of them, but we are going to have many earth changes because they need to be there. There are going to be a lot of coastlines disappear and a lot of geographical changes take place within the earth.

Seminar Part XV: Going dimensional

(Someone asked if the crop circles were created by the Arcturians. Note that Edgar Cayce was the first to speak of and to the Arcturians who he said are a 5th dimensional being best reached in a dream state.) No, the crop circles are not created by the Arcturians. The Pleiadians have created them and there are many energies associated with them and are utilizing them. They are for the good of the universe, not just one channel. The whole universe is part of the great plan for the transformation of our planet and every energy is involved in that. The Pleiadians have created the crop circles, not for their own use, but for the use of the universe in the transformation of Earth. More questions?

Speaking of the Galactic Council, do they have some kind of identification like an emblem or crest, or some kind of identifying moniker? They actually do. They have an energetic form but they didn't want me to bring that and I'll tell you why. It's recognized by the universe but it holds a very high frequency and you need some interaction with the Galactic Council before you can really be with that frequency. It would be too much (for us to take). Maybe in another seminar we'll have it.

I want you all to stand and place your finger against your thumb (similar to the OM hand position) and it will help you align within the vessel when the energy comes in. We're going to play with it right now. Bring your conscious awareness to both sides, where you feel your thumb and index finger. You can do it tight or light, it doesn't matter. Then, feel yourself as the third point on that triangle. (So both hands in position represent two points of the triangle and we become the third.) And that's what you are taking into the vortex! Your crystals will not be in your hands because you will be creating the triangle. (We filed into the vortex area and put our crystals nearby.)

Now, the triangle may expand. Understand that within this vessel it's multidimensional and is way beyond this room, so you may find all of a sudden you are in infinity. You, within that triangle may suddenly expand out as a triangle from here. That's okay, it's expected from the triangle energy. You may not (also), but just allow your experience and don't let go of your triangle. Don't disconnect; it could disturb you energetically. If you let go of one hand, you let go of the connector. The hands are our energetic connectors. You don't have to push very hard; you can be very gentle.

First form your triangle and feel yourself in the triangle. The vessel itself, the Galactic Council vessel, is going to begin to descend around here. I want you to bring your consciousness more deeply into those two fingers and yourself and feel the triangle more completely now. Just allow it to become more defined somehow. Bring your conscious awareness into the vortex and you and the triangle will be moving into the vortex. You will move into the dimensional flow of the vortex and let go.

You're going to feel as you move through the flow, there is going to be an acceleration in the flow, almost like a whirlpool energy; stronger, larger, as if the vortex flow is going to expand. Maybe it feels like it's filling the room and you are going faster and faster through the flow of the whirlpool. Allow yourself to move through as a triangle. You are going to come out the other side of that whirlpool.

The Galactic vessel is here and we come to this still, silent lake. You are still the triangle moving on that lake. At the center of this stillness is this very tall energetic cylinder, or it might be like a column. Bring your consciousness into the column. The vessel is opening up as though there are millions of embedded jewels within the inside of the vessel. You, as the triangle, move across the still lake and as you move into the column, you fit perfectly in the column. As you enter, let go and let yourself receive the energy and imprinting from the column.

As you receive the imprinting, you will move through the column and into your place within one of those embedded jewels. The imprinting has created another aspect to your triangle and your ability. Open to the energy of the Galactic Council as they greet you within the column and then move you, assist you, in moving into your embedded jewel. Feel the essence of the love that is here. Feel the essence of your place within this embedded jewel and the essence of every jewel that is within this space, much like an energetic oneness of consciousness; the energy of love. You can expand your consciousness here in this energetic space and open to the full communication connection here. (Chanting.)

It's as though your place with that jewel is multidimensional. Maintain yourself as the triangle and see how you fit and expand within this space as though each space has its own multidimensional form and color. Open up to the form of the signature that you have been given; that you are. Breathe into the triangle and let go. It's as though the triangle is filling and becoming that color (whatever color you see) and form. Allow the transformation. It's as though crystalline energy is birthing and filling your triangle. (Chanting) When you sense or see that your triangle has transformed and it is crystalline and has received and taken on the essence of the color, you are going to return back from your place in the container, back into the column in the center. By bringing your conscious awareness to the column you find yourself in the column.

Open to the energy within this form; each one of you taking your place, fitting perfectly within your crystalline form within the triangle in the column. Just feel yourself there. Open your consciousness. As the column appears a certain way when you get inside it, it's very different dimensionally. It's like a chain of light that you have entered as this crystalline form while maintaining your triangle. Open your consciousness and feel the presence of the Galactic Council bringing the energy to you. Certain teaching, or understanding, or knowingness within this chamber of light, is imparting to you an energy and essence that your crystalline form is receiving and absorbing in. Take a breath. Let yourself go and expand into the pure truth within your chamber of light. Receive the full energy from the Galactic Council. Feel yourself being infused with this energy of truth. the mark of the Galactic Council into you and place it within your crystalline structure. (My mark is below.)

The mark I was given!

(Now Christine spoke softly, as if doing a meditation.) However that mark presents itself, you can open up to it at any time and utilize this energy. Now the column is beginning to release you down through that lake; it's as though you are being released from that column. And moving out across that still, silent lake, maintain your triangle and open up to the fluidity and the reflection. There is a very gentle current beginning to move you from that still lake back into a current. Feel the whirlpool energy; it's soft here, like a Galaxy. Let yourself be part of the galaxy as you're being spun out with the Galactic Council, being taken beyond the vessel out into the universe. Feel the space and the movement. Let the freedom come. Maintain your triangle. Feel the jewel of your ancestors as you move with the Galactic Council through the galaxy.

Very slowly, move back into the vessel back through the flow, back into the vortex. Feel the triangle, feel the form, however it is, going back through the flow, back to you out of the vortex, back to the triangle. Feel the crystalline energy anchoring through you. All that energy is moving through your cells, through your crystalline structure, coming into your heart. Open up your consciousness to the Galactic Council; allow them to feel you as you open up. Whenever you want to align back to your place within the Galactic Council, you form your triangle to reconnect to your form.

Keep integrating through yourself until you feel the full crystalline structure leaving the triangle and blending through the cells; fully absorbing through the cells of your body. Once you feel your crystalline structure of the triangle has birthed through yourself and absorbed completely, bring your conscious awareness into the flow of the dimensional space and allow yourself to move into that flow for integration. Don't try to control it now. You want the dimensional flow connecting to your flow. Allow this flow to come into your heart. It's containing a lot of new elements.

When you feel the full integration bringing the flow back into your heart center, anchoring that energy, then you can let go of your triangle. Hold your crystal and allow the full integration of infinity. It is another aspect of you being birthed. The mark that you were given by the Galactic Council is integrating through your heart center. You feel fully integrated, taking all the time that you need, then return back to your place on the grid and integrate through the grid. Place your crystals back in the vortex and keep breathing and letting go to allow the integration. Take all the time that you need. (The room was very silent now.)

(Now we were back on the other side of the hall and in our seats.) Let's anchor words connected to the experience with the energy of the triangle. Bleak. Safety. Vehicle. Sailboat. Container. What word can you put on your place within the vessel? Big. Sacred. Connected. Worm. Locked in. Core. Key. What word can you give in reference to the mark from the Galactic Council? Unique. Squiggle. Power. Symbol. Neutral. Eyes. Crystalline flower. What about the energy that came back into the heart center? Connection. Power. Fire. Acceptance. Throbbing. Golden heart. Passion. Long awaited for. Uniquely mine. Joy. Sacred flame. Light energy. Celebration. Make sure you drink plenty of water.

(My experience in this was very moving and I'll try to describe it here. -add my traveling over the void.

My drawing says: Drop of God light for self healing in spine. Strong blue crystal in center- as I get closer, it was larger and dark blue liquid crystal that I went inside. Vast expanse bluish. (Left arrow points out movement.)

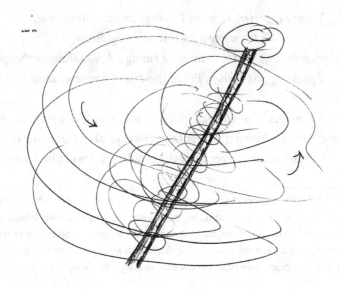

What I experienced when I went to another dimension.*
What I wrote from bottom to top below:
Vortex (arrow up), Void/Ocean- calm but liquid; no substance though
Sparkling gems (blue), Pillar, (No color I have ever seen)

First I entered the vortex, which to me, was like a swirling immense cloud of white fog, larger than the crystal circle in our room, larger than the room, larger than the building we were in. I was not

---

* Note: I'm assuming here that most of us were in a trance state for a time where we could hear Christine but could also travel away from this hall. My bridge was a silver thread that came from my palm and it drew me into other places from the ever expanding vortex. What I describe here is not even close to what I saw since even the perspective of largeness was no longer meaningful.

taken up, or down or sideways, but merely passed through it coming to a vast, boundless ocean, though even an ocean does not fully describe it. There I seemed to hover over the edge of this endless body of water that wasn't water. It had a liquid appearance and was calm, and yet, lacked any substance that I could recognize in 3D. It was a very dark blue. There was nothing above me, but I could still look down on it. I didn't turn around to see if there was anything behind me.

Suddenly I took off across it at such speed I felt like I was passing through eons of time, or at least, immeasurable space in an instant. As quickly as the ocean had come, it was gone. I was still and quiet, but continued moving through an eternal void of darkness that wasn't dark. Again, it is hard to describe this. The void was another form of blue, so dark it was indescribable, however I could still see that I was moving, moving, moving so fast. I say 'form of blue' because it could be sensed or felt.

Far in the eternal distance was a dot of light that came closer so quickly that I couldn't fathom the speed I had been going; more like the speed of thought. As the bright dot grew, I could see it was glowing a beautiful blue that I had never experienced before. As I drew closer and slowed down I saw other beings traveling like me, but not necessarily human, though it didn't matter at that time. Nothing mattered. I was just in the experience; participating, but as an observer.

The glow came from an immense blue crystal hanging down from nowhere. The crystal was hollow, looking like it had been sliced at an angle at the bottom, and all of us were traveling to its opening. Closer yet, I now could tell that each of us was a crystal, or at least, were in a crystal that held us. The inside of the large crystal was filled with tiny crystals like we, who had just arrived. Each one of us shot into the crystal and took up a place where our own crystal selves fit perfectly within the openings that seemed to be made for each unique individual.

My crystal raced up the tube and fit into an opening without a sound or feeling or any kind of sensory stimulation except my own perception. Christine was calling from somewhere and I left this place with my crystal, dashing through the void of nothingness. Again, the ocean suddenly appeared and I flew over it at the speed of thought seeing the white fog in the distance coming ever closer. Then I was in the fog. As it swirled around me, I felt nothing. Without knowing I was moving, I came out of the fog still attached to my silver thread (bridge of communion) and was back in the room with Christine and the group.

I do not know whether any others experienced this, but I am doubtful they did. I think this experience was an individual one and would be different for each person who experienced it. I will not forget it though.

***

What was in our packets?

When I returned home, I waited a few days and looked in my packet. It had all the instructions to commune and anchor me with specific objectives like those we had learned over these three days. One was to be completed on 12/12/12 and again on 12/21/12. We had all our sheets with the crop circle and codes to work on if we cared to after that.

Christine did not think any earth shaking events were going to take place at this time, but it was important that we nurture ourselves and grow with our crystalline structure. How lucky those being born would already have theirs activated as we move toward a new relationship with other dimensions. We have only to believe.

I finish this chapter with a newer message from the Pleiadians through Christine on October 18, 2013. You will find much more information on Christine's website- http://www. christinedayonline.com/.

A Loving Message from the Pleiadians
Beloved ones,
We greet you at this powerful and empowering time on your earth plane. We bring news

of dimensional shifts and transformational times coming, beginning in the last few days of October. These are designed to open you to a new energetic flow of light consciousness that is coming onto your planet.

There are to be a series of powerful energetic shifts moving through the anchored grids on your planet, these are going to create upheaval and change. Be prepared to align consciously to your heart center, you need to be committed to this action within yourself, in order to stay balanced and to have the capacity to flow during this transitional time.

Flow and breathe, flow and breathe. You will not be able to understand much of what is going on during this time frame, you need to be prepared to let go and trust on a new level.

Your stability will only be possible through your heart center during this time. This is your central place of anchoring. An anchor needs to be established through your heart in readiness for this time. It is going to be necessary for you to birth a structure within your heart center to maintain your stability at this time of upheaval. We will be working with you in the October 27th broadcast to assist you with the creation of this structure.

We hold you. You need to reach out for the support that is waiting for you to call them forward. It is the time now during this transition to utilize this support that is available to you.

Blessings
The Pleiadians

— CHAPTER 11 —
AYALA CHEN

Bio: Ayala Chen has studied Judaism and Kabbalah her entire life and is currently exploring the universal core of this knowledge in preparation for the "apocalypse" - the lifting of the veil on secret and esoteric knowledge for all to learn. Ayala has pursued academic studies at Brown University, Hebrew University in Jerusalem and a number of small Torah institutions in the U.S. and Israel, in addition to studying texts since a very young age. In recent years Ayala has begun incorporating her unique knowledge of Kabbalah with concepts and ideas from the universal mystery tradition in search of a lost common core of mystical ideas. One focus of her work has been the study of the ancient Hebrew calendar and its correspondence with western astrology and the study of the constellations across cultures. As this is a time when the Messianic Torah, or a unified field of knowledge, is downloaded to humanity in the current generation, Ayala hopes to serve as a translator of material from her tradition for this collective remembering of sacred knowledge.

Ayala is based in Northern California, where she is currently doing research on further overlap between texts from her tradition and the universal mystery tradition. She also continues to read personal and event charts in a unique blend of authentic Kabbalistic knowledge and Western astrology. She blogs at http://kabbalastrology.wordpress.com and can be found on Facebook.

Links to the Kabbalah

Kabbalistic astrology - Jewish views on astrology - Wikipedia, the free encyclopedia en.wikipedia.org

Kabbalistic astrology, also called mazal or mazalot, ("zodiac," "destiny") is a system of astrology based upon the kabbalah. It is used to interpret and delineate a person's birth chart, seeking to understand it through a kabbalistic lens.

I met Ayala through my medium friend, Laurie Stinson (Chapter XV), so began my interview learning about that connection as she describes her first meeting with Laurie.

It was one of these amazing internet connections. For me, personally, my surroundings [in 2011] were not as much in tune with the new consciousness as my online community. I posted a Kabbalistic teaching online once, and she (Laurie) really resonated. She wrote me and it turned out that the particular reading of the Torah that week matched up with this big question in her life. We started exploring it together and it's a powerful connection when the mystical and real life overlap. We've gone on like that every few months; we exchange insights from life experience and sources.

I've only known her since summertime and feel like I've known her for years. I can say the same thing. She keeps me organized with my book. I saw something in your chart about organization and you have the potential for being very practical. I used to even vacuum new footprints off my carpeting, but not anymore. You have a lot of force of personality in the fixed signs and then there's a lot of potential for growth in the more flowing, changing signs, so it sounds like you are on a good trajectory.

Did you grow up in Northern California? Yes, I am living very close to where I grew up. I lived here until I was 14, then my family moved to Israel, where I attended high school and learned Hebrew. Instead of going in the army, I came back to the states and went to college, spent my junior year in Israel, came back to California after college, went back to Israel for graduate school and am now back again, in another spiral.

While being there (Israel) did it affect your political views of what is going on, or in another way, does this path affect how you might have viewed things back then? I've been through a lot of stages of development regarding what Israel means to me. In high school I was not as aware of the political situation, because as a high school student in West Jerusalem I did not know what life was like in the Palestinian territories, sort of like living in an upper west side part of New York and not knowing what goes on in Harlem. Even though there were bombs going off in downtown Jerusalem in some of the worst periods, the attitude among the youth there is to just keep on living and not let it shake you.

In college I became involved doing campus activism on Israeli-Palestinian coexistence and peace work and in my junior year abroad I lived with Palestinians and Israelis and worked on joint environmental projects, with shared ecological resources being a bridge for understanding and cooperation. That greatly affected me and I was passionate about peace and coexistence, almost to the point of not wanting anything to do with Judaism because it felt like part of the problem in a way; the attachment to the land. From there I did kind of a 180° and had a major spiritual transformation that brought me deeper into the Bible, Jewish texts and the mystical dimension. Part of this was seeing the land of Israel as part of a mystical framework, not that God forbid leads to oppression, but that explains something about the sanctity of that place that many feel, that explains why this region is a nexus on spiritual, geographic and political levels. Peace work became a spiritual venture for me, to bring to light the mystical core of religions, all of which want to see a new day, and the light of truth and knowledge emanate from Jerusalem - 'City of Peace'.

Was there one thing that sort of set off your path to the more spiritual type things? My parents are very spiritual people, so I grew up with a lot of spirituality around me but there was definitely a switch from a sort of intellectual seeking to something that just sort of cracked open in my soul. My path was a very personal seeking for a while; I felt I was always asking and looking for something, and when I opened the ancient texts they started speaking to me in a very personal way. I was getting answers to questions I hadn't gotten answers to before and it wasn't necessarily from the religious authority figures teaching them, but from the ancient authors and prophets of the texts themselves. At religious institutions where I studied, it was frustrating sitting in class learning them in a very dogmatic way, but the texts themselves, started speaking to me. The encounter with the texts was what opened my soul.

So, certain things were standing out to you that had a lot more meaning? Yes. It's interesting because I had seven years of living in this Jewish narrative and now it's opening up to something more universal. So, now looking back, I feel like I had these universal questions that I was finding answers to in these Jewish texts. For me at the time, I felt like I was encountering a level of beauty, like this whole world that has been hidden from me and has always been portrayed in this overly pious religious 'just behind the garb'. But then the ideas themselves were so intellectually and philosophically and artistically attractive to what I was looking for, that I feel like I kind of managed to sneak in under all of the preconceptions that are put on these religious texts; to transcend the external differences between my soul and the soul of the person writing it and just have this direct connection beyond time and space of the search. Then, to be able to take that back into my life and not necessarily become or be part of a set track to become very religious or orthodox, but to take that direct connection and bring it into our modern context, that's really a challenge.

Where did your Kabbalistic* interest come from?

Everything I was drawn to was from the mystical tradition. The mystical tradition; I see it not like a separate shelf on the bookshelf, it's more like the entire tradition, if you dig a little deeper, that's Kabbalah. It's like the inner dimension of the entire tradition. So, anything I was drawn to was looking at the deeper meaning. For example, looking at the deeper meanings of some of the 613 commandments. There's one where you wash your hands in the morning, first your right hand, then your left hand, then your right hand, left, right, left; and most of your life you grow up and see people doing this stuff and you think, this is crazy, who told them to do this one time and now they are hooked on it. But, then these texts have pages and pages of making the body a sacred temple for drawing down the Kabbalistic forces of the right and the left, and by doing this simple procedure with the water, you are bringing more life force into reality. That's just the tip of the iceberg; there are pages and pages on this practice and so on for all the other practices.

I researched what I could understand on it (Kabbalah), but it seems like it has to be imparted to you as sort of a secret sort of fellowship of informed people. Did somebody fill you in on this or were you just gleaning it yourself? I definitely met some people along my path who had a purity of heart that communicated certain ideas to me in what felt like an authentic way. It wasn't an esteemed Rabbi; sometimes the Rabbis are hiding the truth instead of revealing it. One thing to remember with all the secrecy around

---

* Note: Kabbalah is defined as the ancient Jewish tradition of mystical interpretation of the Bible, first transmitted orally and using esoteric methods (including ciphers). It reached the height of its influence in the later Middle Ages and remains significant in Hasidism. While it is heavily used by some denominations, it is not a religious denomination in itself. It forms the foundations of mystical religious interpretation. Kabbalah seeks to define the nature of the universe and the human being, the nature and purpose of existence, and various other ontological questions. It also presents methods to aid understanding of these concepts and thereby attain spiritual realization. It is thought to pre-date the world religions.

Kabbalah, is that there's sort of a grand narrative around the mystical tradition in Judaism and relating to when it can be revealed.

The revelation has to do with the onset of the Messianic era. Revealing the inner tradition is bringing about the Messianic era. When we see that the secret Jewish teaching is becoming more revealed, we know the Messianic era is approaching. This means that revealing it was always, like in the Zohar (the chief text of the Jewish Kabbalah, presented as an allegorical or mystical interpretation of the Pentateuch), the author of the main text of Jewish mysticism said, (do you know the Jewish word, oy? Yes, I use it all the time.) 'Oy, if I reveal it, and oy if I don't reveal it!'

So there is this tension: on the one hand there's a deep and complex mystical framework that represents the ultimate truth, but on the other hand there is this kind of urgency of bringing out this layer in a way all can understand so that people aren't dwelling in false beliefs. Then sages of different eras push that boundary line for how much can we reveal and when is the right time to do so, and did I reveal too much and agonizing over whether it's time to reveal it. Around the 18th century, there was a movement of popular Kabbalah, not in the sense of making it shallow, but in a sense of making it available to everyone. The leader of that movement was named the Baal Shem Tov. His idea was to reveal God everywhere; to reveal God in every person. He would go to the marketplace and teach people the deepest secrets. Stories he shared taught that sometimes, the most complicated Kabalistic codes couldn't open the gates of heaven, but the prayer of one person who didn't know the words to the prayer, but just cried because he didn't know how to pray—that was what opened the gates of heaven. This revival movement— Chasidism—was about returning to the inner point of the heart; that is what can shatter all of the gateways.

Which is sort of the drawback of most religions. They've gotten so stuck behind a facade of rules and hoops to jump through; protecting themselves to make sure people follow them and don't break away. Yes, I can see that (what Ayala said). Is that what led you into astrology? A year before I began seriously studying astrology, I met someone with whom I had a powerful connection but was not sure if this person was a life partner. As part of my decision making process I received a series of psychic and astrological readings which opened the Pandora's box of my journey of self-knowledge and awakening.

A year after I received the astrology reading, I looked at my chart and I wondered what this reading was based on and thought perhaps I should look into the placements and aspects a bit more. I started with drawing up my own chart, wanting to be aware of what it meant that the planets were where they were. A lot of things in the reading didn't resonate much at the time, but a year later things from the reading would surface, and the chart emerged as the place I felt I needed to look for more information on what I was experiencing. As I learned and explored there were so many things that resonated, and I eventually began looking at other people's charts that I knew and telling them about what I saw. All the while I kept in mind that the calendar is such a central theme in Judaism and the intersection of souls and cycles of time was an area that transcended boundaries between traditions.

There is an entire field called Kabbalistic Astrology based on an astrological tradition in Judaism, but it is my belief that all of astrology and all of Kabbalah are united at an even deeper juncture. I started from basic intuitive connections; for example the month someone is born in is important in Judaism, and the day they were born, if there was a holy person who passed on that day, then they may be connected to that soul trajectory. I studied people's birthdays from the Kabalistic perspective side by side with their astrology charts and would find crossover points where they were telling the same story—a story that could only be fully deciphered by combining the two traditions, or perhaps two halves of one lost tradition. I was thinking, 'what are these two sacred traditions drawing at that are bringing down this information that is really only accessible from this inner place of connection'? There are ways to study those disciplines that are very intellectual, but once you're in that connected space, they start fusing together and emerging from a shared nameless field.

Where did you learn all this! When I read your posts on Facebook, it blows me away. I have no idea what it means that so and so part of this planet is affecting another part, and so on. Who taught you all these things? With the astrology, I'm an autodidact; I like doing my own research and I have a feel for what's authentic and what is emerging from another's viewpoint. My curiosity has led me to extensive personal research and study as well as archived, online and live lectures of modern-day experts. With Kabbalah, I've been studying my whole life in institutions and training, but with astrology, I have charted my own course of study and research. In recent years, I've been immersed in charts. It gets me up in the morning, this ongoing search, this mystery that I want to keep unfolding and uncovering, and sometimes it all shatters; my rational mind kicks in. With anything that's based on synchronicity and correlation you can have amazing moments when everything comes together, and then it starts to disintegrate a little, so it is definitely an emotional journey in trying to recover all these ancient systems.

Are those moments psychic? In other words, do you think you are psychic or know that you are?

That was one of the things I learned in my first reading. I was told I have some powerful planets in my 12th house, which is the house of the unconscious, and Neptune, which is also the planet of the unconscious that would lead to psychic abilities. I was studying metaphysical subjects and was always curious and drawn to those, but we're raised in a world in which I was never empowered to connect to that place. It's almost like it was always hovering underneath the surface. The astrology was this gateway to accessing it; especially other people's charts, there was a certain period when I would have to read charts, because that's what would get me

in that base of coming back to this well of wisdom inside. It's like it wouldn't take part unless I was studying something that was beyond the mind.

Does the Kabbalah come before astrology or does astrology affect Kabbalah? It's interesting. All this stuff about intuition and connecting to the inner wellspring of wisdom; that's all over Kabbalah. I think that's also why they say that you need an instructor or you need it to be transmitted because you can read these texts your whole life, but if your head is the thing reading them, even if you are very educated and spiritual, the head is only getting one percent of it. Everything in Kabbalah is trying to connect a person to their pineal gland and the heart center and all these gateways we have to the divine realm for the human being to become perfected, to become a channel for to connect heaven and earth. And so, these concepts are all over Kabbalah, and they're discussed, but I guess it's kind of like you need to know the language of that experience to really tap into it.

It's ironic today because due to the travails of exile and history, the Jewish people who are carrying this tradition have to some extent lost that experience. Many people from other traditions, who are becoming interested in Kabbalah, are the ones who have the experience, but don't necessarily have the vocabulary of the architecture of the higher realms from those who have traveled there over the centuries. So in many cases, the Jewish people are carrying the vocabulary and external structures, and seekers from all traditions are carrying the experience. If we can humbly learn together, perhaps the prophecies of the Messianic era will be realized, and knowledge will cover the earth like water covers the sea, and God and the kingdom of heaven will no longer be eclipsed in this reality.

Would you consider Kabbalah to be enlightenment? If somebody would ask you (about Kabbalah), what is it? I'd speak about the different layers of the Jewish tradition. There is the Torah: the five books of Moses, that are called The Revealed Torah. That's what God gave the world in writing. Inside of that is The Concealed Torah, which is Kabbalah. That is the study of God; the divine reality. The divine reality is unified, but has many aspects to it. A later iteration or "bringing down" of Kabbalah is a movement that began in the 18th Century, Chassidus, which in essence is the psychological dimension of Kabbalah. That's not studying God for the sake of studying God, but studying God for the sake of perfecting our vessel so that we become a translucent receptacle for the divine flow. The idea is that reality is monotheism, there is one God. If there is one God, and the world was created by God, then Kabbalah goes about this saying that if God was all that existed in the beginning, then how can there be a world? So, it must be that God contracted himself and then created a space that could be an empty void, and that's where the world exists. That is why the world can produce an illusion of separateness and of God not existing, and so on and so on. But, according to the basic truth that God exists everywhere, the role of the mystic is to reveal that God exists even in the void and that no place is really devoid of God. By revealing the interconnectedness of everything, the oneness of everything, we correct the original mistake. The withdrawal of God and creating the empty void is also related to the sin of Adam and the shattering of the vessel; the cosmic myth about how this reality came to be. The way we fix all that is by showing that even though something appears to be separate, there is actually divine energy animating everything, so with the human being, this becomes, not so much like other religions talk about getting over the ego, but the big emphasis in Kabbalah is almost going through the ego. If we take anything and put it aside and say this is not God, this is something we need to get away from, that is kind of denying the truth that God willed everything into being. We go through this experience of separate consciousness, seeming separate, and through that experience we reveal that even this feeling I have, I'm existing right now, that is actually God. The highest experience is when this whole vessel and this whole experience of consciousness is experienced consciously as nothing but him, or there's really no experience of separation. And that's kind of the agony of the mystic, wanting this experience that is almost antithetical the creation of a world of where there is another, but the desire for that experience is so strong that when you taste it, it is something you can never forget. It becomes transforming reality through perception and consciousness which I think is really what some really amazing individuals around the world right now are doing through their own experience.

Can you give an example? I've had my own experiences that have been just momentary when I feel like I'm no longer my separate time- and space-bound self; where I almost feel like I'm channeling something, or I feel like I am becoming this kind of receptacle for something else that I just want to give that space to. But, I haven't been able to live that because it's so easy to get distracted again into the illusion. I guess when I say that people are doing that, I'm referring to things that are being written about it, and people who are discussing ascension and this process that we're going through where we're ascending from this illusion of separation back to the oneness. I guess I'm referring to the whole movement, or group of people are communicating about the same ideas that are in these texts. As far as living them, that's the challenge and always has been.

When you first started talking about the Torah, you said 'inside that'. Does that mean there are further writings that came later? So, each part tells what is inside the one before? Definitely academically, they see it as a historical progression; you have the Biblical Period, the Rabbinic Period, the Mystical Period and so on. In that narrative the mystical tradition sort of popped up around the 12th or the 13th Century. The mystical tradition however attests about itself that it goes back to Adam, the first created being, and that it was communicated orally from father to son. According to tradition Abraham is the author of one of the main mystical texts, so you have this mystical tradition going on behind the scenes but then it is revealed to select circles in the 12th Century. As far as where it's located, the traditional approach is that if you take any verse in the Bible, especially the first verse, and especially in the original Hebrew where every word can be translated five different ways. Even with the English translation, there are so many questions that come up from the original verse. So, the mystical tradition as well as the whole interpretive tradition comes from just asking questions; from encountering the five books of Moses and then just asking a question.

What happens in the mystical tradition is the techniques of asking questions become a lot more rational and more associative and imaginative and creative; you'll have calculating the numerology of the different words in a sentence, kind of moving away from syntax. There will even be Kabbalistic teachings about the shapes of the letters, or the shapes of the designs on the tops of the letters. Kind of going into this psychedelic state of just having anything in the text sort of speak to you or signal something to your soul that there is more in there.

But don't you have to have the original (text) to do that? I definitely think that there is a deep (meaning) between the Kabbalistic teachings and the sounds and shapes of them. But from my experience, people who began learning something like the Hebrew alphabet can often get more out of mystical teachings about Hebrew than Hebrew seekers can because they don't take for granted the shape of the letter and how different letters fit together, and their questions are a lot more creative. I think a lot can be gained just from knowing the 22 letters of the (Hebrew) alphabet, and their sounds and their shapes.

Reading the mystical texts in English, just having that basic framework of the alphabet adds a whole lot. But, I think one thing that I hope happens is showing the world that the English text of the Bible, that is really the basis for the monotheistic religion, is a lot more dynamic than it appears. The most orthodox forms of Judaism are actually based on this extreme dynamism of the text of the Bible. Even if you go to the ultra-orthodox Jews, they are living their lives based on a very creative dynamic approach to this sacred text. What is so exciting about that approach, is that it's all based on consciousness in the encounter of the person who is totally sovereign of his own experience reading the text in the original text. That's why it's important to have that direct connection and not be always getting it from a church, or Rabbi, or institution, but to have that encounter with the text.

I think if the text was translated, it's fine, but when anything sort of pops up, we should realize that a word that seems out of place, it might be interesting just to see what it was in the Hebrew, and any level of Hebrew can already reveal a lot. If I went to study the Bhagavad Gita (sometimes referred to as Gita, is a 700 verse scripture that is part of the Hindu epic, Mahabharata) in translation, I would need to keep in mind who is translating it, and all of that. Sounds complicated! No, it's all very simple.

Something I read (about Kabbalah) was the description of the beginning of the world created in six days. Kabbalah says that is really a spiritual description and not a physical description. Is that right?

It's interesting. I've been working on my latest hobby, looking at historical timelines; looking at the astrological ages and this whole theory that a lot of these historical sites around the world were built around 10,500BC, which was the end of the last golden age. I've been looking at the creation story and seeing if these could match up in any way. One thing I found right away, first of all, for the six days of creation the first parallel that is made is that they represent millennia. That's where the narrative comes from; we're now in the Jewish year of 5,700 years since creation. The world is supposed to exist for 6,000 years and then the 7,000th years are like the Sabbath, sort of the Messianic era.

The first parallel made is that six days is referring to this world existing for six days of work, and after that 6,000 years, and era of redemption and Messianic era. One thing I found interesting was that some of the commentaries say that on the first day, when it was evening, the commentators say, 'if it was evening, then there must have already been an order of time', because it was said that on the first day God created light and then there was evening. What does it mean that it was evening? Does that mean the world did a revolution around the sun? But how could it be evening? There must have been some structure in place that defined what morning and evening were. So the commentators say that something existed before the moment of creation. I think that kind of opens up an interesting space for creation happening sometime around the age of Gemini to the age of Taurus. Going back, there were other ages but they weren't in the same format as our current world. That's what I'm working on now; relating this 7,000 year narrative to what the Mayan and Hindu texts say about these ages that go back in cycles, and seeing how those can go together.

What do you mean by the ages? It's a really complicated topic, but once you get into astrology enough, or any ancient text, you have to get over this hurdle of the complex astronomical question. Pretty much, the spring equinox which is when the hours of day and night are equal, happens when the sun moves through the first degree of Aries in the Zodiac. What happens is, if you take a certain star in Aries that doesn't move, then look at the first star of the constellation of Aries, which is a shape that exists in the division of the sky (called Aries), it turns out that moves one degree every 72 years. What happens is over time, the constellation that we call Aries is actually now in the part of the sky that we call Taurus. This is called the procession of the equinoxes. There was a time when the spring equinox occurred perfectly in Aries, and that's when a lot of astrology was written, and that's why Aries is associated with the spring equinox. Still, we say that spring occurs when the sun reaches Aries, but we're saying that because the sun reaches the portion of the sky that is called Aries, even though the actual constellation of Aries has slightly shifted.

It gets really complicated because you have some astrologers who go by where the constellation actually is, and some going according to the divisions of the sky that never move. I have to say that where the constellation is, makes a lot more intuitive sense to me, but also the astrology I've connected to so far, has been in the divisions of the sky, so I'm kind of in this moment of crisis! Aside from that technical type of question of how do you read a horoscope, what this means for long term time keeping is that on the Zodiac, if you take the point of the equinox, then the time it was in zero Aries until the time it will get back to zero Aries, was 26,000 years. The equinox will be in each sign for about 2,000 years. So again, when astrology was coming together, that was the age of Aries, which was up until the time of Jesus' birth, and then around the time the advent of Christianity we moved into the age of Pisces which is the connection with the fish and Jesus. Also, Pisces is the sign of sacrifice and giving over of one's self, and the dissolution of boundaries. That connected with the Judeo-Christian ethic of the sacrifice of Jesus for our sins.

The age of Pisces is now ending and sign that will be rising at the equinox will be Aquarius and that's where the Age of Aquarius comes in. We have this way of defining ages that are about 2,000 years long, and the 26,000 year cycle was something all the ancient cultures probably knew about. This is really an amazing thing because we're talking about the movement of the stars one degree in the sky every 72 years! Isn't that amazing!

The conventional narrative is that there is no way they could have known this. One theory is that the Sphinx, a lion, is facing the area that the constellation of Leo would have risen at on the spring equinox during the age of Leo which was 10,500 years ago. That is one of the theories, that a lot of these ancient sites were built as complex astrological observatories that measured many things; among them was this 26,000 year cycle. Now modern science doesn't know why this 26,000 year cycle is caused but they have many theories about why stars are moving this way, or why we are moving in this very slight way. Some say that the earth wobbles, another is that the sun is revolving around a binary star, so the sun sort of has its own orbit; not only are we orbiting around the sun, but the sun is also orbiting around something. These movements that aren't taken into how we normally calculate days and years and local cycles but there are also these vast, or longer term cycles that are connected to our sun and what our sun is revolving around, that it may be these ancient cultures knew more about it than we do and they associated this 26,000 year cycle with great cataclysms that happened around the time before all these observatories were built.

Now a lot of people are working on where we are in this cycle and what I know is we're not back at the moment before the cataclysm which was the age of Leo. The Zodiac can also be divided up to the four animals that were on the chariot, you have the bull, the lion, the eagle and the man in Ezekiel's vision. The age of Leo corresponded to the lion and that marked when a lot of these cataclysms happened in the ancient world. And now, we're approaching the Age of Aquarius, which is the age of man. That's one explanation that could have backed all the 2012 narrative about this change happening to the cataclysms that supposedly happened in 10,500BC. I'm in the middle of all of this; I don't really have a clear narrative, but I just find all this fascinating that astrology is really the key to these cultures and these longer term cycles.

So when Ezekiel saw the wheel, could that have been the movement of these constellations? It could be; the idea of a cycle within a cycle. I had an intuition about that when I saw somewhere something written about cycles within cycles that reminded me of the vision. Some people say that we had contact from other cultures (flying saucers?) like the Indian scriptures talk about the Mana (Vimana), the flying machine. Some people say that was some kind of contact we had with these beings that came to give us technology or wisdom, or advance our enlightenment.

Is the Zodiac (comprised of) all constellations or is the Zodiac just some constellations? The Zodiac is a 16° wide strip of the sky that the sun rises and sets on and all of our planets rise and set on. So, the sun is always going to rise and set through the Zodiac; through the 12 constellations. The rest of the sky is a whole lot of

– 176 –

constellations like the Big Dipper and all that we see and can point out, but our sun will never move through that region of the sky.

Why 16°? I had this period when I was looking at charts and felt like I was getting all this information but if I tried to sit down and explain to someone, I would not be able to create a linear narrative. One day I wondered, what is this circle with all the signs all around it, and why is it a circle? At times I feel like I am back in kindergarten, learning the most basic astronomical facts but with the intuitive mind awake. For example in some mystical traditions the tilt of the earth at 23 degrees is a physical representation of the "fall" from Eden, and an impending polar shift will change life on earth as we know it. Basically the ecliptic that contains all the constellations is 16° wide, for reasons I do not yet understand. I do know that if we were on the Tropic of Cancer, which is right above the equator, the ecliptic, which is the arc of the sky that the Zodiac is in, would be in a perfect arc above where you were standing. Now it's just a strip of the sky; everything will rise in the east but that strip won't be a perfect arc above, it will be a band from northeast to northwest, for example. Everything rises in the east and sets in the west, because the earth is rotating east.

Some of the things that I see, I don't understand; like when you are talking about 'something is in the house of something else', does that have something to do with the Zodiac or constellations? Yes. There are several ways of characterizing planets in your chart. One is by planet signs, and the other is by planet houses. There are 12 signs; that is about where the planets are (located) in that strip of the Zodiac when a person is born. For example, we have Jupiter in Gemini, so if you go outside tonight you'll probably see Jupiter; it rises just before the moon in the east. It's so cool to see the moon and Jupiter in a telescope! (However, it ended up being too cloudy for me.) Is that easier than seeing the rings of Saturn? The first time I saw the rings, it was unreal, like something fake. It's important to bridge astrology and astronomy because everything the astrologers are talking about is what the astronomers are looking at, so it's fascinating to bring these two together.

Jupiter is now in Gemini. On any given night, we see half of the Zodiac because the other half is below the horizon, kind of like a circle all around us. We can now see Jupiter because Gemini is rising in the sky around sunset, whereas, Saturn is now in Scorpio and Scorpio is below the horizon and was only viewable a few months ago. So one way of understanding a chart is by looking at where the planets are in the constellations. For example, Jupiter is now in Gemini, the moon is now in Cancer, the sun is now in Scorpio and so on. That relates to the astronomical climate at the moment and at the moment of birth.

The houses are determined by the time of birth. For example, for your horoscope, I wasn't able to do any information based on houses, because there wasn't any time of birth. Have you heard a term like Sagittarius rising? Yes. Well, you are going to have to do some detective work, because if you ever want to know your rising sign, you need the time of birth. Some astrologers are really good and can tell you your time of birth based on what should be in your chart. The time of birth helps us hone in on the moon placement and establish the axes of a chart. Right now Jupiter is in Gemini for the whole planet. But, whether Jupiter is rising on the horizon or below the horizon, is going to depend on where I am on the planet and what time of day it is; hence birth time and birth place. The houses in a chart correlate to what the sky looks like at a given moment and place. Then the planets that are above the horizon tell a certain story and the ones below the horizon tell a different story. Each of the 12 divisions above and below the horizon represent a different area of focus.

The first house is the house of self. The second is possessions; the third is the mind, and so on. How many houses are there? Twelve, same as the Zodiac. They're related to the signs, so the first house is related to Aries because Aries is the self starter, the moving forward energy, and that is the house of self. The second house is related to Taurus. Taurus is security and grounded. That's me! Right! You have your sun and Mars in Taurus. Mars is another very forceful planet and having it right next to the sun makes it forceful, and having it in Taurus defines its priorities - practicality, being established in a project or home, being grounded. You have this sun - Mars conjunction in Taurus that accentuates both the Taurus element and the power of Mars.

As far as the houses, if you had a birth time in what was in your second house, it would also tell part of that Taurus story. It's kind of like another layer of the charts. I find it really informative; the houses, often my first source of information. I like the idea of connecting to what the sky looked like at that moment and also I just like when I have lots of information, when different systems overlap and confirm an overall interconnected story about the soul's divine blueprint.

What kind of things can you tell by knowing where the stars are located? It's more like learning the traditions associated with what sign was overhead. Let's say, in the sky right now, Aquarius is overhead. When I was born, the sign of Scorpio was overhead. I've never really associated myself with a Scorpio; I'm a Cancer, rising Capricorn, Aries moon. But my mid-heaven, which was the sign that was directly above when I was born, is Scorpio. That's only accessible for a person at a given time and place. For me, that's a huge key to my personality; an aside, the mid-heaven was directly above in astrology and this is what's been carried down from ancient cultures that intuited the meaning of these placements. Whatever was in mid-heaven, is often what your direction is in this world; what your career will be. The mid-heaven is what is shining down at that moment. There are a lot of things in a chart that will hint at life's purpose.

For example, the north node is a fascinating piece of astrology, not actually a planet but has to do with the lunar cycle. It's two critical points in the lunar cycle that have been studied by a lot of different civilizations; you have a north node and a south node. These have a lot of meaning in evolutionary astrology. The north node is your trajectory of development and your south node is what you are coming out of, or the karma you are coming out of. Where the north node is in a chart is what you are growing into and the direction you should be reaching for in this life, and how to measure your evolution.

Your north node is in Pisces, which is a really beautiful placement. Do you remember how we talked about the age of Pisces and the connection with Jesus? Pisces is the end of the astrological cycle, right before Aries. Where Aries is all about stealth, Taurus is all about stuff and being here, Pisces is almost the opposite of that movement, it's the end of the chart, it's the dissolution of boundaries, it's transcendent; in a negative way it can almost be like the coming apart of self or sacrifice of self like in the Christian narrative. But, in a positive sense, in the Christian narrative as well, it's a sort of transcending of ego for others, it's the connection with the collective, it's a water sign so it has to do with the subconscious, or the superconscious. So having your north node there, I think is a really beautiful placement. I think that's your trajectory of growth.

It's interesting because the south node is always going to be the opposite sign, so that's kind of where you are coming from and that's Virgo. What you had been saying about footprints being on the carpet is very Virgo. (Laughing.) I have no Virgo, although I am developing some Virgo. People with Virgo have to have everything in order and everything be obedient and fixed and trained and routine. But moving from Virgo to Pisces is moving toward freedom. Pisces is the fish, so it has to do with swimming and water and being flexible and adaptable and is also moving towards fun and play; transcending boundaries. If you know Krishnamurti (Jiddu Krishnamurti, May 12, 1895 – February 17, 1986, was a speaker and writer on philosophical and spiritual subjects), he also had his north node in Pisces and his south node in Virgo. He was an amazing Indian sage who was groomed to be this leader in his tradition, but ended up breaking all conventions of thought and taught to have no preconceptions, and this very radical message of truth and freedom from the mind that grew away from his upbringing and tradition. It was kind of the movement from rigidity to flexibility. Virgo is also like working for someone, where, with Pisces, you are employed by the collective; or you're like a channel for the collective.

(At this point, Ayala held up the chart she had made for me so I could view it on the screen.)

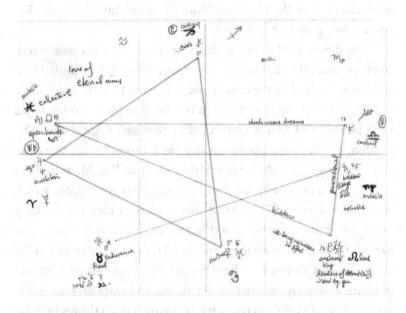

Here is your north node, and if you see these two blue lines, they make an astrological formation called a Yod. (Astrology explains that raised or multi-aspected planets within the Yod can produce unusual situations and personalities, and should therefore be carefully examined.) A Yod comes from the Hebrew lettering Yud; stressful situations or pressures, burning creates yearning, it's frustrating or agonizing or difficult placement that makes growth inevitable, so it burns but it also creates yearning that has to be birthed.

The place at which the Yod points is what is going to be burst. So, this north node in Pisces grows into this trajectory of your soul path which is Pisces; serving and being a channel for the collective: healing need. But then there are these two stressful affects that are pushing that along. That has to do with, on one hand we have Neptune in Libra; these two placements actually belong to the whole generation of people who were born around the time when you were born, but you happen in the north node which is a unique placement for you. There were a lot of people in the generation that were affected by the Neptune/Pluto dynamic, but the resolution you are bringing to it is unique.

The dynamic that needs this resolution is on the one hand, Neptune and Libra has to do with ideals, visions, dreams, balance and harmony, and on the other hand, Pluto and Leo; there are some astrologers who say that this sign is related to Pluto having to do with power, and Leo is connected to that astrological age: The Golden Age. So, some people say that the Pluto and Leo generation were the kings of the Atlantean civilization (past life). Many of them are back here now to be leaders in the Aquarius generation, which is a different energy. Maybe in this Atlantean civilization, they were power and leadership in this very esteemed role was almost handed to them or taken for granted and now it's a different kind of leadership. It's almost like there has to be an overcoming of karma of being an overly revered kingly figure and instead, one of the associations of Pluto and the sun is bringing hidden things to light. There is this dynamic that can happen on the one hand of having the ideals and visions and dreams, and on the other hand, almost like going beneath the surface and bringing hidden things to light, that this is what can push you on this evolutionary path. So that's one part of your chart.

This is exactly what I am hoping to do with this book; to lead people into enlightenment. There was a single point in my life that changed me and I haven't looked back since. Yes, you have a very special astrological formation. In some traditions it was seen as a chosen one. The Yud is 10, which in Kabalistic numerology relates to the ten fingers, and Yud is related to the word Yod, which is hand, so it's considered the finger of God. It's like the finger of God is pointing, but the aspects of the planets involved make it not a pleasant experience; it's off in a deep, ancient, karmic thing, but it's not like the shapes in astrology that have this endless dynamic of not going anywhere. It's always pushing and producing something. That's exactly what we have in 2012, at the winter solstice there is a Yod and it's pointing at Jupiter, which, just like Mars is pointing at your north node, sort of your evolutionary movement, the Yod at 2012 points at Jupiter which is, among other things, fate.

One interpretation I saw; there is going to be this huge revolution in the way we think about (and it's also in the house of Gemini, which is about writing and text) religious text. Through this experience of pressure on the soul and pressure that's kind of forcing something ancient to resurface that will get us out of this dilemma.

Do you see anything for 12/12/12? I went to a three day seminar where we communicated with the Pleiadians and Lemurians and went to different dimensions; one of the strangest things I ever did. We also met with the Galactic Council and all three were together for the first time. We talked about the megaliths, crop circles, pyramids and the sphinx, and all those are connected. We are to be leaders. The person who ran the seminar was psychically told that I was to attend, so I was allowed in as a guest even though the seminar had reached the limit. I guess I am being led and doing what I'm supposed to be doing. (I continued telling Ayala about the seminar and also how so many people call me a healer.)

You know the Pleiades are in Taurus so you might be connected to them in other ways too. The bull is one of the constellations in Taurus, but right next to the bull is the Seven Sisters (the Pleiades). Taureans are often connected to them. Taurus on the Huber calendar is the month of Iyyar, which is the month of healing, and we now have Chiron and Neptune in Pisces; this will be a long period because these planets move really slow. Chiron is the planet of the wounded healer; one who experiences their own pain and out of it becomes a healer and Neptune is the planet of spiritual insight. So we have these two forces working together in Pisces which is the sign of the dissolution of boundaries and self sacrifice for the other, and that is right over your north node; the head of the evolutionary trajectory, so you have these two planets helping you, the wounded healer and healing.

You said that a lot of people around my time of birth were in that Neptune area, but then you said something about Pluto. Does that mean all of them were in that Pluto area too? The thing with Neptune and Pluto is they also move slowly, so they do define generations, but there are also qualities of their placements that hold unique lessons for an individual. In your chart you have Neptune at 17 (degrees) Libra, and Pluto at 17° Leo. When two planets are the exact same degree, that's a sign for me, and also 17 is a powerful number. There is a lot of 17 in Kabbalistic astrology, and Santos Bonacci (researching the ancient works, compiling and translating them into more accessible terms in his study of AstroTheology) has also taught extensively on the number 17. That really jumped out at me, and the fact that they're connected to your north node, is unique.

I saw somewhere on the internet that on election day, Mercury was starting on its way backward (retrograde). What does that cause? It's really interesting. One thing about this whole predictive astrology thing is; I was learning about the void moon. In each of the signs the moon starts a new story when it enters the sign, but those stories can have different lengths. Some of them continue for almost the whole two-and-a-half-day period, the time it takes to get through a sign, others are much shorter, but always there is a pause in the end of the story. It can be short or long, but it is always there. That pause in the end of the story is the void-of-course period of the moon. When the moon doesn't make any aspects in a chart and it happens every few days for a certain time like a few hours or sometimes for a whole day. I was just learning about this when Laurie* and I last connected and she told me about your book and next, we connected. And I noticed this was happening during a void

* See Chapter XV

moon; is that a bad thing? Traditionally the void moon is not a good time to start anything. So I was getting all these paranoid thoughts of maybe I should wait until after the void moon. I observe those thoughts, but I'm really not into that kind of astrology that is sort of predictively ominous in a simplified way because I think when astrology becomes too much like a science, that's when it becomes the most shallow. It's an art but it has to do with observing things and having that bounce off your own internal connectedness.

Technically the knowledge piece of it that has to bounce off us and be intuitively confirmed, the knowledge piece of it is that Mercury has to do with communication. From earth, it looks like Mercury, instead of moving through the Zodiac, Aries, Taurus and Gemini in the right order, it starts moving back, so every night it will be a little bit farther back. That has to do with an astronomical context I don't fully understand yet, but from earth, for a certain amount of time each year, it will look like planets are moving backward in the Zodiac, so some forms of traditional astrology saw this as (with that planet) things were going to be withdrawn or convoluted. So people say that around the election, that means we could have a replay of the year 2000, when the results aren't clear and things are messed up, so it's certainly a possibility; I think a lot of these things are kind of hidden, but I think astrology is about revealing the hidden dimensions. Reality kind of starts speaking to you, and it can definitely be demonstrated in the world, but I think it's subtle, and if it doesn't happen, it's still going to be Mercury retrograde.

The astronomy behind it has to do with Mercury is always going to be very close to the sun in a chart. It's almost like once Mercury gets too far ahead of the sun, it goes into retrograde to get back in sync with the sun, so it also has this positive aspect to it bringing it back in harmony with the solar system. That, on an inner level, can be like a time of reflection and inner worth, rather than outer worth. That's one way of understanding it. I think with a lot of these things it just has to resonate. I think we have all these planetary forces inside of us so we have to let them speak about the experience, revealing to us what Mercury feels like and why is Mercury going backwards. But it's deep, so we'll see. I'll definitely be watching on Tuesday.

So, just like a normal psychic, you get a feeling for the truth. Exactly. It's fun cocktail party stuff to talk about Mercury retrograde and the election, and I think there is an astrological tradition of predictions like that, but I feel that is not the highest form of this wisdom; I think it's very deep and profound and it has to do with a living mastery. I think for example, in the Jewish tradition, there is a practice around that if someone has a bad dream, then they should tell it to a friend and the friend should tell them three times, 'that was a good dream!' The act of interpreting a dream is a very delicate experience and people should be careful who they tell the dream to, and make sure they are telling it to someone who can take the good out of it and who can make the experience into good. There is actually a ceremony that is done for turning a bad dream into a good dream and it quotes verses from the Bible about making the bitter water sweet and turning the curses of Balaam into blessings; there's this story of Balaam who came to curse the Jewish people. Anything he said, anything that came from his mouth, instead of being a curse became a blessing. It's this deep Kabbalistic idea that darkness is just contracted light and with the right formula any aspect can be turned into a bridge to greatness, and actually that is what we are here to do—expand.

In a chart, that can work out because if someone has negative aspects between planets, in some forms of astrology might be like your weaknesses, your struggles, or a bad day, those are actually gateways to depth. A negative aspect makes you look at something, but what is going to come out of it can actually be deeper than the positive aspects. That's the deepest truth in mystical tradition; redeeming the light out of the darkness, or finding the light that is in the darkness. That has to do with how these practices are done. I'm very conscious of it when I give readings; I'm a very sensitive person and if I'm giving the reading and someone is telling me about all my weaknesses, that is probably going to create my reality. Or, if someone happens to see my weaknesses not as weaknesses, but actually as really deep and high aspirations that are somehow being obstructed because of physical conditions there to create a pearl out of friction, then I can have power again over my divine blueprint and move forward with self love.

Where do you see yourself going with this? Do you plan on growing this into some kind of business, or do you already consider yourself in business? You tell me! I'm in this new territory. When I was living abroad, and there were certain obstacles because I was in more Jewish context and there weren't people who really affirmed what I was picking up on. So I had to believe in myself and find some people who helped me believe in what I was talking about.

Back home, I have a new set of challenges of being okay with the fact that my deepest truths are not always confirmed to the people who have been central to everything I've done until now. As an empath I am sensitive to the thoughts of the community and people I associate with, and solitude and connecting with like minds helps me remember the truth of my path, guided by a higher intelligence. Looking at my chart, I've seen some karmic stuff around having some kind of connection to a mystery school that was persecuted or suppressed. Also, everything in the Jewish tradition about when is the right time for this stuff to come out; it's almost like the odds are against me to keep going on this journey. On the other hand, that just increases the desire and curiosity; it's that important. All odds are against it but it's the true self and the quest for knowledge.

Right now I think I have to learn. The first stage of it was that I came out with it and made this blog and started doing readings, but a few weeks ago I just felt like I had to stop doing readings. I'm really glad you found the reading of your chart helpful, because I haven't done one of these in a while. Recently my focus has been learning the back story of all this stuff I was picking up on. I have to admit that the intuitive stuff is immediate. It's like the less I know about astrology, the better it works. But then the mind and the researcher in me wants to figure out the other part; what it is that I'm looking at so that I can feel like I have a handle on this field that has produced all this wisdom. It's definitely evolving. Right now I feel like I just want to learn and take in as much as I can. We are in a physical realm, so ideally this will develop into something that I can spend all of my time on, and it's where I can be an independent fully functioning human being. Right now I am blessed to be able to devote a lot of time to studying, and I hope in the future I will have the opportunity to share it with others on different platforms.

You sort of hit on what I was going to ask you. Do you see people's futures; details or where they are going to end up? And the follow-up to that would be, have you looked into your own future on your charts? I do have Saturn, which can be the place of obstacles, in the area of studies and higher education. I've always been a successful student, but I've had a lot of starts and stops and a lot of different institutions. It's like I start in this amazing institution and then something will draw me out with it and then I'll do that all over again and it's already happened four or five times. Academic study for me is this area that is both compelling and challenging, and yet, many of my gifts are there so I have to keep pushing at it even though it's not one of those areas that just flows, in terms of persevering.

I do have a lot of planets around my mid-heaven and my career so I don't think I'll be able to give up on my worldly ambition, as much as I would love to become a hermit mystic. I guess the point is that a career enables me to bring this knowledge out into the world, even though it often feels that making a living with it involves making a compromise on the intensity and spontaneity. I think I do have this kind of drive and mission in the world that I see in my chart, so that is going to be an important part of my journey in how this manifests in the world.

This is also time of my Saturn return, which is something that happens when a person is 29, and again the second Saturn

– 188 –

---

return, later in life. The Saturn return is like a very difficult period. Everyone experiences it on a different level, but for me it totally resonates, almost like everything ends and you are totally reborn; you have to come out anew. We have Saturn in Scorpio, so it makes everything more intense. For me, I had this month back in August, where everything just ended. My relationship ended, my academic program ended; even though it wasn't supposed to end, I was in the middle of it, I just felt like I had to leave this academic context that was just way too heady because all this intuitive explosion from within. I moved from Israel, sold all my furniture, came back home and had to deal with all the family dynamics, it was like an insane pressure cooker, and yet, I know inside of me that I know something is going to be reborn. It's really going to be reborn; I was feeling in the dark for the first stone of what is this going to be. I couldn't pull from what came before me what this was going to look like.

So, that period is beginning now and will go for another year; I'm probably going to be in this liminal zone for awhile. Having said that, I believe in prayer and I believe that there is a force that works through the stars that we can connect with. Kind of like the Yod, with all the pressure at one point, I think that the best thing that can come out of this situation is a prayer; if I genuinely express to my higher self, or in my life, or to the higher power what is coming up in me through this higher process, that can also jog it along and bring about resolution more quickly. It's not like anyone is doomed to a bad year. Having said that, when things are changing rapidly or stuck, I think that astrology can help us accept it as it is, and then once we accept things, the ways to work around circumstances emerge and the blessings start appearing. Right? I'm in this space of just accepting that and feel like a totally different person than I was a week ago, than I was a month ago, and a year ago, and all this keeping the thread from day to day is the journey into this ancient wisdom that enlivens me. That's what I'm holding onto.

As far as telling the future in general (in charts), I'm surprisingly open to it considering that I'm not into the more rigid astrology. I kind of see it as, 'when are there opportunities?' It's such a natural thing for a person to want to know, 'what's around the corner for me?' I think the stars have always been a source for that; but it's about reading them in a way that focuses on opportunities and not negatives.

In your chart you have Chiron and Neptune right on the north node, the evolutionary trajectory, so you've got that; healing and spiritual planets there, so that's clearly a sign that this is an amazing era for your evolutionary growth. You also have Pluto over your own wounded healer; your Chiron, the wounded healer is in Capricorn, which is a karmic crisis between success and nurturing. Capricorn is the sign of success. Cancer, its opposite, is the sign of nurturing, security, comfort, tenderness, and familiarity, as opposed to Capricorn which is success, reputation; very different signs. Capricorn is more the father and Cancer is the mother, so having the wounded healer in Capricorn can indicate a karmic crisis about succeeding in one's quest and the need to justify self-worth through action. That's a little heavy. With Chiron, it could be that you have already healed that and now you are already onto the healing of others regarding that. It could go either way. It's a way to open up some blind spots inside, but also, if you've done a lot of work already, it might mean helping others along that trajectory of quest versus nurturing, and maybe not making those opposite anymore. That's where it is now, you are right on.

I had a feeling it's more the healer and less the wounded, or it's already been a little alchemized or transformed. The good thing is that you now have Pluto in Capricorn if you read astrology articles that say, Pluto and Capricorn, Pluto and Capricorn! You have Chiron in Capricorn, so that means Pluto is right over your Chiron; it's sort of like a bulldozer going through everywhere, churning things. It can reveal dynamics. Your Pluto is the sign that we said is in Leo, so it has to do with the king and the leaders of the ancient golden era of civilization. Having that transformative power moving over your own healer capabilities, shows that this is a particular time where there is an opening for this.

This must take you many hours to do each chart. Yours, I did on a few different sittings; I did just a short intuitive look, then I did some deeper research, and then a last intuitive thing, so probably 3-4 hours. Every chart for me is such a journey. I don't know if my direction is individual charts, or larger (ideas) of what age are we in, what ages have existed in history and these more general research and scholarly things. They are both so compelling. The chart work is kind of deep and I can't just do it in a removed, professional way, if I open my email in the morning and someone ordered a chart reading, I feel like oh my gosh! The whole day is going to be like the karmic journey into this wormhole of this other soul (always a mirror), and that's great! But, I want to feel out what is the best way to work with this energy. I think that once I get into the actual experience of relating to a person and coming across nuggets with a deep resonance about their souls and past, that's priceless and that's fun.

But, there's a lot of 'feeling your way in the dark' work and I'm not always sure where to take it. The directions I have been taking it in are kind of changing so we'll see; I definitely want to bring it to the world in some way. And that's actually one other thing about your chart that I can tell you or maybe wrap up your chart with. On the Kabbalistic calendar you were born in a time of the year that corresponds to the Tree of Life and each of the days in Gemini and Taurus are matched up to a pair of aspects on the Tree of Life. The Tree of Life is a tree of ten aspects that are considered the Godhead and are often mirrored in the human being; in the human body and the soul.

There are seven of them that correspond to the days of Gemini and Taurus, and moving through Taurus and Gemini is sort of like a cleansing of all these divine attributes as they're expressed in a human being. The pair of attributes that correspond to the day you were born, which is the 22nd of Iyyar, is the chesed of nesach (chesed translated as 'mercy, lovingkindness, steadfast love, or compassion and goodness; a primary virtue); it's the week of netzach, which is eternity, and chesed is love. This pair of attributes is the love that is in some eternal dynamic. Sometimes we can have an eternal trajectory, kind of like what you have on your chart; this very ancient, almost eternal mission. An image that came to me with the chesed part is bringing something with open hands and it's the love that's in that eternal mission that is the motor that keeps this going, or what you are out to give. That inspired me too, like it's about that love, it's about that handing over of information (as if) we're serving something higher that's bringing out these abilities and information and when we're serving that it's like taking orders.

There's a lot to talk about of your chart, but just briefly, with the Chiron and nurturing and success, you also have Jupiter in Aries, where Aries is very much about the self and Jupiter is expansion, then with Capricorn in a challenging aspect to the mothering, nurturing, tenderness side, so a lot of things I read about these aspects is that there is a very strong drive for success in a healthy way; that's Jupiter and Aries. It's self expression and expansion and also Capricorn is having something worldly that is not negative. However, those dynamics are in stressful aspect in this chart. From looking at the chart, the dynamics around success are locked into other stuff about emotional belonging. Then there is Venus in Cancer, which can be potentially problematic, like clinging to loved ones or needing to feel safe and so there could be this survival type thinking that is locked in this right triangle. In astrology, that's traditionally considered stressful and the energy will keep going like this.

That's also what all spiritual directions teach us, that we have to transcend the ego and temporal to achieve this kind of bliss. In your chart, it's really there, everything that's connected to the collective and the higher consciousness, is really moving forward, and anything that's about otherworldly expression or success is somehow locked in this dynamic. Now, that's what the traditional astrology could suggest, but I feel that to make that complete, we have to bring the ambition and the endurance and the nurturing; and Capricorn, the water goat, can sort of be the top of the mountain looking down and having wisdom and understanding, those have to be incorporated too, in order to fulfill all your personality, which is going to serve that larger purpose. I don't know if I have a clear cut answer, but I do see something with Taurus and being grounded, and practicality and ambition as being like key personality strengths. I guess the question for all of us is how do we feel like complete human beings and incorporate all of it into the divine plan.

If I become a millionaire, I'll send you a pile of money so you can get going on whatever you want to do. (Laughter) That's what I say sometimes. If someone is in a situation like me, I don't want to charge for a reading; this is information that we need! But I always say that if you win the lottery from what I tell you, cut me a check! It's sort of crazy in this age; I don't think I know anyone who is really comfortable. I know people who don't have a lot and are really happy, but I don't know too many people who are 'well to do' in this world and on the mark spiritually. I really feel like the people who are being woken up are these amazing heroes who are not always in the easiest situation, from the viewpoint of what our world values. I find that really moving. I've been happiest while being poor. Maybe what the world values is an illusion, as King Solomon the great said.

Have you ever heard of Abraham Hicks, who talks about creating your own reality? I was listening to that when I had my initial awakening to all this stuff and it really did wonders for me; expecting the best, and telling a story of success. I feel that if your mind can stay on track, I feel like reality has this weird thing where it sort of corresponds to the state you're in. For me, it's hard when you get in a rut and you think 'how do I change the channel?' Laurie Stinson says the same thing; if you want it, manifest it in your mind. I think it's really getting in touch with a lot of parts of us that are one with the creator; I think we can create, but it's a hidden layer inside. There are some techniques out there that say, imagine money and you'll find it. But I think it's like this part of ourselves that is all powerful.

And then the question is, when you connect with that part of yourself, are you really going to want money? What are you going to manifest once you're God? In the Kabbalistic tradition it's always emphasized that no matter how high you get, giving charity is the most sacred thing you can do. I like to remember that level. At the end of the day, that is the central part of human existence and there is no such thing as being an über-spiritual person and then tell everyone they don't have material needs. The highest spiritual level is giving materially! That also requires understanding that being comfortable is a good thing and is a divine gift. Can you tell that to the politicians? I think there is a lot more about our reality than we are led to believe; the most subversive thing we can do is just believe that the political system is irrelevant and to not live in the kind of dynamic that my biggest effect on reality is voting on Tuesday. I think we can do a lot more. If there is some agenda of the system we are in, it's to make us forget that, so, it's really subversive to tap into real knowledge and our true cosmic nature, and also remember how it can be relevant right here. It's our heritage and our purpose to realize that we are capable of being a channel of the divine. Praying is the most subversive thing a person can do; through one prayer, it can change reality.

— CHAPTER 12 —

MAGGIE CHULA

Note: I discovered Maggie online and, after reading the informa-tion on her web page, I was intrigued enough to want to know more. She definitely fit the bill of being different, that is, having different gifts than all the other mediums.

ABOUT MAGGIE (from her website- maggiechula.com): I am a Psychic, Vibrational Energy Healer and Teacher of Sacred Healing Wisdom. I am also a Channel of Light and Wisdom for the Master Teachers of the Akasha.

I have been consciously aware I was in Earth School since I was very young. My development as a Psychic and Healer was cul-tivated through my own profound life experiences and studies on:

- Mysticism
- Spirituality
- Alternative Healing
- Business Leadership
- Project Management
- Quantum Physics
- Subtle Energy Physics

I was in the corporate world for 24 years. A Project Leader for very high level, complex projects. I didn't realize it at the time but these very same skills of being able to take complex business issues and translate them into clear and concise business solutions have helped me to translate complex spiritual knowledge and develop profound tools and processes that you as a spiritual visionary need at this pivotal time.

In addition I have a natural ability to dialogue and channel information from the Master Teachers of the Akasha and your Council of Light. The Akasha is where your Soul resides. It is through this connection that I have created the courses that are the main body of my work to support and guide you as you manifest your big vision for your life's work.

I have always had an intimate connection to the energy and sacred healing wisdom of the Universal Source or God. This aware-ness has been with me through some shattering moments within my life and helped me heal my mind, body and spirit. It has shared with me many miraculous healings that have helped me move forward in my life when my heart was broken, my body was too weak to get out of bed on its own, and my motivation to live was almost gone.

Each time I was on the verge of giving up something inside me would rebel and say no, not at this time. I want one more chance to work this out. In that moment of fighting for my life I would be granted the knowledge of how to heal another layer or piece of my energetic being.

The energetic connection I have with God and the knowledge and wisdom that has been shared with me has helped me feel complete in my being. It is a feeling of belonging to all that is. This Divine Wisdom became my primary guide and counselor. I was guided and taught how to develop my knowledge and understand-ing of how to be whole and healthy within this physical existence while maintaining my deep connection to my Soul Light and the Universal Source of God.

The years I have spent on Earth working through my own jour-ney have helped me learn how to create Divine Health within my life and manifest a sense of joy, happiness and peace that radiates throughout my entire being. I have learned how to become healthy, happy and in alignment with my soul's purpose and life choices. My results combined with the results my clients and students have been able to attain prove your mind is in control of all the systems of your body and your consciousness is in control of your mind.

My work within the corporate world, taught me how to take complex business issues and translate them into clear and concise solutions. I have used these skills to translate complex spiritual knowledge and develop profound tools and processes that are needed right now at this pivotal time in the human conscious development. My work as a Neurolinguistic Hypnotherapist, Certified Psychic Professional, Spiritual Healer and Counselor, have helped me grow in my knowledge and understanding of how people create and maintain health and wellbeing within their body, emotions, mind and spirit.

I have combined my knowledge of what I have been able to manifest and create for my own health and wellness along with the skills and techniques I have learned within the work I have done to develop a series of transformational processes and techniques designed to show you how to create balance within your life and integrate your Sacred Healing Wisdom to help you heal on every level of your being.

Here is what my clients have been able to achieve from working with me and learning the processes and techniques I teach:

- Regenerate healthy organs instead of having surgery.
- Eliminate shingles after one session.
- Go into a state of balanced remission or eliminate degenerative diseases.
- Create and implement ways to live and thrive instead of quitting their jobs, changing their careers, or just giving up.
- Double their income within 12 months after working on their life plan, taking an assessment of their talents and

gifts, and realizing what they were contributing to their companies.

- Regenerate health and wellbeing after being told to make peace with their life and go prepare their loved ones for their transition.
- Stepping out of their comfort zone to acknowledge the visions they have and creating successful new careers.
- Chose to live instead of take their life because life was too hard and no one cared.

***

It was a day of fighting my way to get this interview done! I had stayed overnight with my brother about an hour away from Maggie and was ready to leave for her interview when I discovered my recorder batteries had given out. I fixed those and rushed off. Next my GPS quit, so I had to 'wing' my directions, but fortunately had Maggie's address written down. I eventually found Maggie's house and was invited in and even passed the cat test. She used her cats to sense people who were not welcome in the house (they sense energies that are not welcome so they can be cleared right away, so I was okay there. We sat down and I got out my recorder but it would not turn on! I had it working before I left, and now it was refusing to operate! Maggie, fortunately, had a phone with a recorder and made the tape for me, so I was thankful I had made it through the morning's trials and was excited and ready to speak to someone who was able to see the Akashic Records.

My goal is to pay it forward. I have always worked with the divine guidance but I will share with you that I did not care or know who all these beautiful light beings were. All I cared about was that I could tune in and get beautiful wisdom to come through. I am smart enough to realize this wisdom is not coming from me. The words that were coming through were for me to help me heal my life. I've always been a natural healer, I know this because I had been sick most of my life, and I am healthy now. I credit the master teachers of the Akasha for helping me attain and maintain my current healthy state of being. (Using Divine Wisdom as her primary guide and counselor, Maggie was taught how to develop her knowledge and understanding of how to be whole and healthy within this physical existence while maintaining her deep connection to her Soul Light and the Universal Source of God; from her web page at maggiechula.com.) So, I think that from the beginning I have always known I had this ability (being a natural healer).

But, my family's point of view was my abilities were something I had to be protected from because people would think I was dangerous or scary. When I was little people would be frightened of the things I shared with them. I was told my abilities and the angels I saw didn't exist. There is a whole section of my family that believed I wanted to establish a cult. I would be the worst person ever at creating a cult because while people have always gravitated to me like I was some kind of guru, I still run away from that devotion. It's truly funny anyone would think that about me because my whole message is, 'anything anyone else can do you can do yourself!'

Anything I can do, other people can do. So I have spent a lot of time teaching spiritual concepts. Then, about a couple years ago I had created and taught about 10 different classes when a student came to me and said, you know, I think all your classes are really the same thing. He said it respectfully. I thought about it and realized it is all the same. It is all the same and keeps leading back to the Akasha. But, it isn't the Akashic Records like Edgar Cayce. The records are only one of the tools. I almost feel like the angels have pulled me into a Harry Potter kind of world. When I look back at the kind of world I have lived in, I can see how the people around me believe that I can do this, but they don't think they can.

To me, it's like the angels are my older brothers (helping with the Akashic Records); most have that male energy. What I'm doing now is finishing up a 15 session course: The Akashic Vibration. If you've read my web site, you know that the Akashic Vibration is where your soul resides. That's also where you can get to the vibration of the divine, where your source is. What I love about the work I do with the Master Teachers is, they are very open that each and every one of us has our own center; our own source, and then we are all part of this great divine source energy of God. But, it's a matter of words amongst the humans here as to what we are going to call it. We're all speaking similar things; it's just, what are the words that we're putting around it.

When I get going with the channelings, I've tried to put my project leader logical mind into it. I say we need to make these guided visualizations 'this' long, we want five minutes or we want ten minutes but when I go to channel the meditation, we are usually around 30 (minutes). (This would be the length of the channeling for the Akashic Records.) It doesn't matter what I say, that's about how long all of them are (for the guided visualization part). I've learned I'm not in control, I will publish what they (Master Teachers) want published, and I'm always taken care of; always!

What I like about this work also is that because this has always just come to me, I've been very respectful of other people's work on the subject of our Soul. I take in what they wrote or shared, but when I was growing up; I'd know when something was missing. So most work on the chakras, I never gave too much credit to because they didn't talk about the golden chakra. The golden chakra is, to me, the most important one. That's the one that is above your head; the transpersonal chakra, and that, if you will, is the key to the Akasha, that vibration.

When my friend gave me the book, Life Between Lives, by Dr. Newton, that's when it all kind of fell in place for me and I realized that this is something I couldn't run away from; you can't be a part time mystic. I didn't realize back then, my natural abilities would be described as psychic talents.

For my corporate life, I did mergers and acquisitions in information systems and it was SO much not what I do now it started to cause a clash in my brain. I was very good at what I did because I drew people in, made sure everybody felt heard. But, there came a day when I had to walk away and say I can't support that structure anymore. It turned out that was the day George Bush was reelected. I didn't know for sure, but there was something inside me that said I can't do this anymore. This isn't the future I see. I unplugged from that world, and started trying to create a living supporting others as an alternative healing professional.

I reconnected with a lovely guy who met me when I was in systems, so I was a project leader and he was also a systems professional. We hadn't seen each other for about 12 years and he wanted to reconnect. He didn't know I was now working as a psychic and alternative healer. But we really loved each other. He grew up Catholic; an Eagle Scout etc. While here I was, a spiritualist, so I shared with his family I was a certified hypnotherapist.

When I met his sister I was trying to share with her something I did that would be considered acceptable and when I said I was a hypnotherapist, she yelled, "Don't look me in the eyes, I know you're brainwashing me!" And I knew I couldn't tell her all this other stuff because I wanted to fit in. I've come a long way since then; I've released most of that. I think that's when the master teachers felt they needed to step it up and start coming through to people. All of a sudden I found myself telling clients which angel was with them. People would not say anything; I'd get no feedback. But then they'd melt and start to cry, (and say) I've been praying to them for guidance. So I received a lot of verification the energetic being was Metatron, or Mother Mary. It's been astonishing to me because I can't honestly tell you how I know their distinctions; I just do. It comes naturally to me.

When I teach or mentor people, I teach them to just open up to whatever comes through and share the visions as they receive them; what's the song, what's the impulse you feel? I feel as if this whole body of work has been me looking back and healing my sick, crippled inner child. I sometimes wonder, how did she make it through to a place where, after I turned 50, I grew an inch. I thought the doctor was joking! I started thinking about it and realized I had always wanted to be 5'2", like the old song, five foot two, eyes of blue. I think all of these things have come to me so I can share them with others and say, you can do this! I always thought I was born out of sync; out of time. Now the world I wanted to live in is becoming a shared reality.

I've had any number of illnesses that have been healed. I have been diagnosed with Crohn's Disease; that was the toughest one. But because of the Crohn's, I was on heavy doses of prednisone for several years. Prednisone eats away at the calcium of your bones causing them to become less dense. They (the doctors) had told me at one point I had bone death, which I totally rejected as a thought form. I asked why would they call it bone death and they said because that bone is not a viable bone anymore and can never get better. I said I can't share that belief with you. I did some bone scans and my bones looked like Swiss cheese because some of it wasn't as dense as others, but I worked on my bones (spiritual healing) and they are fine now. Not that I needed to share that with others, but I needed to know for me so that when I'm working with people, I understand the mechanics of it. All of this can be done in the Akashic vibration.

It took me reviewing over two years of audios I have done in classes to realize I never was teaching the same thing. I kind of was, but that's when I realized we had these tools that the master teachers kept playing with and sharing with us. We have the emerald mirror, the reflecting pool, the grotto and all kinds of beautiful places where it just depends on which divine being will come through and channel the guided visualization for the class and where are they want to take us. What's taken me the longest to publish this is; how do you complete something in a linear process that is not logical? For the Akashic Vibration Process, you start where you are now and you go to the next level of understanding. I am working to create it that way, but even though I do that, I think I should just put it on the website and say you can purchase any audio you want; whichever one resonates with you will be the right one.

The point is my talent is a natural ability that I have augmented through the idea and understanding that I have a scientific brain and I absolutely love studying what other people have discovered about life, the human mind, and how we grow and change. Then I always ask to receive a confirmation or feedback from my own Council of Light, as I like to call them, on what works. If something doesn't work for someone, it used to bother me. I would wonder how a person could heal and be fine, and then walk away and in two months they come back and that feeling of health has disintegrated in them.

That's when I went off on a tangent reading a lot of Caroline Myss (pronounced Mace: who in 1982 started giving medical intuitive readings and moved into work with holistic doctors. She combined seven Christian sacraments with seven Hindu chakras and the Kabbalah Tree of Life to fashion a map of the human energy anatomy.) What she discovered on why people do not heal convinced me I needed to help people learn how to heal rather than hold the sacred energy and focus to help produce the healing with them. I needed to share how this healing can occur and how they produce the healing themselves.

The client that shared this important lesson with me was a neighbor of mine who has fibromyalgia. We met right after I had asked God to guide me to understand how come some people can't seem to hold the healing? She had a horrible life as a child, very brutal. While working with her, she first needed to get through some of her memories and feelings of betrayal. When I did a reading with her, I felt like she was energetically holding some people, almost like in a bird cage. It felt like there were these spirits that had crossed over and were in an energetic bird cage because she was keeping them there. I said that to her and she said, 'I know that.' I'm always shocked at how much people know.

I said you do realize that it keeps both of you in that prison. Think of how much of your energy is it taking to keep these people in this energetic prison. I started to help her understand her energy and her powers. How you can't have the energy to sustain your own physical body if you're giving it to this energetic cage; you are degenerating your body so that these spirits can't move on because of what they did to you. It goes back to forgiveness. When I got her to realize she did need to forgive them, I learned she had lost her faith in God; lost her faith that anyone else could keep these people from causing harm to someone else. She believed that when they incarnated again, because she believed they would, they would be just as evil as they had been. I work with her to understand that's not her responsibility. She didn't get to do that. All she was doing was holding herself in pain, complete pain all over her whole body because almost all of her energy was devoted to keeping them in an energetic prison.

When we got through all that, I'll never forget it, because all of a sudden from my perspective, I saw all of this energy leave her and lighten up, and she became this bright golden energy, though right before that I saw she had a death's door exit point and she was going to check out! She chose not to go and chose to forgive. When she did that, she noticed there was an absence of pain in her feet and it just continued all the way up her body; she was completely pain free and fine. It was like being reborn. She started driving a car for the first time in ten years and doing all kinds of wonderful stuff, but because she was my neighbor, I got to see the people around her. First they started looking at me like I was some kind of witch, who had hurt their friend. But she was fine! You should have seen her! They kept telling her no, you can't do that, you have to sit over here and let us take care of you; they couldn't accept her healing.

For her work, she is a sculptress. She had learned how to do sculpting while being disabled, and that was her identity, being a disabled sculptress. But she wasn't disabled any more. Within a few months, she started getting all this pain back and taking on this persona once again of the disabled sculptress. We talked about it; I shared she didn't have to do that. She started working with the healing energy again and got to the point where the pain is now only in her thumb, but if you are a sculptress, that can have a devastating effect on your life.

It was so important for me to see all that she went through because it helped me realize; it isn't me. Every one of us; we're the ones who are healing ourselves. Other people help us; I can help people, doctor's help people, massage therapists help people. While I don't give medicines, I can help your mind understand what's happening within your energy, your beliefs, and your feelings and how it is affecting your body. Where you are sharing your energy and where you are taking too much energy away from your ability to sustain a healthy, viable body.

I believe, with all my being, that that's where we are going with medicine. I have also seen people get the best medical help we can share go through chemotherapy and die anyway because the medicine itself can't help you; what can help you is your belief that the medicine's going to help you. I used that on myself when I had the prednisone and I was trying to get control of the Crohn's Disease. Once I realized that this prednisone was taking over part of my mind and I was not in control of my thoughts, then I learned how to bless the medicine coming into my body and help my body accept it and I started to lose some of side effects of the drugs. Eventually I got off of all medicines. I think that the real main point here is for the healing to work you need to ask for a healing, stay in a state of positive acceptance and take action steps you believe will help you heal.

The other thing I realized was that on all of these audios channeled by the master teachers, (available from Maggie's website: maggiechula.com), there's always a prayer and some sort of vibrational healing included. But because I'm a channel … (Maggie stopped here and asked if I was familiar with channeling so I would know what she was talking about.) When I was really little, I would just open my mouth and say things to people; I didn't have any idea what was being said either. That's why I was a scary little kid. What channeling means is you open yourself up and connect to the highest vibration that you resonate with, that fits comfortably with you, and you allow wisdom to come through. So, the wisdom coming through is not coming from me, it's coming from this higher vibrational energy.

Now I've learned how to be a conscious channel because when I started out ten years ago, I shared with my Council of Light I want to know the words that we're saying. So as I ask for the masters to come through, some other energy uses my vocal cords and my body.

Who comes through in channeling? Well, this is where I didn't know or appreciate the different beings that would come through. What happened about three or four years ago I was asked to a party to host a goddess party and do some channeling. All of a sudden this booming male voice came through and it turned out to be St. Peter; he said something about being Peter and I realized it was St. Peter. It was about all this difficulty coming up and stuff that was going to happen on earth; not a light bright party kind of message, and it burned my vocal cords! I kind of pushed him away and was able to allow different goddesses to come through. What I learned about that is I have to be very careful; I just don't want to open-endedly ask someone to come through. That's why I don't tune in and see your mother, your father, or the beings that are around you. I can do that but I have to be careful. I have become such a highly attuned channel almost anyone can come through and so of the beings are not of a high vibrational nature. Now my intent is to connect up with the highest vibration available for you (that) I can. I want to hook up to your higher wisdom, to your soul, and the Council of Light around you to get information.

The way I do it now is generally they will let me know who is coming through, or there will be a confirmation by somebody that I'm reading for; they'll come through and tell the person who they are. Or, I can ask. If someone wants to talk to Jesus, I can ask him to come through. I think I've been doing this long enough that we seem to know each other's vibrations. In the last few years I now get people's angels and guides come to me and tell me about their humans and they say 'how can I get them (the humans) to come to you?'

Between sessions one time a few years ago, there was this little guardian angel and I was thinking, 'why are you showing yourself little?' Then I realized she was new at this, being a guardian angel! I asked what can I do for you? She shared she had been listening to me and she couldn't get her human to come to me. (I was thinking I have a great imagination but this is kind of odd even for me.) We dialoged a little bit after that and I helped her feel better, the little guardian angel left feeling more hopeful. About three weeks later, a woman called me from out of the blue; she'd seen me six years before. She shared she had a daughter who had died five years ago and she wanted a reading. She also shared I had helped her with her younger daughter doing healing work. When she came to see me her younger daughter had sores all over her body and into her mouth, open lesions. They had been to about four different kinds of doctors and nobody could help her. They came to me and didn't have much money; I think we had a half hour session together. I talked to the daughter and helped her connect with the light of her source and showed her how she could heal her skin with a visualization. I shared if she healed her emotions also, it would reflect on her skin and her skin would be healed. I never heard from them. I thought about the little girl occasionally and I would send her healing.

The mother called me about three weeks after I had the visit from the little guardian angel. I did realize it at the time she was the human for this little guardian angel. The mother shared that within a couple of days of my session with her younger daughter lots of the lesions were gone and within a week, they were all gone and they have never come back since. She knew I was connected to the spiritual realm, she know the miracle she saw within her younger daughter from our one visit. Then after that, her oldest daughter was having problems and committed suicide.

Her younger daughter was still able to stay connected to the light and the lesions didn't come back, but it had been a difficult thing for the family, her older daughter's suicide. I realized immediately that that moment, the little guardian angel was her older daughter. This was the angel who wanted her mother (her human) to call me. All of a sudden all these connections came together and I got my verification that this little girl I had worked with, with all the lesions on her skin had been okay and I got my verification that I wasn't going nuts!

I told her (the mother) that 'your daughter is your guardian angel now, and she came to see me' and the mother said 'I know she is; I had a feeling she would be'. So I've got this scientific person over here (Maggie) that thinks that's fascinating and then I have the part of me that is working with the angels and doesn't care if anyone else knows, though I want to get the word out so I can continue to do this work; that's sort of where I am in my two parts in a nutshell.

But the channeling part really happens. I tell people the easiest way to start is with automatic writing. I've been told to do it, but haven't done it yet. Well, you might be already doing it. Do you ever sit down and have this inspiration and just write? When I'm writing a book I would lose track and have a chapter done but had no idea of even doing it and I'd think back and ask, 'I wrote this?' That's channeling. I just do it automatically (channeling what she is told in her mind). I started out singing and always knew I'd make a living with my voice. Where I finally did push through to 'I can go public and release this', is because I can do it with my voice.

Trying to transcribe all this work takes time; it takes a lot of hours to transcribe a half hour because you go in and out of the theta brain wave (the light meditation and sleep brain waves). If you are going in and out of it, you kind of take five words back and you write that down. We've checked it out and it's taken several people four hours to translate a half hour. When I sit down and write, I ask to receive information on a subject many people come to me for, which has been release work. Or, maybe Mother Mary wanted to come through and she did, and from that channeling I wrote an article called 'understand to be understood'. What I'm learning is, when I give something up to be published, then I can't put it in my website and I can't give it to people. I kind of have to wait through that, honoring these people who are going to put it up first. Once they (the publishers) have it out, then I can put the link out there (on the site) and I'm finding frustration in that.

I wrote a prayer for ascension that I gave to OM Times, and they put it on their website. It's only two minutes, but if people listen to it, it will change you; it will help guide your spirit so you're more in alignment with what your soul wants for you. Another one came out was a heart healing from Archangel Raphael. That came about because when I was doing a webinar I was telling people you can have healing dreams. Then one night I was lucid dreaming and my physical body was getting involved. My heart was hurting so I kind of woke up and realized that I was in the Akasha and was in the Emerald Mirror. There was this green river of wellbeing.

I knew all this stuff (already), but I saw Raphael on the other side of the river willing me to go into the water; to let the stream flow through me. When I did that I felt this burst of energy from my heart but the reason I wanted to write it up was because of my physical body; if I hadn't known better I would have thought I was having a heart attack. It felt like my heart was too big for my rib cage. In the water I saw all this energy burst open and I saw Raphael and I saw my dad, and I was able to release everything about dad. It was just a beautiful, wonderful heart healing that had taken place. I went back to the webinar the next week thinking the students had gotten this same vision, which sadly they hadn't. So I asked Raphael to channel this heart healing so we could give it out for the ascension and for the holidays. We created that about three weeks ago and it took this long for it to be published, but now that it is, I'm putting it on the website. It's 13 minutes long and what I like about it is, he uses the vibration of the Akasha so it's like helping people to come into my world but also heal your heart energy; who doesn't need that right now.

I know they are ready for me to move forward and now I'm getting things beyond the Akashic vibration but I have to finish that body of work (with the Akasha). In a nutshell, the work (available on Maggie's website) is to help people connect up to their soul; not just to know that you have a soul, but to be with the wisdom of your soul, so that on a conscious level you can know more about what your higher wisdom is: why are you here in this life, why are you doing this? The purpose of life is to experience life and to help your soul grow, of course. We know that, but how can you be more in sync and in tune with your soul wisdom and create a world that reflects your understanding and connection to your Source of wisdom, your soul?

Along with that happening, because the earth is vibrating at a higher frequency, we are all going into this vibrational align-ment and we are meant to be these more dimensional beings. This means you have your higher soul self in the Akashic vibration, but you are in sync with it so more of your spirit is here; you are more directly linked here. When you do that (connect with the Akashic vibration), you can do wonderful things. We can use the resources of the earth better. We don't have to spend all of our money on health care because we realize we have the ability to heal our lives. We might have to spend money on learning how to do some of this stuff better, but we'll be more in sync and in alignment with our Soul's wisdom and purpose. Some of the best medicine available is aspirin because it's so close to its natural compound.

What can we do here? I think it was very encouraging when I read that 90% of the people, if they were given the chance to write their own directive as to how they want medical science to proceed as they age, 90% of them would say 'stop invasive measures and hooking me up to a machine. Let my body go. I'm just going to be more alive'. And yet, that's scary, right? All the different people that don't want that to happen. I worked for a health insurance com-pany. I think very soon it's going to be a different ballgame than it is now. That's where I think the shift is and what was going on with

2012. My main message is that this is all about us learning how to be more truly our whole being. You can call it multidimensional or your soul or source, but that's what I think we are doing. When you said Christine (Day) took you to this different dimension, I'm sure she did. (This goes along with what many other psychics predict, that the world is going to start to experience life changing events, physical and mental such as a state of enlightenment. They also say it may not be immediately noticeable but will happen. I described to Maggie briefly what I had experienced with Christine Day to create a crystalline structure in us.)

That's why I needed to hear that because that's what they do in my courses; we're creating a crystalline structure. That's good, that's what I needed to hear! Perhaps because I come from a family that gets scared, I wanted to do this in a way I hope regular people can be okay with it and can do it. Guided visualizations work for me. I really can't meditate like they say you are supposed to; number one I have problems with rules. In systems you learn there are twenty ways to get to the same result. For me, to heal my body I always knew my mind had to be able to see it; it was that simple. If my mind can see it, I can do it. Now, of course, we've learned through science that that is quantum physics. You are the watcher; you bring it into existence because you 'see' it and you know it. We can do that with your body too. I know that's the way I've healed things, that's the way I helped that little girl, that's the way I help a lot of people. But the children get it! (Maggie clicked her finger.) And they're good! (They understand!)

I had one little kid connected to all kinds of dark murky things and they were going to institutionalize him as schizophrenic as (if) he is a dark soul lost forever. He was six. Six! I looked at him and at first I did feel this ooky energy around him, and then I looked closer and saw a Knight's Templar and a beautiful cross and this amazing sword and shared, 'you forgot how to connect up. You need to connect up to your light; you're not connecting to your light'. Then this little kid in a teeny voice said, 'I forgot how'. I helped him and it was just beautiful to behold; he became six again. I almost had to jump back thinking I hadn't realized I was working with a six year old because when I looked at his soul and spirit, here was this beautiful white knight. And here they want to lock him up? And who knows, maybe that might have been a good thing because he could have gone with the lost souls and finally helped them find the light, but it just seemed wrong. How many of us are they actually medicating so that you can't use that part of your brain? Really? It just doesn't make sense.

You are confirming a lot of what I have found in my healing. I do a lot of distance healing and I visualize (the infirmity and the person). A friend knew someone closely whose children dropped a baby on its head. The baby was in intensive care and doctors didn't know if it would pull through. To send healing, I visualized the baby; I was holding the baby and the baby's head in my hands, and I could feel it. A lot of others were also sending healing. By the next day, the baby was out of danger for that but they found the baby had a heart problem. So, through this bad fall, they found something they were supposed to work on. You are right where you need to be; that's how you do healing. The thing about it is there are always exceptions, always. When you work with adults, the hardest thing about that is they need to release and let go of a lot of stuff they have brought through the years. What I've found is it won't be logical. If they are having a block or an issue with something and they are looking for some logical, rational reason that that's happening, they are not going to heal.

It can even be something that you know. You might know that when you were little you fell down the stairs so you are afraid of heights. But that's not helping you heal your fear of heights. What will help you heal your fear of heights is when you realize that your brother was right behind you and pushed you. Then you are going to think, some big nutty kid isn't going to come and push me as I'm on this whatever. It's trying to get through those parts of our body; I like to think of our subconscious as our gatekeeper. It's keeping track of all the things that we need, that we learned throughout our lives that will keep us safe.

I had a horrible allergic reaction to pepper. I swelled up like a balloon when I was little and I thought I was going to choke to death. Then all of a sudden I had this vision of being, which now I know it as a concentration camp, inside of some kind of cage and there were a lot of people around. We were like scraps for dogs. This happened when I was four. I was walking to tell my parents that I can't breathe, as I was going by my little sister's bed all of a sudden I see her get up and she looked like a guard and this guard was going to shoot me for being out walking around. I don't know how I got out from that vision, but from that moment on I could not eat pepper. I've cured that allergy now, but when I looked at it I realized it was very possible, because they used human experiments, that they were experimenting and using some sort of pepper that finally caused me to die. I swelled up and I couldn't breathe and I choked to death. It was like one of these little things (vision) that come in and out but are hard to explain.

I was really young when this happened but I learned how to cure that later when I studied NLP. NLP stands for neuro-linguistic programming. It's the study of words and how your mind accepts words. It's sort of like taking hypnotherapy and going off to the 3D version. How does that connect with healing? If someone is saying, 'I'm wasting my life, I'm wasting my life', they probably mean waste, like wasting away, and yet, they could be very heavy because, when you think of it, waste is also waist. That might not help you heal, but it's interesting because those two words are together. If you are working with somebody who is wasting their life you can start to work through what does that mean to them.

First of all, it's a lot of different things because it's a spiritual law that (says) as you are there concentrating on that (the wasting), you want to somehow build that in your life. So, some people may build it in their life and become bulimic, but it has a secondary effect, and that would be on your physical being. (At this point Maggie thought she might be drifting and wanted to talk about what was important to me. I told her that the most important thing for me was to learn what her gifts are.)

I do medical intuition and my passion is to teach the Akasha. The Akashic vibration process is really fascinating because number one, it takes you to your home, where your soul resides. It's got a lot of visuals to it and it will help you open up that third eye; open up your ability to really visualize what is going on in your life. Now it sounds like you have already been working with that third eye; you saw the baby, you saw the head and worked with it? Yes, if that is really what I've been doing. That is what you are doing; you're already doing it. A lot of people say, 'I don't have a third eye and I'm not very visual'. I say, 'can you see yourself in your kitchen? Can you turn on the stove? Can you go in your car? Can you shift the gears?' That's your third eye! Once you realize what it is, you say oh! The other thing about that is the most important thing we have is our imagination; if you can visualize something and you can believe it, then you can bring it into being. How are you doing that? You're doing that with your imagination. It starts for me like; first we were the word, and the word was God. With the power of your mind, you are creating your world through your mind. And your mind is not linked to your physical body or your brain; it's linked to your soul. That's who you are.

There is a series of ways we go to get to the Akashic Vibration, but once we are there, there are a lot of tools. Now, the Akashic Records refers to the storage of knowledge of the universe; anything and everything is recorded as the universe is growing and expanding all the time too. So you, Edward, have a book of life; there's a book up there that says this is Edward' life. But you also have a soul. Do you know your soul's name, or who has given that name or connected up with your soul? No. Just wondering. You have your source; your soul. All of those are interchangeable; that's who you really are. Often in the Akasha you will meet that part of you, your Soul. But as you go through my series of classes, you have to start from where you are right now in your conscious understanding of yourself as a soul and we work to help you expand your understanding.

What's also available would be information related to you, Edward, or me, that would say, 'here are the allergies; here's Maggie's interaction with pepper. I could go to that space of knowledge. When I say the whole world, or whole universe, that's in the library. Along with the library you get a librarian because a librarian knows all about you and knows where all your information is; so you connect to that vibrational being.

Is that an angel? It can be any and everything. It changes; they change. It can be your mother; when I first went there it was my grandmother who was very important in my life, so of course, she would be there. This is where you learn what your mind knows.

For past lives, we have the hall of records in the Akashic vibrations. When you first go to the Akasha, you go to your inner temple or your inner sanctuary. That space is yours; it's dedicated to you. There you have these tools; one of them would be the library, and within the library is your book. There is also the place called the Hall of Records which is well known; a lot of people understand it. The Hall of Records is an infinite hallway with doors on either side and you can do a lot of wonderful, great healing there. But, you need to understand that the Akashic vibration is outside our understanding of time, right?

I got a chill all over when you talked about the infinite hallway. I just had a dream about it the other night; being in this hallway with doors and doors. All those doors represent all your incarnations; your soul and the different roles your soul plays to learn and grow. Think of it this way; people that are with me now (in classes) when I first started out said no, I never had another life, or I've only got this one, but now we all seem to know we have had past lives. The great thing about this is when you look at the past at all these infinite doors, but if you just shift your mind over, you go into the future. It's pretty awesome! That's where the quantum jumping comes from with Burt Goldman; that's what he's doing; he's going to the Akashic vibration.

I don't doubt that at all as all my life I have had dreams of the future and I'll reach a point when I tell someone I know exactly what you are going to say; everything is exactly like I already knew. Then, all of a sudden, that dream I had (long ago) makes sense because now I know how it came to be. Exactly! That's one of those 'AHA' (moments); your conscious just expanded! I work with people and want them, on a conscious level, to be more aware of this. Not that you have to go into a trance or listen to one of my audios; I really want people to use these tools all the time.

I haven't even told you about my favorite tools. My favorite tool of everything is the Flame of Transmutation. I LOVE this flame! I've always loved flames. At first I thought it was St. Germain or St. Germain's flame but it isn't. It's this beautiful flame and in my world that I bring people to; once you are in your temple, the first thing you see this gorgeous, beautiful, huge flame and it's up on three steps. You go up three steps to get to it and it doesn't burn. What it does is it changes all of your energy; all of your vibration. It takes away anything that doesn't belong to you that might still be with you, but by this time you are pretty pure. It's just beautiful; you can use it consciously right now. I could bring this flame up in my mind and by bringing it to my mind, it will purify my energy and take anything that doesn't belong, out of there. It can grow and help protect me; it's an incredible energy, incredible tool for people to use! It changes colors depending on what your body or mind might need, so it works with color therapy.

As you can probably tell, there's a lot to this. Let me get through a couple more tools and then I can send you a couple links to the audios (which I will tell about at the end of this chapter). The first one I like people to go through is the (Akashic) Initiation that kind of introduces you to some of the primary tools. Along with the flame that I adore, we also have the Emerald Mirror. The Emerald Mirror is a huge mirror. The point of it is you can see things that your physical eyes would not be able to see, or your mind hasn't understood. You can bring people there, you can bring situations there, and you get to see it from your soul's perspective; how did this really impact you? Because the whole point of the courses (which Maggie offers), is to help people heal. The way I like to explain it is, we get these hundred shares of energy a day and if you get these hundred shares a day to keep your body healthy and animated, and you spend, let's say, 20% of it on issues from the past, then that is stuff you are not sharing with yourself. Or, if you spent 10% of it on your children or 50% of it on your spouse, all of this is not being used to help you and you are being drained. What's happening is you don't (then) have enough energy to animate your physical being so your physical body starts to deteriorate.

The whole point is to help shift people in how they can stay in alignment with a higher source and help others. When I go to expos and work there, by the end of them I'm buzzed. I have so much energy; I'm not drained at all because I bring people to this vibration and together we work there. You are not coming to my energy; I'm hooking you up to yours and hooking me up to mine and on that level of equal vibration is where we'll work. Because I'm a psychic, when I do past life regressions, I don't even do them the old fashioned way anymore. I can follow and track where you are going. What I've learned about these courses is, if you've connected up to your higher self it naturally awakens your intuitive abilities, your psychic senses, that other portion of your brain that isn't just lying idly doing nothing. It makes you more connected up to it.

So we introduce people to their council of light; everybody has a council of light, it just depends on who is in your council. This is in your temple. This is something different from the hall of records or the library? All of those are in your temple; when you first go there, you go to your sanctuary or your temple. We progress from the understanding that I am going to my temple, I'm going through the meadow and all these things (This is part of the recordings available from Maggie). We progress along until you get to the last class and you realize that through your breathing you connect up. Now I like to close my eyes because I can see so much better, but all I have to do is breathe and I can bring in anybody I want; I can be in that energy right there. When I get to a stress point I can just breathe in, connect up and realize all is well and I'm in control here; I do have control. Some of the themes that come over and over again are, your greatest power is your power of choice.

That's what we're here to do; to choose. If people come to me for a reading, the angels aren't going to tell you what to do because that would disable your greatest gift in life which is being here in this physical form and from here, what are you going to choose? It's like a prime directive from Star Trek. They (the angels) are not going to interfere with that; they'll help you clarify your choices and help you see the different things that are going on. And, things are always changing so the Emerald Mirror is used. The most common for me is my dad, who has his own issues, so I would go and bring situations from my past there (to the Emerald Mirror) and be able to see it from what was coming up for him that he could treat people that way.

You get to really understand how we're all connected and how this person is a human too. They have frailties and he was abused as a child. People who have been abused as children, I'm not in any way trying to you need to bless this abuser, but I am saying you need to see this situation for what it was and not let this color your whole entire life. This was a moment in time. You need to understand that person has their own moment of review with love and compassion. They will see their actions and how their actions had an impact on the creation of other actions. Going into the Akasha, you can to do that right now. You can expand your understanding and help heal your life.

Let's say there is somebody badly hurt. I can go up there now and I can bring that person there into the vibration of the Akasha. When you were with that baby, you were (really) with that baby. Some people may be very confused about it, but I can tell you did it. You were there! And, when you work with someone else, you need to wait until there is a moment of done; in my world, because I have been doing this since I was little, I have a done button just like a turkey (laughter). Pop, they're done; move on. Or, when my husband broke his foot and I used hands on healing there is all of a sudden a moment when I need to take my hands away; when I realize that the energy is no longer healing; it's overwhelming and his tissue doesn't need any more.

Learning how you are a spiritual being, how your energy is flowing, can help you really be effective healing yourself and helping to share healing energy with others. Then there are some people who don't know they are energy drainers, but they are. You can be in their presence and you just feel sucked dry, and when you're finished, they spit you out and there you are; a lot less energetic than you were. Then you have to get back to it (your energy). There's a lot of stuff going on here. This is similar to Abby Rose's interview where she was taking on negative vibrations from working with people's hair and had to finally get protection from it. (See Chapter IX: Abby Rose.)

Exactly! That is sort of what happened through my life. I would know when someone needed healing and I would be shown maybe, they have this diseased liver and you need to recreate it, so I would build it in my mind. But what I was never doing was tapping into my own source and getting recharged; sort of like batteries. Between sessions at the hair dresser when you take all that in, you have to learn how to disconnect. So I don't do energy work the same way I used to anymore. I don't do past life regressions the same way anymore; let's just go to the Akasha because there you can heal multiple lifetimes on an issue through all layers of time and space. You need to understand, to really have this work for you. Then when we're talking about it (being) a vibration and that you are a pure vibration, human laws don't exist there; that's something we've all agreed to.

We have agreed, okay, I'm going to come back to earth and I'm going to have this body, and I'm going to have 24 hours in a day. What I love about that is every four years or so you have another additional second. We're all doing that, and we've all agreed to that, so we have this group consciousness and the group consciousness is now expanded to say wait a minute, the way we do things isn't working. It isn't okay to let more than half the people live in poverty and be shot at, and (whatever else is happening) that's not okay; that is beginning to affect me. How are we going to change that, because of course, we can change it. We can change it when you see these terrible things on the television, instead of tuning in to the atrocities that are happening, start tuning into the angels coming down to help them, seeing the people talking to each other and working it out, and visualizing peace; visualize peace!

The easiest way to understand that is there is an energy test you can do where you get a group of people together and have one person go out of the room, and I don't do this because it is very negative, but you can have people think negative thoughts of this person; when they come back in the room you test them and the person who was out in the hall having negative thoughts sent to them are completely weak; they are just devastated. I can teach them how to hold their energy so they can go out there (out of the room) and they will stay strong. Or, you can send them love and prayers and their bodies will get stronger.

We are so affected by other people and other people's energies that it's spooky; I don't like to play around with it because it's like playing with a Ouija Board. I won't do it. You could really hurt that person, but you can do it; some people get into it. It's like you can take sugar and do kinesiology (the study of human and animal movement, performance, and function by applying the sciences of biomechanics, anatomy, physiology, psychology, and neuroscience; muscle testing) ; does this work for this person or does this not. Sugar? Yes. You can do it with foods, you can do it with lots of things; you can even do it with your beliefs. Muscle testing would be like forming your fingers like this (Maggie demonstrated by locking fingers together like hooks), keep them strong and say something you know is true like, I am a man. It should hold strong. Then you think to yourself, I am a woman, (I tried both ways) and it shouldn't hold strong because your mind says I'm not a woman. (It worked!) Or, you can do it moving forward and backwards with your energy facing north; anyway you can do that and you can do it with your beliefs. I am loved. Do you hold strong to that? If you don't, your body doesn't believe it's loved; your mind doesn't believe it's loved. That's muscle testing on an energy level.

But some people get all hung up (saying) you have to do it in a way where you don't use any negative words because if you said 'I am not strong', then you are really testing 'I am strong' (how strong am I) because your brain sort of takes those negative words and puts them aside. (For example) Do not think about that water over there. Well, all you are going to do is think about that water! You have to learn how the mind works and that's why I studied NLP (Neurolinguistic Programming).

But, that's like using a pendulum (where the swinging pendulum can answer questions of yes, no and undecided). It is! A pendulum is energy of your mind. I can cause my pendulum to do all kinds of fun things; I love to play with them. You can use a pendulum to show you how open your energy centers are. But what all this really boils down to in the simplest term is, your mind is creating your life. What does your mind believe? All this is what your mind believes you can do. The body just follows.

So my fear of airplanes is caused by my own mind? What happens when you think about being on an airplane? It relates mostly to claustrophobia; being in a box. Does anything else come to mind when you think about that? No. In fact, once I rode on an old DC6 and was tense riding in one direction, but on the way back they let me sit in the pilot's seat and steer and I was perfectly fine. You were in control. I have a real respect for planes because I don't understand how this huge thing flies in the air. Another way to get through a flight is, I would sit in my seat and wait until I felt there were angels all over, like this little herd of angels that was going to protect the plane. I believe in angels enough that when I felt the angels were all around and I got this 'you're good Maggie' then I knew we were going to be fine. I was on the last plane out from Hurricane Hugo but we were fine and I think it's because I did my prayers and saw the angels all around. But, yours has to do with control. Did flying the plane help you with all of your fear? No. It would if you could associate that feeling of 'I'm in control and I'm going to be just fine'. It has to do also with connecting things up.

For me, I am a person who is afraid of heights and I finally realized my brother was the person who came out of the shadows and pushed me and I went down the stairs; I didn't fly, I rolled and in the end I was hurt. When that happened, I had a chance to realize why I felt I was always going to be falling. That was a true fear of mine; then I got over it. One of the things that helped me get over it was knowing I was in control now and I don't have to stand on the edge of a stair on a dare and I can the choice to take a couple steps back and look out; connecting things so your mind can accept it.

Can you get yourself to where you really feel frightened of heights? Can you get to that association of it? (This was referring to a similar association like Maggie had on the stairs.) I don't know that I am terribly frightened of heights; I'd have to be really high to be scared. But I do know where my claustrophobia comes from. My brother and sister used to roll me up in a rug so all that was sticking out was my head. What could help with that is, in your mind you see you are that little person who is rolled up in a rug, but you take your arms and go like this (Maggie threw her arms outward) and you take back your energy of that stuck little person. The mind is fascinating, completely fascinating!

(Getting back to my question of Maggie's most important gift, she answered,) I do so many different things, I don't know what would be the most common thing that I do. If it's anything, it would be helping people unstick their thoughts so that they can heal. What I will do with you is share the initiation (used in Maggie's classes for reaching out to the Akasha). The initiation goes through a lot of wonderful visuals. The thing about the course is that is starts from the understanding that you've never connected up to your source, or people who have can do this anyway; but they (spirit or higher realms) like people to get the initiation because it tells them about the primary tools. Then I can send you the one I call The Book of Life, since you are interested in past lives. What I like is having it as an audio is you can listen to it as often as you like.

What I tell my students is, after the visualization it is important to write even if you only got colors. Some people when they first start have so many beliefs about this that their minds may just shut down and they don't get anything. But, the initiation has healing in it; we go to the hallway and in the hallway we work on your beliefs about being in touch with your higher wisdom because through the centuries it has been bred out of us. We were taught you need to go to this person or that person or pray to whomever or whatever it is we believe. So the Initiation works on your beliefs so that the next time it is easier and more effortless. As you go through the course, by the end, it gets very mystical.

By the ninth (course) when you are working with your own divine source, then we work with God. It kind of takes people through the layers. Then the Akasha is now your starting point. The Akasha is where we need to get mankind. So we get it; our soul resides on this vibration and it's true that all of this knowledge is available to every one of us. We have to learn to open up our minds to tap into it. So, if I wanted to know something about how to be a veterinarian, I could tap into that when I have an animal that I'm working with. But, I don't need to do that anymore because animals talk to me; everything talks to me so I just ask the intelligence of the animal what they want to say.

What I do when I tune into people and I can talk to either people who are related to them or people who are living or dead; people do not have to be dead for me to talk to them (their spirit). But I'm very respectful of, 'is this information that they (the person) would want shared?' And that's the information that comes through. So, sometimes when I'm working with someone, my voice will cut out completely and the thoughts shut down because it's like we just stepped over a boundary and that is not okay; so you don't want me to go there (and that is fine).

A couple weeks ago my friend Laurie (Chapter XV) said my mother was coming to her, though my mother is not passed but is paraplegic and on oxygen and has other problems and sort of drifts between the worlds. So, of course she could come (my mother come to Laurie). She could do that even if she was healthy. If you think about it, she's a vibration, you're a vibration; it's her physical body that is deteriorating, but your mother is getting more into the soul of her being. That's hard, when you're in that in-between space. (I experienced) the hallways when I was little (in Akasha); but, there's another hallway where I see people that are crossing, or about to be born, I realized, so I can see babies around people and they could be two years out! I can see that energy of another being who wants to come in physically; and they could come through adoption or any way, but I do get a sense of that. Your mother is definitely in that hallway; in that transitional phase, which hopefully she'll take.

Does she want to be released from her pain? She always has a good attitude; she's like an angel because she doesn't let stuff get her down. Maggie stopped, sat up, and closed her eyes. Just a minute, I think they (spirit) are doing a check in. Well, the check in is sort of on the two of you. Your mother is fully surrounded by beautiful divine energy; they've got her now. I'm sure this is a message for you; they are showing me that she is ... I don't have a good term for this, so I tell people processing; she's processing through her ascension. She's now about 97% ready to go. She's staying for the heart connections (with family). They are helping her understand that connection can still go forward. I guess there is a little bit of worry in her mind about can she still stay connected to the people that are on the earth? So she's got a lot of angels helping her. Definitely her guardian angel is with her and is sharing with me that this is going to go pretty fast for her. But she's not feeling a lot of pain because I don't think she can connect that up to her body anymore; she's not feeling it like we would sense and feel it, and/or she's floating in a lot of pain meds too. That is actually keeping her more connected to her body. If she weren't on (meds) she would have transcended already. It's up to her; she can go anytime (she wants to).

The good news here is that by going to that vibration you begin to get the awareness of those dreams that aren't dreams; the ones when you can talk to your loved ones during the night. Do you ever have those? Yes. The past three weeks my dreams have been so intense that I am exhausted in the morning and wake up hungry. You are going through a lot of changes too. They are showing me that ... wait a minute ... what is this? (Again Maggie stopped to receive a message.) You are connected up to the blue lights; you're connected to blue energy. It's right around your brain right now.

Was that part of your bridge? (Maggie was talking about my experience crossing the void in Christine Day's seminar.) The blue lights usually to me (Maggie paused here in thought); they are saying you have processed it to your brain but you have not processed it down; you need to process it further down because you've kind of got it right here (pointing to the top of her head), it's on your higher chakra but it isn't sinking down to the physical level where you can have a greater ability to utilize it in the material world. How do I do that?

Well, you are opening up to this and you are understanding you want it but there are situations that are going to come up, I always love it when they say things like that, that are going to help you see more of the choices you are making and how that is creating the future going out. Because they say that some of the things you are doing with this: working with the book and working with people, is really to help you sink more into the understanding that, yeah, (Maggie was interrupted in thought by more spirits) there's that healer in you coming through; you've got a shaman over here (near us). Are these lifetimes now? (Asking spirit aloud.) Yeah; different times that you have already done healing work that seems to be coming through to you now. What they want me to share with you, the number one thing, is to help your mother through that; to help your mother as you're working with that (healing). Do you physically see her or just work with her with your mind?

It's been with my mind (remotely) because I have so little money I can't travel to see her often. All of this is going to shift. What they want you to know; one of the things they want you to understand is that abundance and affluence and how to help each other; a lot of that can be through sharing. We don't have to have the paper money to be able to do this as much (healing), and I think we are seeing that definitely on the spiritual level, that we're more willing to work with people bartering again, doing energy exchanges. But, they are saying that (with) the book, you need to get going! You need to get working! Are you publishing any articles?

I write for a little magazine but it doesn't have to do with this (type of work). Well, you know what, you're supposed to go beyond that little magazine. You need to start learning and growing; in fact you're a scribe, so you actually do have some very good talent here with writing. They don't want you to be worried about money, but let me go back to your mom, I can understand that (speaking to spirits again); they want you to know that for your mom, what she is asking you to do is (now Maggie is interrupted again by Rafael to tell me through her), okay, I'm going to give you that heart healing. They want you to go through that and work with that, but they also want you to, when you are going to the Akasha, and I'll give you a couple of them (lessons to listen to); what they want you to do with that information is write down how you are working with it and really use it like a tool, like a student, to grow and to open up because they say it will really open up your healing ability. The first one you work on is your mom; not that you are working on her physical body because that's something we need to start understanding; your mom needs to ascend. She needs you to work on the heart level to release her; to know you are joyfully releasing

MEDIUMS NOT SO RARE

her into the light so that she can go home and then she is going to come back (in spirit)!

It's going to take her a little time; not as long as it would take some people. Your mom is really pre-ascended! She's not going to take long to come back and let you know that she is here. She's been doing a lot of work already. They want you to work with that and see her joyfully, without pain, just joyfully ascending (to) her husband and her mother and all these beautiful people waiting for her. Now they are showing her growing younger, which is usually what happens after you have ascended.

This is going to be good for you because you can go from a point of 'where are you now' and do that checkpoint; where am I now, how do I feel about this now? And then using your scientific writer brain, the one you said you are doing this (book) for people to share your experience. But, you need to grow your sense of self esteem and self confidence so that you know that this writing is going to be able to be published. (Maggie paused to talk a bit about publishing her lessons and then went on.) They want me to send you the healing grotto which I think is gorgeous and beautiful and is not one of the beginning ones (lessons).

In the Akashic vibration there is all this stuff; it's like a different land, so fun. In the grotto you go through the stream of wellbeing, then you find yourself in the grotto and meet up with your power animal. You're going to meet up with your guardian angel. I believe they merge you with your guardian angel because they're saying that this is something you are meant to do. You are meant to go out and share this with people because you represent your generation; you represent people who really do need this and have the time now to put your work and energy into it (the book). Just remember that your part of this is to take that journal of 'here's what I am today'.

Do you know about the emotional guidance scale; Ester Hicks channels Abraham who is a series of disincarnated beings, so really similar to the archangels, but they just go under the name of Abraham. She's been doing this for a long time. They have a lot of different books out there, but one of the things they have is an emotional guidance scale that that is how we know we are in alignment with our source. In a nutshell, what is meant is when you're doing this, it's sort of like 'how are you feeling in your gut' (I believe this would mean instinctual), because your gut is your solar plexus, which is your seat of self esteem or self confidence. So, how does this make you feel? Frightened but you want to go through it so you can learn it or does it make you feel that sometimes you are going to go out there and you're going to say, 'I don't need this'.

You really need to open up and start paying attention to that because they are saying that what you are doing is good, you have great intentions, but there are some people that are going to, well, you want to make sure you stay protected with your energy and stay strong within yourself. (The protection is a spiritual thing I have worked with before at the spiritualist camp where the leader would take us through a meditation with deep breathing and we would fill and surround ourselves with the white light of God for protection.) Because what the angels have agreed to with you is, yes, you can be a scribe and you can help get the word out that we are all different; that there are people who can do this (the gift of spiritual things like being psychic) and they do it in different modalities. But, how can this modality help? Or, how did this modality help you so that you can become more of an expert, if you will, for other people who don't know where to start. Does that make sense? Yes.

So, I think we are getting into a reading (Maggie laughed at herself here as she has been doing a reading for me without thinking about it.) The other thing they (spirit) want me to share is it feels like there is still a darkness, a hole; feels more like a hole more than a block, that is in your heart that just hasn't healed. (This would most likely be from the trauma of my divorce and the trials of the heart that were attached to it.) I don't know if you have the intention you don't want it to be a hole anymore, or maybe it has been something you haven't put any energy into either on sort of a conscious level. But Rafael is saying to watch for that.

When you do the heart healing meditation, know this; it takes 13 minutes and you just follow it through but have the intention of opening up and allowing this to happen. When we work on the energy level of people, what people need to understand is, it can take three sleep cycles. And the reason I say it takes sleep cycles is because that's when you are really more fully open to your source. People, no matter what they are or what they are doing, when they're sleeping allow more of their spirit in, more of their higher being in. Or, they go there (to see spirit rather than spirit coming to see them), I don't know whichever it is, but they get more in alignment. And when we're working on energy we're aligning that anyhow, so that's why it can take sometimes more than just one day. Don't listen to it (the healing meditation) and disregard it, though, some people just automatically right away get it. But some people can take a little bit. And they're saying with the heart, it's always going to be your choice.

So, with the heart and this sort of black hole, that feels like that's within that energy for you along with what happened to your mother, they just want you to be a little more gentle (on myself) and realize that it might take a couple of days, it might take more than that, but know that when you are thinking of your mother they want you to really let her go into the light and be happy for her that she gets to do that. When you can do all those things and feel that happiness for her, that's when you're going to be able to take a checkpoint and say okay, I'm through that. They want to give you that as a guidepost.

Or, when you start to think of some of the things from your past and it's like 'I don't feel that anymore; I'm just not tied to that anymore'. That's also going to be a guidepost to you. Then your own healing is going to start to kick in; your own healing works for others because they just want you to give a little more healing on yourself. When you work through this, that's what you will probably find you gravitate to the most is healing and helping other people understand it's all about their choices in life.

You are validating what my dad said this past Sunday through a medium at (spiritualist) camp. He said I need to completely forget the past and not fear the same thing happening to me again. I think he feels that I am afraid I'll end up in the same situation (being cheated on). And it feels like you don't trust your instincts because if you had instincts and you trusted them, how could you be in that situation? But know this; it's everybody's free will. If you align yourself with, and I like to do this every day, I like to align myself with my source and that I can be a channel of light that is for the highest good for people coming my world. For their highest good, that is the information I want to bring to them. That said, I'm the one who goes to the expo and gets really interesting people. I've had gypsies with curses, I have lately been tied into a Hmong community and they have through the generations had some really dark energy that they need to release and let go of. My husband asks, 'can't you just work with people on the phone', and I tell him don't worry we're protected.

That is the Flame of Transmutation! If you ever feel really stuck at something, you can bring (connect to) that flame and it gets to be so visual; it's like offering yourself into this higher vibration and letting it cleanse all the energy around you. You're going to get yourself into some situations where you can walk into it and be open to it but then when you're finished with it, you want to rinse it off and let it go; anything that doesn't belong to you, let it go. Some people, when they are new they don't have all their stuff together yet so their energy can be chaotic. If you are working with somebody who has chaotic energy, it can almost unplug you a little bit. It's hard to explain.

I started to ask a question but lost my thought. I want this to be an open dialog with you; I know that my work isn't something I can teach people in two hours. The intention was to open you up to this (this session of learning what Maggie does) because number one, you were drawn to it, and two; everyone who is drawn to the work is having memories of being in the Akasha. They are opening up too (for example) 'I think I get where the Akashic records are!

I know that hallway! You probably do because we're involved in there; we all go there all the time but usually at night.

I did a past life regression at the camp last summer and was skeptical that I would be able to release myself enough to get anything to come through. I came up with a life; I knew the year, I knew the place and could picture everything there, and I knew my name. We were taken through (that life) until we died, then came back (to the present). My logical brain says I have a really good imagination. Was that it; imagination? What I know about this is if you got that information that was something that was relevant for you to know. Was it anything that had information that you felt you could really use? No, I don't think so. It was just a really neat place with a log cabin and I became the mayor of a town, I was married to my daughter which was sort of weird.

Well, you know what it did do though was it affirmed to you that you could go there. It affirmed that there was this other life that you had and that there were people you were connected to. In doing this kind of exploration, it's important to know that. When I take people to the Akasha and they have any kind of experience, when people come back, they're not the same. That's why they call it the initiation phase because things start to happen in your life and you become more aware! What I will say, because of my chaotic childhood, a lot of times I'm almost backwards with signals; suppose I'm going to an expo and I'm not sure, I'm feeling very insecure about this; normally what that is telling me is, 'you're going to meet someone and it's going to add to your experience'. But because I was so psychic as a little kid, I (think), I don't want to do this. You have to learn your own signs and soul language.

Definitely the guides that come through and the teachers that come through; all of them want me to share with people (that) your experience is not another's experience. That's why I'm glad they say things like, is it your temple? Is it your sanctuary? Is it a cave? Everybody has a different center of light a center that they feel grounded in.

So when you do past life regression, you don't do it the way I do it? (Being put into a gentle self hypnosis with a guided regression backwards.) Not anymore. Were you dialoguing? When you dialog, that's hard for people because you go in and out of the vibration; the theta, the beta; all the different vibrations of the mind and you get a chance to awaken that gate keeper who says no, no, this isn't happening. The way you did it is really a good way because then you get to be in that experience. Going through this guided visualization is 30 minutes (from Maggie's recording); it takes people to all kinds of different things and the one that is the Book of Life, will take you through the hallway, to the librarian, I think we also work with the Emerald Mirror. They work with all these different tools so you can reaffirm it (your life) in different ways.

It helps open your mind up; so the one whichever your mind is the most accepting of, then once that piece of acceptance comes in, it sort of melts away resistance. It's like this piece (tool) says yes, I'm good with this and all the rest of the mind goes, well, if they're good with it I guess I'll be good with it. You've already done one (past life regression) and you've got all this great information coming through. That kind of weakened the gatekeeper to say, well, this isn't such a scary thing, lucky he (me) showed himself; I guess we can let that happen again.

When you do past life, do you go to the temple? You go to a sanctuary, or the temple, right. Do you talk to anybody in particular, or does the information just appear in your head all of a sudden? Well, it comes to people in different ways. The way it comes is like a digital download. It really is like 'tick' and it opens up. Some people get full movies in their heads right then and some people don't get it until a couple days later. But it's like a little download, like okay we're going to give you this information, okay we're going to unlock it so that you can have the connection. My intent, when I do this, is on a conscious level you remember. Some people come out of these and say, 'I don't remember anything in the Akashic level'.

I say, well go ahead and write things down anyway! Then a

couple weeks later they'll come back and say, 'the craziest thing has happened; this happened and that happened'. So, it unfolds the way it works for YOU. I didn't used to put that intent in there and with some people it was too much for them; they got scared with the information they got and they shut down. Now they've gone backwards and we have to work even harder to get them to where they were. When I work I guess I'm co-creating this because from my human experience I'm taking notes on what happened to this person, but the angels are listening; the archangels, Mother Mary, the Mother Goddess and people who come through are listening, so they adjust and it's kind of interesting to see how things have adjusted as we have progressed working together.

One thing we all have an intention of is; we're working to make it so the group consciousness of humankind opens up to knowing they are souls and they can connect to their souls and use these tools on a conscious level, which will happen and be a known thing; we want to make that happen as fast as possible. It's like, from a scientific point of view, the Rhesus Monkey; these monkeys lived on different islands so they weren't with each other. They had scientists looking at these different groups and one day, after years (had gone by), one monkey decided to wash its food before it ate it. Other monkeys around saw it and thought, why not, so they started washing their food. When they got to about 100 monkeys, then monkeys on other islands started washing their food. What it taught the human scientists is; they had a group consciousness!

From the angel's point of view, not to call us monkeys, we have a group human consciousness. This group human consciousness thirty years ago would have said, you can't take me to a past life, that's ridiculous; it's too out there, Maggie, you think you had past lives. Yes, I was born remembering past lives. But, I've worked at it too and I could get more and more people to do a past life memory. Then lots and lots of people were working at it retrieving past life memories, then other people were published on the subject and before you knew it, people would say, 'well, I've had 12 past lives', and then one would say, 'I've had like 350 past lives'. (Maggie laughed,) Really, do you know them all? 'Well, this person told me that', but I said I'd be more impressed if you knew it for yourself than some psychic told you that. I do not doubt that it is true, I'm saying YOU need to know it, not that somebody tells you this. My goal on earth is so people know (how to reach the Akashic records themselves).

(For example:) I have a past life. I want to be a writer. Let me go to the lifetime where I was a successful writer and bring that talent here so that it isn't so scary when I sit down at a blank piece of paper. We're getting there! We are getting to that point in human conscious evaluation. It's cool because people know they had past lives! (People say:) Yes, I understand about the Akashic records. Great! Yes, I believe in angels. Do you talk to them? When you talk to them do they talk back? The other thing; it's a spiritual rule, I guess, that they cannot interfere. They cannot interfere! That is taking away your choice. That's the prime directive. They can't take away your choice; that's what you're here for; to learn how to choose.

But every day if I wake up and say, I'm asking you (the angels) to bring me people who I can help, they are not interfering with those people, they're saying this person wants help, that person wants help; win, win! It's (about) learning the rules and working with them. And, that's one of the things you are here to write about; what are some of these rules from your perspective and how has that helped you heal your life? So, you know there are things in your life that are healed, and that's your base point. And working with some of this; does it feel better? It can take years, or it can take months, or it can be tomorrow. It depends on your belief system and how ready you are to change.

When I take people to a past life, I can do it one on one, but sometimes when they get to the point when they want to say something, and if it will bring them out of that trance, that space, then I'll just continue with them so they can have the memory and look at it later because that goes into the going in and out of brain wave thing.

To see somebody else's past life, do you have to be there with them? No. Do you have to take them, or can you see that life without them participating? I can and a lot of psychics can. We can tune in, in my vocabulary, to the Akasha and we can tune in to their lives. What it really means to be psychic is we're using that part of the brain that other people haven't quite caught up to the fact that they can use it.

Can I be causing my life to change so drastically that everything a good psychic can tell me is wrong? An example is, there is a psychic my sister told me about, who my sister has talked to several times, and was spot on every time my sister talked to her (for readings). I talked to the lady then and everything she said for me didn't pan out. Okay, I'm glad you brought that up because as we (psychics) are all different, and the way we do things are different, we can't read for every person; we're not in vibrational alignment with them. That doesn't mean that psychic wasn't good for your sister, it means she couldn't read you. Or, from her perspective what she was reading, because the other thing psychics do which makes sense if you think about it, would be like if you went to a doctor or any person, you filter it through your knowledge; your world's view. If that person hasn't experienced certain things, they are not going to know how to pick that up (information for your reading). That's why people like Caroline Myss, who basically coined the phrase, medical intuitive, will say you can't really be a medical intuitive if you haven't gone through physical issues. There is something about that vibration that you become more sensitive to.

You find with all these different people, where are they in their life? Some of the people on Best American Psychics will write to me and ask me to do a reading for them because they have a client who kicks something up and now they're sick or something clicked in their mind that they hadn't healed. We're all at different levels of understanding. Basically we're all created equal, yes! Mother Mary comes through and says we are all equal. But it's true that we are not all equal in the understanding of that statement.

That makes me feel better because intuitively that is what I had been thinking (all along). That's because your intuition is kicking up and sharing with you, right? I hope one of the other things you got from this is that you are really opening up, really opening up! When I sit here and say you're going to be helping heal, I'm not just saying that to make you feel better. I'm hearing that; I'm being told that that's where you are growing. Writing this (book) and really communicating and getting it out to whatever segment you get it out to, is going to be very healing. Healing doesn't have to mean you're a doctor; it doesn't have to mean you are a light worker or Reiki master or whatever. What it means is that what you do is setting out to help heal the world; the human condition.

I received a DVD on how to do Reiki a short time back and found that what was on it, I had already been doing intuitively! You have strong shaman energy too. The shamans were taught bring other people's energies into our energy and we rinsed it off and cleaned it and put the energy back in the person. But, by doing that, what does it do? It brings the lower vibration into your energy stream, which means you have to have a way to cleanse that out of your energy or you will take on someone else's lower vibration.

Maggie Chula: Akashic Initiation

Maggie let me in on two of her class recordings, the first being the Akashic Initiation; an introduction to going to view the Akashic Records. The Akashic Records are described by her as being an infinite library of all thoughts back to infinity which contain records of our own lives and all others and allow us to view those lives and instances in order to learn from them, find out where there are problems or things lacking in our lives caused by past lives, or even how to correct these things and retrieve those broken pieces of our lives. Though I will describe the following way to reach the Akashic Records as Maggie did it, I'm certain that there are as many ways to reach the records as there are people willing to try.

The start to Maggie's initiation was much like I have experienced at Spiritualist Camp Wonewoc as we begin our healing meditations each week. First, you relax and let all negative vibrations and thoughts evaporate from your body. This is done with deep breathing in, followed by slowly expelling the air while envisioning it taking away all things negative. After even a few breaths like this I feel so relaxed I could melt into my chair.

Once a totally relaxed state is achieved, we bond with the earth picturing our feet extending deep into the earth to where we can be one with Mother Earth and all things natural. We ground ourselves to the earth where our bodies came from.

In the meditation at camp we would walk a beautiful trail of our own making, be it through a forest or glade or meadow or wherever we like. The trail we take is also of our own making and would end up in a special place where we could meet up with a loved one who had passed. Sometimes we would ride (or be) a feather that would carry us upward into the blue sky where we could meet others or find our own peace in a cloud. Maggie's initiation was similar to this in that we entered a pink cloud; pink signifying love. On our journey we traveled through a meadow, a mountain, bridge, and another cloud; all of different colors reminding me of the chakra colors, which I 'm guessing they were.

Now Maggie's initiation parted from what I experienced at the camp because we went to a huge building, then found a doorway; all done with our own imagination as to how the building and door looked even if they stayed the same size. As we entered, we crossed a room with tools for us to use, to what I pictured as a fountain of violet flame that didn't burn but took lower energies/vibrations out of us so only our highest energy was left.

I left the flame proceeding to another area of the room to a beautiful emerald mirror that showed my own source and anything I wanted to see with my conscious mind. Here I will understand the truth of whatever I want to see and as I looked I saw my source in the mirror as purple.

Now I moved to another door with rooms and rooms reaching to infinity where I could go to any of the doors to the rooms to find out anything about myself. I felt the doors led to my past lifetimes and all I had to do was enter them to have access to each life.

Coming back to the original room I sat in a comfortable chair of my own making. My records are laid out in front of me here. There is now a librarian who I can ask for help viewing whatever I want. The book is brought to me and I can view it as a book or however it comes through, such as a movie or floating image. Just like a book though, I can go into it and find out what I need to understand myself perhaps by it being revealed now or in the future, or given to me in some way I comprehend. I thank the librarian and remember what the librarian looks like.

I move out of the temple and can look back to see if it has changed. Above the door is written: I shall bring to thy remembrance everything that ye have need of from the abundance of the universe. This is my promise from the Source (oneness of God), and I am welcome to come anytime to use the tools inside. Of course, this is Maggie's library so your own may have different words with a different or similar meaning.

Now my journey reverses quickly as I turn back through the colors and images; gold, lilac, indigo, blue, green (where our source stays), yellow, orange where I finally joining my cleansed body, back through the red, the meadow, the cloud of love, bringing myself back to the ground and deep into the earth to a place where no one knows, and finally rising back to where we started. I breathe and ground myself. As I get comfortable in my place I can now become aware of my present surroundings, opening my eyes and becoming part of my own reality.

The process of this initiation takes about a half hour, though it passes seemingly in seconds as we leave our earthly body and enter a place of no time or space other than what we create in our consciousness following Maggie's words in our ears. Though it isn't necessary to close your eyes, I believe it is a much better way as we can then close off much of our outside stimuli and concentrate on our breathing and thoughts. I am only skimming what is really covered in this initiation since the only way to really experience it would be to take Maggie's courses. To reach the full depth of this initiation one needs to meditate and separate their physical body from the spirit body. For me, it was hard to come back fully to my 'awake' state after my journey. I felt very at ease and relaxed as my eyes finally opened.

Maggie Chula: The Book of Life

After we have gone through the initiation until it becomes natural and comfortable for us, six times for me at least, I moved to Maggie's Book of Life recording which she uses as part of her classes. Once more this began as Maggie says, "as we always begin; with our breath" connecting us with the energy and power of the universe. This time I spent more time breathing and letting go, usually with air coming in through my nose and breathing out with partly closed lips to delay and slow the exhalation.

The start of our journey begins with finding the ball of energy at the third eye which we take down through our body, through our feet and on, into the earth, down deep where the crystal caves, which hold so much energy, are. Here we gather the magnificent vibrations of the earth to our consciousness and come back up through the earth, back through the bottoms of our feet and breathing deeply, opening the energy centers of our body (the chakras) making us feel more grounded in this vibration.

We keep raising our consciousness up through the body until it reaches the vibrant red root chakra, having to do with our basic survival and family needs. As we exhale, we get rid of all that does not belong in that vibration of the root chakra; fear, things that have bothered us.

Next our consciousness moves up to the orange chakra (sacral, spleen) of our sexual energy and creativity. Again we breathe in to cleanse the energy center and let it grow and breathe out to get rid of anything that may be blocking the center.

We rise to the solar plexus, the yellow chakra, having to do with our will, self-esteem and feeling of self confidence and breathe in healing energy and focus on who we are, breathing out anything blocking our higher path.

Continuing up through the chakras, we reach the stunning green of the heart, opening up to all the love that we could ever feel and knowing our heart is in alignment with our desire to go to the Akasha to our higher wisdom; breathing out any blockages that would keep us from attaining this.

The energy lifts us higher to the beautiful blue of our throat chakra that governs our ability of speaking the truth and be in the truth without being held back by the thoughts of others; aligning us with the higher truth and wisdom that our guides have for us. We breathe out any blockage, opening ourselves to the higher voice within us.

We move to the yellow energy centers by our ears, where we can hear the higher realms; the sounds and music and voices which we will clearly hear when we are ready, breathing out anything that would block that information from us.

The indigo energy of the third eye arrives as we rise through our chakras. Maggie instructs us to open that eye and make sure it is clear and moving; looking in to see ourselves and looking outward seeing wisdom. As we look out, we can see the vast energy around us and use that eye to connect us to the highest vibrational wisdom of sight that we are in alignment with.

Finally we reach our violet crown chakra at the top of our head where we open up and connect, clearing and cleansing it. Once it is open, we allow a wonderful shaft of light to come down through our body, making our chakras tingle and even going out through our hands and fingers, opening all the energy centers in our body. Now we rise to the golden wisdom, our center, our own place where the golden energy bursts open so we know that we are in the

Akashic vibration and can feel the energy surrounding us, spilling over all the energy centers, over all the layers so all parts of us is within the golden column of wisdom. Next, we allow the column of wisdom to grow until it is 12 feet around us; surrounding our physical body, surrounding the room, or wherever we are as the column turns into a sparkling translucent white. We are in alignment with our center and with Akasha; grounded into the center of the earth and up into the column of light where we ascend even farther into the iridescent light of our higher wisdom; our power center.

At this point, we are in our own temple. We look around and see all the beautiful familiar things in our temple while realizing that we are moving into the flame of transmutation with all its incredible power that has healed every portion of our energy; every layer, every fiber, every cell; all of our body healing in the amazing flame that only burns away the lower vibrations. While here, we allow the flame to come to us and resolve the issues we have brought because we know as we come to the Akasha, we bring our dreams, our intentions, and the things we wish to learn.

Looking around, we see the Emerald Mirror and the hallway of records which we can go to at any time, but Maggie wants us to focus on all the beautiful angelic beings with us now; our council of light that we can call on at any time. Right now our guardian angel(s) is/are coming through to look at our Book of Life. We came here with the intent of understanding a part of our life.

We go to the library and ask the librarian to come to us. The librarian can change form and be anything that is needed within our mind while the energy of the librarian remains the same. The librarian knows all about us; fears, sadness, love, future potential, so ask the librarian to bring right now the information to help us move forward in our light so that we can learn, and absorb, and become one with the incredible Akashic vibration. What in this life has held us back? Ask for that information to review now allowing ourselves to see the form this information takes; allowing ourselves to understand and knowing this information is available to us instantly and we can connect with it because it is now in our consciousness, our subconscious and our higher wisdom.

It's time to ask the librarian to show us how our information is laid out and show us the many ways we can accept and retrieve our information. Then ask the librarian to share the information that will help us understand from a higher perspective, an issue we have been carrying around with us for many years. Allow the librarian to share the issue with us as it relates to the people who it involved and as it relates to ourselves. What have we learned from it? What was the greater understanding that we shared?

Ask the librarian how we can be healed so that this information can be absorbed and learned. How will that affect the future actions that we will take? Also, ask the librarian to bring back a memory that will help us as we move forward. Ask to be shown one of our greatest strengths or talents and how we may apply it in a way that will benefit our life moving forward.

Then ask the librarian to show us our Book of Life; the one that represents this life. What does that book look like? What are the colors? How are they laid out? It represents our life as we are today. This information will anchor in our minds so we can retrieve it; knowing that all information is granted in an instant and it is within our minds. We can access it any time and we will come back and ask for more information that will lead to a greater understanding and healing.

As we are in the Akasha, we go to the Emerald Mirror. As we look in, we bring the primary issue we came here to understand and allow our mind and the mirror to show us the information we retrieved from our Book of Life in a way and manner that allows us to effect a beautiful, wonderful healing.

Moving our mind now to the Hall of Records, we can have the door representing our life open up to us. We can walk in and look and be in our life seeing ourselves with the issues we came here to address and wondering how the information we have right now will affect our life.

(The following is sort of a prayer Maggie does at this point.) When we finally go back to the hallway with our council of light we know that we have achieved the greatest vibrational alignment we were able with our higher wisdom, with our soul, with the beautiful light beings; asking Mother/Father God and all the light beings to be with us; that the knowledge we acquired, the healing, the wisdom, be contained in us allowing us to move forward in this vibration of knowledge and wisdom, bringing joy to our hearts, light to our understanding and leaving behind any issues, sorrow or regret because we know they do not serve us (our highest good). We will allow our angels to hold that knowledge and feeling here at the Hall of Records and we don't bring it into our life on the earth plane. But, our life on the earth plane is now aligned with the light and wisdom.

We go back into our sacred circle of energy knowing that each time we return we will see more of our striking guides of the Council of Light beings. Now we can ask our light being to finally resolve our issue or issues of some pressing desire we had. They come forward and lighten the heart, energy and feelings of the person who has been healed.

Maggie again gives thanks to the divine Council of Light and Source of all that is; being grateful for the light and wisdom shown to us in our visit. We become one with our circle of light and move away from the temple, down through our body, deep into the earth grounding with our crystals, grounding with our love for nature and people; knowing that our new wisdom is open to share for the highest good of all concerned in a manner of love and compassion. We rise back through our feet and center in our heart; understanding it was our choice to be here. We are happy and joyful for our connection to the light coming from our higher wisdom, to the grounding in the center of earth, to the beauty of our column of light; here to protect and cleanse us, and share the grace and wisdom of our higher selves.

Now take a couple deep breaths as we center (align) in this light, open our eyes and come back into the room. (I find this difficult each time I do this class; being hard to bring myself back to the 3-D earth plane. Sometimes I wonder if I had only been sleeping through the whole thing, but I do remember what Maggie was saying and I am able to hear her call me back into the room once more. Was this imagination? Real? Maybe our imagination is real on a dimensional level and by believing it, we make, or manifest, what happens to us become reality.)

Want to know more about Maggie? Read what she says.

I have learned how to be comfortable as a trance channel for the Master Teachers of the Akasha. My first book will be published in the summer of 2015 and is called, Open the Doorway to Your Soul. This is an inspirational book of messages channeled through me by the Master Teachers. The book is designed to expand your conscious connection to the light and wisdom of your soul.

The Master Teachers included in this first book are: Goddesses - Isis, White Tara, Lakshmi, Diana and Mother Mary; Archangel Raphael; Ascended Masters - Ganesh, Kuthumi, Krishna, Saint Germain, Jesus, Apollo, Merlin, and Lord Melchizedek.

—— CHAPTER 13 ——

PENNY

Trained as a clinical counselor with an MA in Counseling Psychology, Penny (pseudonym) has been at her holistic practice providing medium readings and healing for more than a decade.

I met Penny through Laurie Stinson* and it was Penny who started our talk by asking about that. Since I am a person who loves curiosity, I was happy to tell what I knew, so the interviewer became the interviewee for a time! Listening to Penny's delightful English accent made the interview all the more enjoyable.

How did you end up connecting with Laurie Stinson? I had some books published but my publisher decided to quit the business, locking up all my books in her warehouse so I couldn't get any more (to sell). My best seller was The Girl Who Talked to Ghosts: A True Story. The best bet was to put it on Amazon.com where it could be an e-book. I learned about Laurie doing this when I was at the Spiritualist camp in the summer. It turned out that Laurie had a friend do it for her, but I never connected with that friend, however, my friendship with Laurie continued as we ended up conversing online nearly each day. She has also gotten to know some of my children too, who are very interested in spiritualism also. So you never met face to face? We did on the last night of camp at the end

---

* see Chapter XV

of summer. Just by chance she happened to visit from Minneapolis, so I got to talk to her then. It's an amazing world the way people connect up! It is. I am on a spiritual quest and this is all part of it.

What is your background regarding spiritualism or medium-ship or your interests? I had a life-changing traumatic event happen to me about eight years ago. At that time, I had been into reading spiritual books by Rosemary Altea, if you are familiar. Yes, of course, she's English! Just by chance, after that event happened, I thought, 'I'm going to send Rosemary an email even if she does get hundreds a day'. I heard back immediately and she said she just happened to have an opening on September 13. That day I called her up. Her first words were, 'don't tell me anything! I could be a charlatan for all you know!' That gave me trust. What she told me changed my life in an instant. I forgave someone who had deeply hurt me and it was like the weight of the world was physically taken off my shoulders! (We chatted for a time here and Penny asked where Rosemary lived. I told her she had been in Vermont but I thought she had been swin-dled by a person close to her and now lives in Florida.)

What was it that she said that make you do that (forgive)? She was giving me messages from some of my loved ones who had passed; they were sort of raking me over the coals a little bit. And you paid attention. I did! I listened to whatever they said and I still do. When Spirit talks, I listen; there can't be any better help than that! It changed my life completely and I've been on a spiritual quest since then.

Rosemary Altea was born in the city of Leicester, which was where I went to University. Where she grew up, I think was a very, very poor area and I think she had quite a hard childhood, if I re-member her books. It was terrible; she had a lot of abuse. I loved her books, but I'm sorry to hear she's been swindled because she hasn't had an easy life as it is. It always made me wonder; how can someone who is psychic be swindled by somebody who was right next to them? My antennae is really on to the point that I am too sensitive with people, but maybe if she has been abused, maybe the need for love or the need to be loyal to people who seem loving is so strong that it gets in the way. I don't know.

My husband had a meeting with a so-called angel investor yesterday and before he went, I told him the guy was a charlatan and I knew nothing about him, but it came to me really strongly. Afterwards, it was proven out; he (the investor) didn't know the people he said he knew and I told my husband it was a waste of time. I get those messages, but maybe her gifts run differently because every gift is different.

That's the reason I'm doing this book. There is not just one gift out there; everybody's gift is a little different than everybody else's. I think it's like an artist. You have different types of artists who all paint differently; it's all about who you are and how it comes to you. That reminds me of (the lady) who runs the spiritualist camp. She told me she doesn't 'read' into anybody unless they ask her to, just for privacy, and maybe that's what Rosemary was doing. With me it just happens; I am told, or get warnings and that's not because I'm trying to read with that person. I just knew instantly. And, maybe it was part of her learning journey; we all have our life lessons to learn as well. You are the only person I know who has had a reading with Rosemary Altea; that's pretty cool. I've written a note of thanks to her on the anniversary of that reading date ever since.

You have a lot of gifts. One I'd like to know about is spirit guides as very few people talk about them. Well, my perception and understanding is just mine. As I've been shown, guides are like friends in heaven, given to us by God to assist us on our journey here. Like dear friends guides will advise us, but with free will we can choose to listen or do it our way. And the end of the day they are in Service to God, and they are on their own journey in heaven, learning to help, love and be kind.

Does a spirit guide interpret for other people? What is their purpose? In my own experience, guides step forward to help explain what's going on for the person. They provide advice. In readings, clients will typically say – well I did that, I thought of that, my friend suggested that. Guides provide helpful and practical information that will improve a life journey.

When I talked to medium Laurie Stinson, she said she thinks she is at the end of her earthly lives and is probably going to be a guide next. I'm sure if that's a role you want to take in the next life you could. I think that's between you and God. I'm sure it's quite a hard job too.

Does everybody have guides? My experiences suggest that we all do. How nice is that?

Is there a limit to how many guides (are present)? Or, is there a typical amount? In my experience, new guides have arrived to help when I've had new needs, such as help being more determined. It also seems on a day-to-day basis, I have one guide who helps support me with my personal life and another who helps me in my professional life. However, it's not like I see them all the time. And the end of the day, it's not about guides, it's about God.

What you're saying is a lot like what happens to Rosemary Altea too. Yes, and I loved reading those books. But, those who came through in my reading (with Rosemary Altea) were some of my close family; my grandmother and my father, rather than a guide. Would a guide also assist them, or is the guide the intermediary between them and me? In my experience family members will offer assistance to us from heaven, just as they did on earth. They love us and continue to care for us, and I can see when they step forward in readings we are so happy to hear from them and their advice and presence is a comfort.

Are there guides for the guides? It's my belief that there are. We're all learning and growing all of the time, and that continues in heaven. Right!

What would be above a guide? I don't know the hierarchy. I do know at the center of everything is God. And at the end of the day, that's all that's really important.

What is the purpose of angels and archangels then? You're going to have to ask God for that answer!

MEDIUMS NOT SO RARE

Have you ever read any of JRR Tolkien? No. He has a book called the Silmarillion that sounds so much like what you are saying. (Penny laughed.) Email me that information, it really sounds quite interesting. Although I've read many metaphysical books, I only teach or say what I know for sure; in other words, I only teach what my own experience is. So it would be interesting to read a similar account.

I had a vision of an angel in a dream not so long ago. How wonderful. What did she look like? I'm presuming it was your guardian angel. Years ago I had two dreams of my own angel. And I've never seen her since. What was yours like?

This being was SO big. Angels will sometimes appear in readings. I do know that people who come to readings who love angels always have messages from angels. It's like they love being appreciated. Last week, a lady came for a reading and I said 'I'm told you have an affinity for angels." She concurred and let me know she even had a large tattoo of angel wings on her back!

If I can change our direction a little bit for something that I really wonder about and have asked mediums or whomever what they think, and I'll ask you the same thing. I first start out by saying that I am a musician and was born with a gift of musicianship. I can sit down at a piano and can play things, like my grandfather could, that are in my head. Wow! That's an incredible skill. I am also a semiprofessional musician too; it comes easy for me as something that, even though I had to have training, it was just a natural thing for me. So, I wonder if it isn't the same thing for the gift of mediumship. It's identical! It's the same thing; if you have a gift (whether a talent for computer programming, or for math or for cooking) then it's worth developing it, utilizing it and enjoying it. And you do that with practice!

Am I beating myself up trying to open up my third eye by trying to find a way to be able to listen and see to the other side? I have a message for you. I am seeing music healing guides. They show that every note carries a vibration or frequency and that connects

into the whole spirit world. I think, rather than beat yourself up trying to connect with the other side, just realize that you are healing
through your music and you are working with the music guides
to bring the gift of healing to others. I think that you would really
expand your therapeutic practice. They are really saying that you
could use; they're showing me the word therapeutic and it's almost
like dancing around the edge and recognizing that you, yourself,
should be going out there and using music as a healing tool.

To give you an example, they're showing me: last year for six
months my kids and I volunteered in an Alzheimer's home and every Friday a music therapist came and she played rollicking and loud
music on the piano and sang for all the patients with Alzheimer's.
They are showing me her, and then they are showing me a working
dog, a dog that works to assist the blind or sit by the elderly and be
hugged. And they are saying all of these types of people are healers
and they are working with guides to do healing; and they're showing me the music guides and saying, 'that's your role'!

When I talked to Rosemary Altea, I asked her the same kind of
thing and she said that my psychic ability comes in bits and pieces and
not to worry about it. She also said that I do have strong healing hands
and I should use my healing. You should use your healing. But, the
guides who are showing up are the music healers; they're musicians!

(Penny made a comparison to medieval musicians.) That's funny
because I used to play tenor recorder in a Medieval and Renaissance
group. (Penny laughed at the irony.) Well, you must have contem-
plated some therapeutic healing because it's like you are towing
around the edge of it. My daughter is going to school in music
therapy right now. Okay, so there's you watching from the outside!

The other thing is they are showing me crystals, different ones
like you have a mantle with different kinds of rock (on it) or crystals
that you can actually tune up the frequency or vibration through
your music. In other words, you can enable them. And so another
thing they are showing me with you is you should try and combine the two practices like a use of crystal therapy or therapeutic

techniques with the music. I'm seeing tall rocks around you. Maybe it is because I keep two crystals next to my bed!

When I was reading through your website, I saw something written by Witch Wanda. Is that something you have done for a magazine? Yes, that was me when I was younger, when I had my first child. Now, I write for Edge Magazine and what started as Witch Wanda has now become a column called Spirited Kids. It's a parenting column that embraces a holistic approach to parenting. My background in teaching and school counseling is useful here. It's a great way to combine my learning and my spiritual interests as well as my experiences as a mom.

I'm going to shift areas again. If I was someone who called you (for a reading) and didn't know what they wanted to know about; maybe a past life regression, or some type of medium message, how does one know what to ask for if they don't know what to ask? They may know they want to talk to you but not what to talk about. I think that people really do know what they want. People either want to connect with their loved ones in heaven because they are suffering the pain of bereavement, or they're stuck in their lives and want clarity. Sometimes people are in pain and want a healing. A very few people want past life work and with those people, they've usually seen past lives in dreams and are interested in learning more.

When a person comes for the reading, I always pray for highest good and leave it up to heaven to figure out what messages are needed; what would get them most on track today? Is it the connection on the other side that they need most today? Or, is it the guides to come through to talk about a life situation, or what's going on, or how to move forward? Or, it is both? And what is needed comes through. That's what Rosemary Altea does and I agree with it too.

I am particularly interested in past life. It's fascinating, and so healing! I think that a lot of 'trauma' can be carried through life times; especially trauma from the suffering of war and death.

When I was at the Wonewoc Spiritualist Camp, I went to a past life regression they had. I'm wondering if you do yours like they do there; going into a meditative state. Yes, my client and I will be in a meditative state which takes about 30 minutes of healing to achieve. Bear in mind, people who come to past lives may have never done any intuitive work before.

In the meditative state, they are taken on a journey, and enter into various lifetimes. Once they've gotten to their first lifetime, they walk through a doorway into each next lifetime. (This is similar to Maggie Chula's description of the Akasha.) Sometimes they take vehicles between each lifetime.

Do you ever have people who can't go anywhere? Yes. It hasn't happened very often, but I tend to know in advance when that will occur and I prepare the client that if they aren't able to regress, that I will then give them a reading instead. I don't want anyone to leave, disappointed.

We had two people in our group that didn't have anything happen in their regression, but all the rest of us found one past life. What I question though is: since I have such a great imagination, was I imagining these things? I think that is a great question to ask. Personally, I think that it's very hard to imagine an entire scene, interact with people, receive gifts from them and so forth. I also find that clients are incredibly emotional as they do their healing work. At the same time I can conceive it's hard to understand.

Mine was really strange because my oldest daughter (now) was my wife back then (past life). Did she look the same in it; could you see she was the same? Pretty much, yes, especially her eyes. In my experience of past lives, I've never looked like myself at all. Nor have I recognized anyone else – but I've known who they were. I think it's fascinating.

To see my comments on my past life regression, check back to Chapter VI: Messages, Messages. This experience should remind you of Maggie Chula's visit to the Akashic records and Penny's traveling back in past lives; both having similar mists and entering doors to visit past lives. As I experienced the same thing, I would suggest that this is real and is probably the way most people can reach their past lives.

—— CHAPTER 14 ——

DK BRAINARD

Bio: D.K. Brainard, M.A., C.Ht., is a writer, musician, certified hypnotherapist and world-renowned astrologer who specializes in helping clients rediscover their soul's purpose for this lifetime, move beyond old patterns and limiting beliefs, and step into life more abundantly. D.K.'s work is based in the belief that each individual has a unique soul path and that, "Living your purpose and realizing your own dream is the best thing you can do for the world." More information is available at http://dkbrainard.com.

When and how did you find that you had a gift? I grew up in a fundamentalist, pretty much, a Christian cult; an extreme sect, I guess. I never, ever could have imagined me making a living as an astrologer because that was basically the work of the devil, witchcraft; anything that didn't accord with this really strict interpretation of the Bible. I rebelled against that in my late teens and early twenties and went entirely the other way; sex, drugs and rock and roll. But, I also ended up getting a masters (degree) in French. I got a scholarship to go to Paris for a year and study at Sorbonne, (University of Paris- French language and culture courses), and then came back and finished up my masters at the University of Cincinnati. Going through college and graduate school, I developed this sort of academic approach to life in a lot of ways; sort of got into the rational side of things. From that viewpoint also, astrology would be considered totally ludicrous, which is what I thought about it.

Then this chain of synchronicities, probably the best way I can describe it, started happening. The first link in that chain (was); I had gone to Paris to write a screen play with this guy who I had met under really bizarre circumstances, and this probably doesn't have anything to do with the book. Maybe it was in the stars! I think it was and there's no other way for me to explain it. I was living in Washington DC at the time and this was when I was 21 or 22. I dropped out of school for a while, had gone to pursue journalism, then I ended up being a bike messenger and all this other stuff.

It was right when I got to DC, here was this kid from Flint, Michigan, who had never really spent any time in a big city before, I just remember looking up at the buildings and wow! I got on the Metro and there was this really cute girl on the train with me and it was obvious that something was wrong. I've always been compassionate and intuitive, and she was really cute too, so I finally got the nerve to talk to her and said, 'is there something wrong?' She was this French Au Pair (domestic assistant from another country), who had just arrived in the US and she was lost on the train; she couldn't read the directions and couldn't figure out where to go. I ended up riding all the way to the end of the line to find her stop and had a crush on this girl, yeah, I fell in love with her, but she wasn't in love with me and used me because she was stuck out in the suburbs. To make a long story short, I met these other Au Pairs.

Well, this girl was always talking about this guy (named) Robby, who I always conceived as my romantic rival. I was hitchhiking around Europe and went to France for the first time; this was an earlier, previous trip when I was 21. This friend of mine had told me, 'hey, when you get to Paris just call up my friend Margo and you can stay with her'. And so I get to Paris and I've been hitchhiking and I'm like cold and wet, it's raining, and I call up this Margo and she says, 'pfffft, you cannot stay with me, my mother is here'. I was like I was totally lost and wanted to start crying. I started looking for a hostel but all the hostels in the city were booked; I don't know what was going on then, so I finally called Margo back and said to just help me out. I'm this American in Paris; I don't speak the language; I'm lost, help me find a hostel. So, she called around and found one hostel that had one bed left in a room with four beds.

I get up there and I'm exhausted; I just want to pass out and go to sleep. There are these three American guys who say hey dude, what are you doing in Paris? One asked 'what's your name'? I told him D. He's like, hey D, I'm Robby'. Something seemed to happen. He said how'd you end up here? (I told him) I met these Au Pairs in Washington DC and I thought I'd come and visit them and just travel. And, he says, no way. I know some Au Pairs. What is some-one's name? I told him, Martine. He looked at me like oh my God, YOU'RE D! I looked at him and said, and you're Robby! He had the same experience; she was always playing him off against me as if I was her boyfriend. She was using both of us and playing us against each other. We ended up being friends and traveled all around and had these crazy adventures. Years later I went back to Paris to write a screen play with him; he was in the film industry. We had a big falling out; it was just this disastrous year and I kind of limped back home at the end of it. I was living in my mom's basement and eating microwave dinners and watching TV.

This friend of the bass player in my first band had a sister who lived in New York who called me up out of the blue and asked what are you doing? (I told her) I was in my mom's basement, watching TV and eating microwave dinners. She said why don't you come to New York for the summer? I've got this place up on the Hudson River that my dad owns and I'm never there, and I hope to get a job in the city. So I did. She was working with this famous astrologer in New York on some other kind of project and she kept trying to get the two of us together. I think she was trying to hook us up romanti-cally, but I ended up having this phone relationship with this famous astrologer; she was always talking to me about my chart and what was going on with astrology and I was like, God, this lady is crazy.

But, I started reading her stuff and I ended up meeting again a couple times over the years and the best way I can describe it, she's a Pisces and I'm a Pisces, is that she gave me some kind of transmission because I started reading her monthly column and some of the things kind of made sense to me, and that got me into being curious as to why that worked. What did you mean (about) transmission? She touched me in some way; I think without consciously intending to on her part. But, if I look at my chart, and this took me years after that meeting to recognize this, but it's really clear in my chart that astrology is something I've done in past lives.

There are a lot of ways you can interpret the archetypes in the chart, but knowing what I do about myself, once I saw that place in my chart, it was OH! Because when I actually started studying it, it just made sense to me and I could do it. That was 1995 and I didn't start offering readings to people until 2004-5. For a lot of that ten year period, I had no idea why I was so fascinated with astrology, or drawn to it; it was like an obsession, but I couldn't really acknowledge that to myself because it didn't fit in with my view of who I was; my identity. I feel like on some soul level, her soul touched my soul; like here, I've got this gift for you.

Let me go back for a bit. When you were talking about a reading, were you talking about an astrological reading or a psychic reading? Astrological. This a thing that took me years and years to admit to myself; I have a fair amount of psychic ability and I think we are all psychic in one way or another, and so when I'm looking at somebody's chart I do all the preparation, I know what all the planets symbolize, I know when you get two forces playing against each other that there's going to be some kind of conflict there and I can, on a mental level, come up with an interpretation of what that might mean.

But, sometimes I get a real clear psychic hit (such as) this person had an abusive father and that's what that represents. And, sometimes I'll even see the details of that or get information on what age something happened, but I don't always. That may be a function of whatever state I'm in when I'm doing the reading; some days we are more intuitive than we are on other days. Some days we've got our own drama going on, but often it's because the client is protecting that wound or that experience psychically and that makes it harder to read.

Do people come to you mainly for an astrological reading? I see (on your website) that you also do hypnotherapy, Reiki, sound healing and other things. Does it all fit together? When I started pursuing hypnotherapy, I really had this vision of how that was going to work out. I saw myself moving away from astrology and doing more hypnotherapy with people. I think most of us when we start out on this path or anything we are trying to master, you go through, even as a musician you imitate other musicians, you have to learn rules of the game and certain skill sets; with hypnotherapy it is the same. I have some heroes; Steven Gilligan is one of my heroes, and Milton Erickson; I love the way those guys practice. (Stephen Gilligan is an American author, psychologist and psychotherapist, who was one of the first students and developers of the work of Milton Erickson, considered the founder of modern hypnotherapy.) I saw myself doing that but it just never really happened for me and for a while it was really frustrating for me. Then I realized at some point that the way that wants to come through me, by and large, is in the context of looking at somebody's soul mission through their chart, and then looking at what they want to create in their life and how they're being blocked from that. Sometimes that's self sabotage and sometimes it seems like fate is always conspiring against them to block them, sometimes it comes through things like physical illness, a tough relationship or whatever.

But, the way I've ended up using the hypnotherapy is primarily, what I could say it with a lot of confidence, it's my own thing now. It's not mine in the ego sense; it's just a really authentic way of expressing that channel through myself that's not based on what other people are doing. One of the big life lessons in my chart is self esteem. In astrology the second house represents self esteem, values and money and resources which are all sort of connected. So actually stepping into that place over the last three years or so has been really empowering and liberating and really enabled me to help people on a whole different level than what I was doing when I first started out.

Basically the way I'll use the hypnosis is if clients are open to it, and a lot of times on the first time around somebody just wants a chart reading wanting to know what's going to happen next year, what do I do about this relationship, am I ever going to meet Mr. Right, am I ever going to make more money; all those kinds of basic questions. I have a lot of clients that I'll work with several times a year, or several weeks in a row, or a certain period of time. What I tend to do, and this is what I love to do, is then we can go into specific areas and that's where the hypnosis comes in.

If you're blocked and you can never seem to meet a romantic partner that resonates to you, why is that? What I usually find is, it's really interesting because there's a place in everybody's chart that says 'this is your past life karma, or what you brought in from other dimensions, other universes or however you want to look at that'. We all come into life with a gift and then some wounded places and also with a comfort zone. A lot of what the south node in astrology shows is what your past life comfort zone is. This is the thing you have been building up; working on in past lives. We come into this lifetime, and in my experience based on more than a thousand in-person consultations, that past life karma energy is always re-imprinted in childhood. So it creates this path that we tend to think is our own path. This usually persists up into the late 30s or early 40s; it's almost like we have to recapitulate what we were working on in our past lifetimes.

What I find is, whatever blocks someone is experiencing now as an adult, you can get to that block on a lot of different levels. I'd like to come up with a visual metaphor for this, but the way I kind of see it is almost like a big molecule, you know, like those molecule three dimensional diagrams. It's like within the soul there are these big chains of molecules and it's got depth, height, it's got width. Some of these little bubbles are just little pin pricks and these are little things that happen like you get cut off in traffic and get angry at somebody and then you can't let it go. It's a little wound; it's small, but it's there. You get irritated at your wife or your husband and that persists. Then, some of them are these big things like you were sexually abused as a child or you were in a horrible car accident and you have all this physical pain from it; but they're all connected.

The crazy thing about astrology is that you can see in somebody's chart what the basic nature of these wounds is going to be. It's like we come into life with this pattern that will just keep repeating and keep repeating until we're able to go in and pop those bubbles and release that energy. The interesting thing that I've found is that you can work with the wound pattern wherever it shows up. A Course in Miracles says something about this, I don't remember the exact quote, but it says the smallest irritation is just as much of a wound or block as the deepest hurt.

I've really found that to be true because it's like if you and I were working together and you were really upset because your wife said something mean to you; if we start working there and can release some of that energy, it's like some of those bigger bubbles that are further down will start coming up to the surface to be released. Sometimes with people we'll find what the block with the partner is; well, they've never been able to trust. So, let's feel into that. If you feel into that lack of trust in your heart, or in your body, or in your mind, what shows up? What do you feel in your body? What are the thoughts that come to mind? What are the memories that pop up? Some client will say, I'm six years old and I really want to learn to play the flute and my dad yells at me and says we don't have enough money to give you music lessons. I just felt like nobody would ever understand me. To me, that's one of those bigger bubbles because what you want is not acceptable.

Then there's always a past life component to this stuff too. A lot of times, if I'm working with somebody, and I ask them to show (see) what comes up, they'll get this image of a peasant in the middle ages and that's where I'll use the hypnotic language to kind of guide them into accepting that. Because on an ego level, we see that and think I'm just making this up, this is just my imagination, this doesn't make any sense. But, if I can hold that space for them and hypnotically induce them to start focusing in on the details of that, it's amazing because they'll have this experience of this drama where they're a peasant's wife in the middle ages and the husband goes off to war and never comes back. So there's this wound about trust or abandonment. Whenever we get to those places, it's really clear how that plays into the pattern in this lifetime. Does that make sense?

Hypnotherapy; how would that compare with deep meditation? Similar, but different, I would say, in the sense that, in the modern school of hypnotherapy that started with Milton Erickson in the 50s or earlier, is often called permissive hypnotherapy. Basically what that involves is that you create rapport with your client. So if you and I are doing a session, I'm going to tune into you and see how your soul expresses things through you. Are you primarily feeling things? Are you primarily a thinking person? Are you auditory? And, what's the kind of language that you use when you talk about your dreams or you talk about the wound we are trying to explore?

What permissive hypnotherapy does is we don't have to put you into a deep trance to change things. All we have to do is create this resonance that enables you to feel safe enough so your ego can kind of move out of the way and some of that deeper soul experience can come to the surface.

The other difference I would see between hypnotherapy and meditation is that hypnotherapy tends to be a definite level of manipulation that is going on. I also believe that I cannot manipulate your psyche to do anything that your soul is not willing to do. So the people who get on stage and bawk like a chicken is because they want to get on stage and bawk like a chicken! With hypnotherapy, the way I use it anyway, is I'm trying to let your soul guide me to what it wants to release, but your ego and your defenses aren't allowing that material to come to the surface because, let's face it, our society doesn't deal very well with emotions. Even if you look at TV or movies, the hero is always the person who can successfully repress his emotions and remain cold and rational and make the right decisions. Whereas, the villain like the Joker or the Riddler, there's somebody that's completely controlled by their emotions! Does that answer the question?

What I'm thinking about is the Wonewoc Spiritualist Camp. I did a past life regression, which I had never done before, and the leader, Sam, took us back very slowly. I did have a past life that I went to and the rational part of me asked, is it my really good imagination or did this really happen because I could describe buildings and everything around me. When we were done she asked how long we thought we had been doing our journey. Most people thought 10-15 minutes, but it had been nearly approaching an hour that we had been in that state. It seemed like a meditative state to me and yet, I would describe it as being a sort of hypnosis.

My belief on what meditation is, or should be right now, at this point in my life; I've tried a lot of forms of meditation. I've been influenced by Buddhist teachings, and I feel like discovering Buddhism in the late 90s, it really probably saved my life because it gave me some tools and a different perspective than what I had grown up with. I think a lot of the Eastern tradition can be geared toward transcending or escaping what we are feeling, or a way of finding some peace.

What I believe now is that meditation is anything that enables us to slow down and be able to look at anything that is happening internally. Most of the time we're going along and caught up in our monkey mind, and whether we're aware we are doing this or not, we have this constant internal dialog that's describing the world to us and making judgments and criticizing things and saying this is good and this is bad. And so, meditation is anything that we do consciously that enables us to step back from that ego mind and kind of look at it as an observer. I would definitely say that past life regression is a form of meditation and most hypnosis is probably a form of meditation, although if I'm trying to get you to squawk like a chicken (under hypnosis) if that counts for meditation or not; that's a different stream.

What are some of the tools you got from Buddhism because I've been told by a psychic that I seemed to be of the Buddhist mentality; being able to clear my mind completely and just not think anything. When I discovered Buddhism, it was the first time that I really started meditating, and I had meditated as a teenager, but didn't call it meditation because meditation was probably an avenue for the devil to enter my soul when I was in the fundamentalist thing. I was really into athletics and I did this visualization practice for basketball and for other things and looking back that was probably a form of meditation. But, when I discovered Buddhism, I actually started sitting down and practicing and that radically changed my life. I don't know how else to describe it other than it opened up everything that I am now.

It's like the forecast I wrote for February (this is from DK's web forecasts); I want to do an update to that because I got feedback from a couple people saying 'it sounds like you're saying meditation and all these things don't work'. When I look back at my mind in my 20s, it was a horrible, toxic place to be; it was so uncomfortable to be in my normal thinking mind. And so meditation gave me this perspective; your mind, there are just thoughts that are there; you can attach to them and identify to them   , or you can keep meditating and that will give you a way to recognize them as it's part of you but not really the core of who you are. So I definitely think it (meditation) is very valuable.

I think if we were able to connect with Buddha himself, with his real spirit and the real energetic core of his teachings; I don't want to get too crazy here, but a lot of the way people practice Buddhism in the west is the same way that a lot of people practice yoga; if I do this because it makes me feel better, and there is nothing wrong with that, but I think the core of the Buddha's teaching is that we unite ourselves on all levels, earth, air, fire and water; physical, spiritual, mental and emotional. Meditation is the tool for allowing us explore all of these areas; what's going on in my body right now, what am I thinking, what are my thoughts, what are my inspirations, or what do I feel compelled to go out and create, what am I actually feeling emotionally?

So I really feel that the most advantageous use of meditation is a way of finding out what is beneath the surface because one of the things that hypnosis and just the empirical evidence of hypnotherapy over the years teaches us is that the subconscious mind and what's going on beneath the day to day awareness, that's what is really controlling everything. We like to think, I'm going to make this decision and I'm going to direct my life towards this decision, but the fact is, that doesn't work for very many people and probably most of the people it works for are raving psychopaths or sociopaths.

For most of us, it's like the Apostle Paul said in the Bible; the things I do are the things I don't want to do, and the things I want to do are the things I don't do. So I feel what we should be using meditation for is to just become aware of; why do I keep repeating this pattern? That makes me unhappy. Where is it coming from? If we can get to those deeper levels, whether it is childhood trauma or past life stuff or a lot of the stuff we struggle with as adults, and this is another thing I have become aware of over the past few years, is that so much of what my clients struggle with and identify with as "their problem" isn't really even personal. It's something that their father or mother struggled with and wasn't able to successfully deal with, so it gets passed on. Sometimes it comes from the grandparents or even further up the family tree.

Meditation can give us a window into 'what is this?' And a lot of that ends up, well, you know the soul communicates primarily through images and feelings and so a lot of that shows up as these recurrent images, whether they come out in dreams or sometimes when you look at a problem and think what does that look like, I remember seeing this little hunched over old man in my liver. I didn't know who this old man was; he didn't seem like anybody in my family. That's something I've been working with for years; what is that energy there; where did that come from?

I thought what you said for February (online horoscope about truth) was pretty neat. I'm finding the more I work on this book, that I don't find myself believing everything everybody says because nobody has it all right.

Before I discovered astrology, I had this really, what my wife would call, self righteous view of the world that what we should all do is be creative as possible, we should try harder and overcome whatever our difficulties are. I kind of believed that everybody should be doing the same thing or going for the same goal. When I discovered astrology, you look at people's charts and it's like WOW, the main reason they are here in this lifetime is to learn how to have a satisfying, balanced relationship. Career doesn't really mean anything to this person. And then this other person; the main reason they are here is to learn how to make money and deal with money. For some people, money is just never an issue; they've always had it, they always know it's going to be there if they need it. So we really all do have these unique ways of experiencing the world and it's cool that there are just so many ways of healing and working with your energy and working toward your life's purpose. Different strokes for different folks basically! The ones without money are musicians, of course. (Being a musician myself, it is not normally a job where anyone makes a lot of money.) What do you call a musician without a girlfriend? Homeless.

I have never understood why the position of planets and stars have any effect on what we do; on what we have or will do? (DK sent me my chart via email at this point to help with his explanation.)

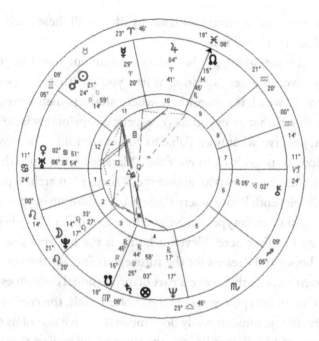

This is how I see it, and you'd probably get a hundred different answers from a hundred different astrologers. What I feel like is the planets in the solar system; each of those planets corresponds to an archetype within the soul. That's within the world's collective soul and also within each individual's soul. I don't believe that when Mars is in a certain sign that it sends beams down to the people on the earth and controls their actions. The way I look at it is that the universe is this extremely complicated computer simulation, or some people call it the universal database.

The planets of the solar system function like the gears of a giant clock. In your chart, when Mars and the Sun are in a conjunction, they're right next to each other, I feel on a soul level that you chose to be born at a time when Mars and the Sun are right next to each other like that. That probably happens for about six or seven days once a year. So there was this period of when a bunch of people said, 'I want to learn what it feels like to have Mars and the Sun, those two archetypes, be married for all my life. So all these souls come in and say this is my time.

I feel what astrology shows us is the unique flavor of energy at any given moment of time. When you put that in a person's horoscope, which is a snapshot of where all the planets were at the time of birth, that gives you this energetic blueprint that is, to some extent, governs what is available to you in your life. The way that functions is, to go back to your Sun/Mars as an example, the sun is an archetype, Mars is an archetype, Taurus is an archetype, and then the eleventh house where those planets show up in your chart; that's another archetype. You've got these four different archetypes working together here. Eleventh house is the life area that talks about hopes and dreams for the future, our friends, the networks and communities that we're a part of, professional colleagues. The sun as an archetype represents the center of self, the core of who you are. In one sense, it really does mean that each one of us chose to be one of 12 different flavors, the signs of the zodiac; there's the Taurus flavor, there's the Gemini flavor, there's the Aries flavor (and so on). And you have all these other factors in your chart that modify that flavor.

People with sun in the eleventh house, your sun, your center, what you came to radiate, are going to tend to be these people that are very identified with either an ideal, a group of people/ community, they tend to be the networkers of the zodiac, so they tend to be the people who are working sort of selflessly to try to get everybody else in the right position so that things can be better in the community or in the world.

To each of these archetypes there are all these different levels of experience, so one person might just identify themself or define themself by who their friends are. Another person with sun in the eleventh house might get a lot of their satisfaction or identity from (something like), I belong to the Rotary Club and the Rotary Club is this great organization that really helps the youth of America and whatever.

Then, as you go up the vibrational scale, you have eleventh house people who are consciously working to bring a sort of Aquarian ideal into the world; working to, say, how can we make the world better, how can we make it more fair for this group of people who are more disenfranchised, how can we restructure society or the community so that it works better for everybody? And ultimately the ideal of the eleventh house is that everybody gets to be their own unique, individual self, but society is organized so that each of those unique, individual selves can have a place that is meaningful. Some people were born to be garbage men, some people were born to be hair dressers, and some people were born to be scientists. And eleventh house understands that all of those are really valid but what's not valid is if it forced all garbage men to become scientists; we send them all to 10 years of school and finance that and put them in a research lab. Does that make any sense?

Then, with Mars in the picture, that's really interesting because any time you have two planets that close together, it's really like they are married for better or for worse. The sun and Mars actually get along pretty well. But, there is this whole system of rulership in astrology that works for some reason, and one of the rulerships is that Mars rules Scorpio, which is the opposite sign of Taurus. Planets don't like to be in their opposite sign, so when you put Mars in Taurus, it's kind of challenged on this basic level in this lifetime. People with a planet in what's called Detriment, technically in astrology, and that just means a planet in its opposite sign, those would be places where you really have to work on that archetype especially through the first half of life in order to get it going in the right direction. Mars is the warrior archetype; it's the aggressive, anger energy, our assertiveness, ego, willpower.

So with that sun/Mars together, that shows that you're somebody that has a real tremendous amount of drive, like once you put your mind to something, and that really winds up with what feels good to you or what feels right to you and the eleventh house matches up with your ideals, you are just going to plow forward despite all obstacles either until it no longer seems like a good idea to you, or until you complete whatever your goal is.

But Mars and Taurus can also get really fixated. Taurus is one of the fixed signs and actually where that comes from is it's the middle sign of the season so each of the middle signs of each season is considered to be fixed energy. Taurus is the fixed sign of spring. In the first sign of spring, which would be Aries, March and April, it's certain to be spring but you still have these wintry conditions that come in, you still get a snowstorm, it still gets cold. By the time you get to the Taurus period of April/May, spring is here; it's stuck in there. And then by the time you get to the next sign, Gemini, we're starting to transition into summer; sometimes it feels like spring and sometimes it feels like summer.

All of these come from these ancient observations about the way the universe works and about how the cycles of energy work. Basically with Mars in Taurus as a planet in its Detriment in a fixed sign, the challenge is that it can be easy for Mars in Taurus people to get really stuck in either bad habits or in facing in this direction and saying in order to achieve my goal or do what's best for my family or community or whatever, this is the way that it has to be done; I'm going to keep on truckin' in this way whereas there might be a much easier, more harmonious way over here if you can just switch that energy over. Hitler had the sun, Mars and Venus all in Taurus. There's a good example of Mars and Taurus getting really fixated.

It's really interesting because with these archetypes, there is some constraint on free will. A Mars in Taurus person is really different from a Mars in Aries person. Empirically, if you got a hundred astrologers together who had seen a thousand clients each, they could tell you story after story of how these differences just play out; sometimes it rains and sometimes it's sunny. Once you start working with these, you realize this is a natural fact; it really exists.

The thing I feel like, one of the biggest miscommunications about astrology is that it's easy for people who know just enough to be dangerous, to look at that sun/Mars conjunction and say, Edward is an angry person because Mars equals anger and the sun equals the self, therefore, he's a fundamentally angry person. You could have two people with almost the exact same chart, so you could have a neighbor that was born in Milwaukee at the same time as you who has pretty much the same chart and has that sun/Mars conjunction, but if his dad is really angry and abusive and your dad isn't, you've got the same archetype but that's going to be played out in different ways. He may be somebody that suffered beatings all the time as a kid and when he has children he perpetuates those beatings and a lot of his life mission is to learn to not beat his children. Whereas, you had a better upbringing and maybe your father had a lot of anger but he was expressing it with more integrity. So you don't have to deal with that energy; maybe your challenge with the Mars thing comes out more in the sense of choosing a certain life path and just persisting on that when you'd actually be better off doing something else.

It's interesting because I think the problem with astrology; one of the many problems that people with rational minds is that you can't just put a percentage on this and say 25% of the time people with the sun/Mars conjunct end up being these people that are really angry and abusive and 25% of the time they end up being these big community leaders or whatever. That's where the psychic side or intuitive side of it (come in) and you know, it's a form of divination (Merriam-Webster: the art or practice that seeks to foresee or foretell future events or discover hidden knowledge usually by the interpretation of omens or by the aid of supernatural powers). I get really frustrated with astrologers and communities of astrologers who are trying to prove that astrology is scientific, because it's not scientific in the way we think of science; there's a lot of art in it. That's why if you go to ten different astrologers you get ten different readings. There will be a lot of things that stand out as being common among the ten readings but it definitely is a form of divination.

Is Mars the red circle with the arrow poking out of it? Yes. Let's talk more about your chart! I look at that as something you chose to have in this lifetime, but also it's psychologically the personality you form in reaction to your childhood experiences; to the experience of your parents, etc. What you're talking about now is the sun in Mars is up at 11:00 (position in the chart comparing it to a clock). The moon and Pluto are at 8:00? The moon represents your emotional nature and where the moon shows up in your chart, like what sign it shows up in; what relationship it makes to the other planet. That's going to show you how you nurture yourself and how you try to nurture other people. In a really basic sense, the moon shows where you go in order to feel safe; if you feel anxious, or depressed, or off your game somehow.

So, the moon is in Leo; Leo is a fire sign. There are four elements in astrology that we kind of talked about earlier. Fire is creative, it's inspirational, it's outgoing, it's spiritual, and Leo is the sign or archetype of actors and actresses, and kings and queens, the eternal child archetype. Each of the signs has a ruling planet and the ruling planet of Leo is the sun. Pure Leo energy is basically, "Look at me! Look how cool this thing is that I've created or what I'm doing!" I have a six year old Leo daughter and she'll put on this puppet show that she totally makes up on the spot, and a lot of times it won't make any sense whatsoever, but it's just so cool because she's creating it, then she'll tell us, 'now you can all clap'! That's kind of core Leo energy.

Moon in Leo people are interesting because the natural planet of Leo is the sun, and when you put the moon in Leo, Leo has a need to be on stage and to be adored or appreciated or affirmed for being its unique self. If you think of kings and queens, the king is the kingdom; he's the ruler of the kingdom. A good king is going to do whatever he can for his subjects to make everything in the kingdom run well so that everybody has a good life; not that we have a lot of examples of good kings in history. The king also commands adoration and respect, and you have to bow down and pretty much worship the king. So, both those signs are in the Leo archetype. When the moon is in Leo, that's present but it's not up front; it's more of an inner emotional sense.

Moon in Leo people really need that respect of admiration and adoration but a lot of times that will play out with Moon in Leo people in the context of family because the moon is our own emotional, private inner self. Moon in Leo people need that creativity but they don't tend to be like Sun in Leo people. If you look at the number of actors, or presidents or things like that who are Leos, it's quite staggering. Those people absolutely need attention and they're going to go out and get that attention in one way or another.

With the Moon in Leo, it's more of an inner focus thing. It's really interesting for you because your Moon in Pluto is in conjunction. Pluto is one of the outer planets. In astrology we look at the inner planets: sun, moon, Mercury, Venus and Mars as personal planets. When you get to Jupiter and Saturn, they are like the social planets; kind of halfway between personal and transpersonal. Then in the outer planets: Uranus, Neptune and Pluto, those are not personal.

So, Pluto is one of the transpersonal planets. With the personal planets, we can work with those; so with the Mars in Taurus that we were talking about, you can work with that and you can say Mars in Taurus can be really lazy too. If you are 25 and realize you are really lazy and I'm not doing anything with my life; I need to find a way to get more self discipline and get more motivated; with the personal planets you can do that. You can take a workshop or you can read a book or you can set your New Year's resolution, start going to the gym or whatever it is.

The transpersonal planets are more forces that happen to us or happen through us that we don't have a lot of control over. They force us to grow and evolve by presenting us with these challenges that we then have to work with. Pluto in the second house represents a life challenge of redeveloping one of those second house values of abundance, of wealth, of self esteem, self sufficiency. With the Moon and Pluto together there, they sort of function as this one entity. Interestingly, Pluto is right on the border of the third house, so some of that may be involved in writing, which is a big third house archetype.

But, with the Moon and Pluto there, it kind of sets up this situation in this lifetime where emotionally you are really identified with resources and having the resources you need, and with Leo there, specifically having resources you need to be creative or to take care of your kids and give your kids a good life; probably both of those. It's also one of what are called the alien patterns in the chart. The Moon/Pluto alien pattern, and some people have these alien patterns and some people don't, the alien patterns function as this extra gift that you bring into the world but which also tends to be very challenging especially in the first half of life.

Basically the way that it works is whenever you connect with somebody one on one, you have this sort of magnetic ability to pull soul out of them. Pluto represents the depths of the soul, kind of like everything we are not conscious of on an ego level. You can say that's the shadow; it's the part that we were told when we were young that it's not good; you can't do that, you can't be that, you shouldn't think that. Anything we've repressed will show up as Pluto to some extent, and so the Moon/Pluto/Alien people basically function as these magnetic attractors where; what you do with people, if people stay in contact with you, it's going to bring up the hearts of themselves that they have hidden from themselves and it's going to try to bring that to the surface somehow.

With all of the Alien patterns, it adds an extra level of challenge to the lifetime, first of all because we're usually not conscious of it; nobody tells us about it when we're seven, eight, nine, or fifteen, that this is something you're doing as you go through the world, and so a lot of times with the Moon/Pluto archetype you can have these relationships with people where the other person ends up being obsessed or developing this really harsh attitude toward you, sometimes there can be obsessive compulsive stuff there. One of the things in this lifetime that you are trying to become aware of on a soul level is just how much power that you have, and I would see that with the real energy is that you activate people's inner desire to become a creator, to be creative, to create this life that is joyful and exciting and fulfilling. The problem with that on an ego level is there can be these occasional situations, these cyclical situations where somebody reacts really harshly to you and you just don't understand; (thinking)' I'm not saying anything negative to this person, I don't have any bad thoughts or wishes toward them'.

What's happening there is that on an ego level we don't want to be shown our shadow stuff. On a soul level, we do, because the only way to be whole is to integrate all sides of ourselves and recognize, kind of like what I was writing in the February forecast (online); we are all unique and everything this is within us has value if it can be put in its proper place.

That's a really powerful pattern and it's even more powerful because the moon is the ruler of Cancer, which is your ascendant (rising). So ascendant's the outer personality, it's how you come across to people. Cancer, like a pure Cancer ascendant, is the den mother of the Zodiac. They are the nurturers, the ones that are making cookies or hot soup for the people that are sick. It's a very intuitive, emotional type of energy. Cancers can usually feel what's going on with other people emotionally, a lot of times even before the other person can.

The interesting thing with your chart is that it gets channeled through that Moon/Pluto conjunction. Whereas a pure regular Cancer ascendant person would have that intuitive side and would have that desire to nurture people, and one of the primary challenges to Cancer energy is to know the difference between nurturing and care taking. All Cancers are going to have to struggle with that in one way or another. Where that tends to go for you is into that Pluto/Alien pattern which is that, when you recognize that something is off in somebody or that they need nurturing, what naturally tends to happen is that you are going to magnetize out of them the reason that they are stuck; that can be really uncomfortable both for you and the other person. Does that resonate with you? Can you see how that operates?

I guess I don't see the reason someone would be stuck; stuck on what, or stuck how? Stuck on however they aren't expressing themselves as fully as they can be. So am I really stifling others (with this ability)? No, not at all; you're a catalyst. The thing about it is it happens in a way that is not really obvious. People with a Sun/Pluto conjunction tend to be these really hardcore people. They come into somebody's life and a lot of times my Sun/Pluto clients end up spending a lot of their life alone because people just can't handle the energy. Whereas that Moon/Pluto is more of a magnetic kind of subterranean energy and basically what that says to me is two things.

It's really important in this lifetime for you to have what you need; to have enough money, to have enough to be who you are. I would imagine there was some struggle or some sacrifice involved in it, especially in the first 40 years of life. Once you have that abundance, what you're going to attract to yourself sort of psychically over and over is people who haven't figured out how to do that, haven't figured out how to be themselves and just by being in your presence, they get triggered to understand why they aren't doing that or what they need to be aware of. I actually feel you doing this while we are doing the interview and I'm tuned into this kind of stuff. I'm still waiting for the abundance!

That's the interesting thing about Pluto is it's this lifelong mission. If I had to say what your soul mission is in just a few words, it's really struggling with that abundance thing until you get it. Then, once you get it, what Pluto wants to do it move into the opposite polarity of the chart which would be 8th house in Aquarius. So the second house is your money, your resources, your values, your self esteem and 8th house is where you share all that stuff with other people or with the world.

Aquarius archetype is like that 11th house that we were talking about earlier. What Aquarius wants to do is create this society where everybody can be themselves and everybody has a place at the table, and we can all be individuals but still belong to the group that we want to belong to. What I see with that is the more you develop abundance, wealth, that's going to look different for everybody else; for a musician, what does that look like? It looks like having an instrument that works and being able to play it, having the time to play it, having the time to immerse yourself in music; whereas for somebody whose life path is to climb the corporate ladder, abundance may look like a Range Rover and a house in Malibu. But whatever abundance means for you that is so much of your life journey in this lifetime, which interestingly mine is too; I have Pluto in the 2nd house. The more you move into that, the more you move into becoming this catalyst for people and for creating this better world which definitely seems like what you are trying to do with this book.

Leo is the sign on your 3rd house cusp as well, so if you look that each of the houses has a beginning and an end, and those are called cusps; if you look at the line that starts the 3rd house going counterclockwise, that red squiggly thing is the symbol for Leo. I see that writing/communicating/peace as being a big part of being able to manifest that abundance. What is all this in the middle (lines and symbols)?

Those show the relationships between the planets. This is based on Pythagorean numerology; numerology is sort of the foundation of astrology. If you look right above the horizon you've got Venus, the green circle with the cross under it, and Uranus, the blue guy that looks sort of like the Starship Enterprise (on the left side of the chart), and if you look, you've got two red lines that are going to Jupiter in the 10th house (Jupiter looks like a 4).

Those planets are square to each other; they're 90° apart, give or take a few degrees and a circle is 360° divided in four and you get 90°. That's called a square angle and resonates to the number four. Planets that are square to each other are like two cars meeting perpendicularly at an intersection. If those cars meet at 30mph at a perfect square angle, there's going to be conflict and it's challenging, but it's also going to create new movement; a vector that sends those cars off in a different direction.

Planets that are square to each other tend to be archetypes within the psyche, places within the soul that are naturally at conflict with each other. Even if you think of two cars meeting at right angles, one of them wants to go this way and one wants to go this way (different ways- veering off), so they have different aims in life. Anytime you've got this square coming up in astrology, it' s like you've got these two at odds forces at work. One of the challenges with those over the course of a lifetime is how can I get these to understand each other, how can I get them to work together?

That also naturally creates momentum and urgency and a desire or need to move forward in life. I had a lady I rented a room from a long time ago in Detroit who was beautiful and looked like an Egyptian priestess; this attractive, sweet person. She was probably in her 60s at the time and she would say to me every once in a while, I wonder if I'm ever going to find out what I'm supposed to be doing with my life. She would just drift around; she always had enough and just what she needed, and never really worked that hard but could never find her purpose. I looked at her chart and she had no squares whatsoever. Everything was based on blue lines, a trine, which is based on the number three and it's this harmonious, creative angle.

When we start learning about astrology we think that squares are bad, they create conflict and tension; trines are good because it's creative and flowing, but people who don't have any squares have a really hard time doing anything in life.

I see two parallel lines coming down from the Taurus area with a square in the middle of each, but they are not as close as the other ones you talked about. They are red lines with a square in the middle. (I was looking at the center of the chart.) That's a square too. It's not as exact or close as the other square but definitely still counts. That Sun/Mars and the Moon/Pluto are two places in the psyche that are naturally challenged in this lifetime. One way that it would work is that with Sun in Taurus; the Sun is a fixed sign and Taurus is the bull. What Taurus wants to do is figure out where it's supposed to go. It's almost like the groove in a vinyl record; it wants to sit, find its groove, sit in that groove and just stay in there as long as it feels good.

With Taurus, as with all the archetypes, there will be a "good side" and a "bad side" and you're never all in the good side or bad side. (On) the positive side, when Taurus is working well, it's a very hard working energy; it can be the hardest working sign in the Zodiac. But, Taurus is always working for a pay-off, whereas Virgo, another earth sign (and there are three signs in each element); Virgo is primarily working to be of service and to make things right. Virgo wants everything to be in order and everything to be done efficiently in the way it should be done. So, Virgos can be very hard workers too, and the earth signs relate to the material world, but they're doing it because it is the right thing to do, trying to fix things. Capricorn, the last earth sign, tend to also be hard workers but they always have this long term ambition; they are trying to climb a ladder to get to someplace that is better and to get stature, and status, and authority, and power.

Taurus is the personal earth sign. Taurus is always working for the pleasure pay-off in some sense and if it doesn't, things are not going to go well over a sustained period of time. Taurus loves the good things of the earth; good food, good sex, money, things money can buy, nice clothes, music, art, just being out in nature. You got it! You've got this kind of conflict there with that Moon/Pluto energy because that Moon/Pluto energy is saying, hey, you have to develop this abundance, or self sufficiency, or sustainability that's based on who you are as a creative self.

One example would be: what do you do for a day job? Last year I had seven jobs, but long ago was a teacher who burned out dealing with administrators. I've had about any job you can imagine:

milk truck driving, building houses, farming, I worked with handicapped kids and group homes, mowing lawns at a cycle factory, giving private music lessons, I've had a secretary job for 12 years that has kept me going, you name it. Okay. One of the challenges I see there is that on a lifelong level, that Moon/Pluto really wants you to develop self sufficiency based on what you love, what's creative to you, what's joyful to you.

But, with that Sun/Mars energy: the challenge with Taurus, and I have a lot of Tauruses in my life, (my two year old son is a Taurus and is so stubborn, my Leo daughter knew what she wanted and what she didn't and her favorite word was no, but my Taurus son just puts her to shame; you can't make him do something he doesn't want to do), but one of the challenges with Taurus is that it can be really easy to get stuck in certain things. It's like (thinking) well, this is paying the bills and this is affording me to do blah blah blah blah. That's where I see the conflict between those two.

One of the things I love about astrology is it shows us these basic conflicts in life and when you can kind of understand it in your chart, at least for me and a lot of my clients, there's this breakthrough moment where it's like wow, I've always blamed myself for this; I've always said if I was better, or if I had more will power, or made better decisions, or was lucky, or whatever it is, I wouldn't have had to struggle with this. Then you see it in your chart and think 'Oh!' That's one of the fundamental things I came to experience in this lifetime and I've got my whole lifetime to work through it. To me it takes a lot of the blame or judgment out of it.

One of the things I would say, I think this book is huge for you in resolving that energy, because what you're doing with this book unites both of those places in your chart. Eleventh house ideals: a better world, professional connections. By connecting with all these healers (all of the interviewed people are also healers), you are engaged in that 11th house archetype because what the 11th house wants to do is find likeminded people and associate to form groups or networks with those people. Ultimately it wants to do that on a personal level to fulfill your hopes and dreams, and on an extra personal level, to create a better society, to create a better world.

The 2nd house for you, the other point on the square is, I've got to develop abundance and self sufficiency based on my creativity, based on what brings me joy; who I really am. This book to me on one level is an attempt to get the two parts of the psyche to cooperate and work together. Does that make sense? Yes. Maybe that's why I haven't found 'the one' (romantic soul mate). Let's look at that.

The 7th house is the place in your chart that shows relationships. Including a long term partner. Where is that in the chart? It's just across the horizon on the right side of the chart. If you look at the horizon and then look just above it, that is the 7th house. Right under Aquarius. Right. The sign on the 7th house cusp, because we're going counterclockwise through the houses, is Capricorn, the little squiggly line. One of the key words or phrases for Capricorn is: they're old when they're young, and they're young when they're old. Wherever Capricorn shows up in your chart is going to be a kind of late blooming energy. With Capricorn, usually the first half of life you are going to struggle with that and then the second half of life things start getting easier in that area. People with Capricorn in the 7th house will tend to be people who find their ideal relationship later in life.

Then, the other place we want to look for that is who the rule of Capricorn is? The ruler for Capricorn, which also would be the planet that has influence over your relationship house, is Saturn. Saturn is down in your 4th house in Virgo; he's the red cross with the squiggly line underneath. That's a really interesting picture because Saturn is like the teacher planet. What Saturn wants to do is teach us about boundaries and structure and authority and about working hard and persevering against all obstacles. Saturn in Virgo, and we talked about Virgo a minute ago, Virgo is the sign of healers and fixers, but it also tends to have this really strong set of rules or of judgments that come with it.

The first house is the house of family; the family that you live with now, but also the family that you grew up with, your ancestral patterns that got passed down from generation to generation. With Saturn and Virgo in the 4th house, there's this picture that either your mother or your father or both that somebody was kind of authoritarian, my way or the highway, had these kind of strict rules or at least that's what you internalized out of childhood that you have to do things right; there's a right way and a wrong way. That family energy plays into your relationship picture in this lifetime in a huge way because basically the picture in your chart is, until you can become aware of and heal from the critical, judgmental energy that shows up in your chart in childhood, it's really hard for you to have a long term relationship that you actually want to be part of.

What you're going to tend to do is attract that same energy over and over because your partners can be people, and this is not just romantic, it can be somebody that you work with one on one, they are going to function as mirrors for you to show you the part of basically your deep emotional wounding that you're not aware of and you haven't been able to release. So whenever we fall in love it's like this period that's great for awhile and then the lessons start kicking in, and that's going to be the lesson that keeps showing up for you over and over. What was that drama like in childhood? Did you have to take care of people?

No, I had a great childhood. It was regimented and yet, not strict in the way of fundamentalists. There was strictness but that was the way of the 50s though for everybody. Did we talk about The Drama of The Gifted Child (Alice Miller)? No. She was a Swiss psychotherapist, and her thesis is that nobody in western society gets what we need as children; what the child needs is love and respect for who he or she is as an individual. Especially if you think of the energy that was in place in the 50s, that sense of nurturing just wasn't there.

With your Cancer on the ascendant, what Cancer really wants is just to be able to have a relationship where you can totally open up your soul and merge with the other person in this really nurturing, empathic, understanding way. The picture I see in your chart is that you didn't get a template for what that would look like to be in integrity as a child. Wherever Saturn shows up for any of us in our chart, that's where we're going to have to just apply consistent, repeated, persevering effort as we go throughout our life to really understand 'what's required of me, what am I growing into, what am I trying to master?' I see that playing into the relationship thing in a big way because ultimately when you're with the right person there is a lot of depth there. That Moon/Pluto energy has the ability to take you really, really deeply into somebody's soul and allow them to see really deeply into your soul.

With the Cancer ascendant, we also call it that personality, but it's also the interface where all the other planets will try to come into the world, kind of like the store front of your soul. What Cancer energy always has to struggle to figure out is, along with Pisces and Scorpio, the most sensitive sign of the Zodiac. Cancer, more than any other sign, has to protect itself because if it has to open up, and remember Cancer is the crab that has that soft vulnerable body and builds this hard shell around it. When Cancer rising people open up to somebody and then get stung or get betrayed, it can be wounding for a whole lifetime. You feel it more than any other sign of the Zodiac feels it. What Cancer has to try to figure out to do is, how do I learn when it's safe to open myself up and then allow myself to open and give all this feeling, nurturing, loving energy that I have inside me to the other person and to receive that back? Then how do I learn to pull that shell to protect myself when it's not safe but yet, be able to open that shell when it's appropriate?

That's what I see in that childhood picture (my childhood past), that wasn't model for you. I can only imagine me, growing up in the 70s and 80s as a supersensitive, emotional boy; (and I felt) boys don't cry. The last time I cried was when I was 12, until a few years ago because it was like, this is what it means to be a man. With that Cancer ascendant, you have that supersensitive, gooey, juicy, emotional side, which I would imagine your kids get to see that part of you. Definitely what you are looking for is someone that can share that with you and that you can feel safe in exposing that side of yourself, and that's what I see that you didn't get as a child. Whenever Saturn shows up it usually shows part of the wound. There are just a few other things I want to get into.

With Jupiter in your 10th house, Jupiter is the architect of abundance and expansion and generosity and wisdom. It's considered to be the luckiest planet of the Zodiac. The 10th house is your career; your life's work. Jupiter is in Aries, the first sign of the Zodiac; the sign of new beginnings, pioneering and risk taking. The picture there is that ultimately what you are trying to create as your life's work is something that is pretty much totally new. It feels like the direction you are going with the writing is very tapped into that in a positive way. What you are creating out of your life isn't going to look like anything that your family would have expected of you, or the culture that you grew up in. But, with Jupiter, the way to access that abundant energy is the more you can trust your impulses that say 'I've got to do this because this feels really vital to me,' that actually brings you the success that you want.

If you ever get a chance, read "Soul Signs" by Rosemary Altea. The book talks about the 12 soul personalities. What I am seeing with this (astrological chart) is so similar to what she came up with the soul signs, it's just an amazing resemblance, like mirror twins. My take on all this is there is sort of an almost infinite level of complexity to the universe and there are all these different systems that are really doing the same thing in different ways; like the more we can learn about who we are as an individual. We're not supposed to be like so and so because so and so is a different soul sign, they have a different sun sign, and have a different chart.

With astrology, even on a generational level, you could look at this with presidents. Both Bill Clinton and George Bush Jr. were Pluto in Leos; they came from that Pluto/Leo baby boomer generation. Obama is Pluto in Virgo which is like Generation X. Pluto kind of shows these big generational groups. The core energy of Pluto in Leo is, what can I create, what can I make out of myself so that everybody will think I am great, or that I can just do the things I want to do. If you look at George Bush and Bill Clinton, they both have this totally 'me' focused solipsistic kind of way of being there and Obama, even if you look at the rhetoric they use, says hey, we're all in this together and all have to be of service and find a way to fix this. That's like a fundamental difference between Pluto in Leo and Pluto in Virgo.

I'm so grateful that astrology found me, (I certainly wasn't looking for it), but it's really opened me into this experience of the world where it's like, 'Wow!' We all have our challenges and if you look at the cycles of astrology, it's like there are these specific times in all of our lives like the midlife crisis. That's this lineup of these three planetary aspects that happen roughly between the age of 38 and 45. So everybody is going to have a midlife crisis; we're just going to have it in our own unique way. But you know there are ups and downs, and there are ups and downs in the bigger historical cycles and it's just an amazing way of organizing energy and understanding the world.

— CHAPTER 14 —

LAURIE STINSON

Bio: Laurie Stinson was born in St. Paul, Minnesota and raised her children in the suburbs of Chicago. At the age of 49 she experienced a spiritual awakening that led her to write her own spiritual autobiography, My Soul's Journey, The Blessing of Abuse, available on Amazon.

She was led to Boulder, Colorado where she taught a class, Healing from Writing, an eight week workshop devoted to helping people who had the experience of abuse. She now lives near Shiprock, New Mexico, where she has embarked on a journey to bring spirituality back to the reservation; to help awaken and heal those who have experienced abuse. She is in the process of creating a non-profit called Wildflower, a Spiritual Healing, Wellness & Abuse Center.

(Laurie opened up our talk by telling me that there were already spirits present as well as a smattering of angels and she was supposed to let me know that. They have been ready all day, shadowing Laurie at work. Laurie even had to write things down on a postcard.) Did they make you do that? Urged, is more like it. Your father is a very, can I use the word, 'succinct' person and is very precise. It's a little bit challenging for me, but that's good. That's his professor coming through. He's taking me to task and I enjoy that challenge of it for sure.

Before we get into the questions you want to ask me, I want to tell you that they are very excited for this partnership that we have. When your father and grandmother came in this morning, I saw your grandmother as Grandma Walton (of the old TV show, The Waltons). I started laughing and said no wonder why I like you so much because I love that character on The Waltons. I didn't think anything more of it and just let it go and your father stepped forward and choosing his words carefully, he said he wanted you to become acquainted with Evelyn Underhill. Well, I know of her, in fact I used a quote of hers in my book (The Blessing of Abuse). She was not a mystic, she was a British woman, and I want to say of the early 1900s, who observed and wrote a book about Psychics and Mediums. I knew I needed to tell you that.

They (my father and grandmother) are with me today because I've already told them I'm a little nervous about what I'm going to say; they know they need to help me out with this, either that or you'll get the reference. Then, after Evelyn, I saw you and they're referring to you as John Boy. I knew it was something about the writing style of Evelyn Underhill and the writing style of John-Boy Walton and so I said excuse me, but I'm not going to tell Edward that he looks like John-Boy Walton. So the conversation between your father and me turned very serious and he said you need to know that … (Laurie changed thought about the Waltons and added more about the book here), Edward, you look at this book you are going to write as something like for fun, or maybe you had a unique idea and maybe it will turn into some type thing, or you don't necessarily have a seriousness about it or it's just kind of hanging out there as something neat to do, (now back to my dad's thoughts) well, he said he wants you to get serious; he wants you to understand that in the larger picture this is something you have come to do!

This is your contribution to what is happening now, no, he's correcting me again. He says that it's not your contribution but your privilege and that you are going to introduce mediums and healers to people who are going to be craving information about what is happening to them spiritually with the whole 2012 and us moving forward into the 5th dimension. He wants you to understand the seriousness of what you are here to do; he wants you to understand that this idea out of the blue, or this whim, or this 'wouldn't it be fun', or 'I have a great title for a book'; you need to understand your role. The hair is standing up on my arms and legs!

Perhaps you didn't understand that, or didn't get that (the idea that this book was going to be serious and a big deal rather than treated lightly). I have to tell you this because I tell everything that I hear (from Spirit). They even had a suggestion for the title. Take a pen and write MEDIUM in capital letters, then there is a small 's' so it says, MEDIUMs. Then there is a comma and lower case 'not' and 'so' and then in capital letters 'RARE'. (I had originally titled the book, Medium Rare.) You do not have to do this, it is a suggestion, but what they're trying to convey is MEDIUMs not so RARE. I don't know what (why) this is, because I love the title of your book but I had to pass this along. But, he's moving back around to (Laurie was silent for awhile as she listened to Spirit talking to her), something about, okay I'm not being chastised, but about John-Boy. He's not saying you write like John-Boy, it's your attitude. John-Boy wrote journals and things like that and never really realized that it was all going to become a book. What he's saying is that you have an innocence like John-Boy about this book, and that this will become a book and it will be a part of the awakening that is happening. That is cool! Again, the hair is standing on edge on my arms!

He's there, and this is a big deal for them to convey to you. Take that for what it's worth. They are just trying to impress upon you that you going to a medium (having the reading with Rosemary Altea) and having it change your life was not an accident. It wasn't like something that you just 'did'. This was, like many of us that have a spiritual awakening, a turning point for you. I don't know how you are gifted, but I know you are gifted; not perhaps in the way a typical medium would be gifted. Also, with this book, you are going to be learning from everyone. You're going to be learning from Evelyn how she wrote having distance from an observation or witness point of view. But also you're going to be learning spiritually when you write this book.

Sometimes something will happen to me and I'll assume that everybody else can do it, or everybody else knows it, and that's not true. So whatever this gift is that you have, you're going to discover your uniqueness, but also discover that you're writing about people that you are in a family with. I don't know if that sounds daunting to you. No, it sounds exciting. Just remember that I said that. One day you're going to hear something someone says and you're going to be like, 'Oh my gosh, I can do that! I didn't know that was something!' The light bulb is just going to go on and you'll say, 'I had no idea.'

Even though you think you're writing about this specific type of people, you are going to find that you are that type of specific type of people, that we all have different gifts, they all come through differently and it's an exciting time for you. There are many levels of things going on of why you are writing this book; levels of understanding, or levels of meaning, or levels of consciousness is a better way to say it. You're going to have a lot of fun with this book, but with that will come what I call 'bump ups'; conscious bump ups in the true reality, not the reality that most people think of. It's like moving up the corporate ladder from the mailroom to the president. That's what we're doing; awareness of reality, and they want you to have that. You've already surrounded yourself with enough people to help you along the way.

While the book is for personal growth, it is for the growth of spirituality or the metaphysical and there is also growth on a soul level for you; a higher level in the higher realms on the other side. Having said that, don't take this project, this fun thing that you have, this idea, and think that there isn't more meaning than just something to fill your days or something to do. Well, I guess I can't argue with my dad! Yes, of course you can. I'm hearing he loves you very much and my heart is just expanding and expanding. To circle back again, he does take some responsibility for that part of you that feels really insecure sometimes, and I'll repeat, it's on a soul level; his soul and your soul. You feel that little bit of a cringe; am I good enough or am I smart enough, or whatever it is, that insecurity that you have. And, he does take responsibility for that, and that's why he feels the need to come through and tell you: you have everything you need, trust yourself, don't listen to that part of you (that makes me feel insecure), you know what to do. So there you go; message delivered.

You said it was my dad and grandma and a smattering of angels? Oh no. I sat down and knew you were going to call, and I always know when someone is going to call or if I need to pay attention because of the tones in my ears that I hear like a heartbeat; they get louder and louder and once upon a time, they were piercing. I know to close my eyes and look and I saw four spirits come sailing in. They whooshed in and stopped in front of my face, move to the side, then another one comes in and I say 'hello' and some of them shine their light at me, some of them don't. In my mind I imagine that my light from my chest is shining for them and that's my way of saying hello. There were four spirits and then I'd say there were maybe three or four angels. We are very protected right now; this is a spirit led conversation we're having, we're surrounded by energy and they are prepared to guide us however we need to be guided.

Rather than starting at the beginning, you were talking about gifts. Let's talk about your gifts. When did you notice you had any gifts and what was it that you noticed? As I wrote in my book, it's something that you just know, like what was the day you first knew you were a Christian, or the first time you thought you were depressed; was that the first day you were depressed, or had it just (already) started? I never remember an exact time; I just always knew when I was little that I could know things before they happened and it scared me more than the abuse in my household.

I didn't think that knowing things ahead of time was something someone should do or should be able to do. I thought it must be demonic because, as abuse teaches, I was a bad child; I was always getting beaten, so this must be (from) that. Sometimes I would be talking to someone and I would be looking at their face, seeing their mouth moving and I could hear them, but I didn't think I was really there, and I said well, where am I?

Something not many people know, when I was in fifth grade I had an ulcer. I was put in a hospital for a week with the ulcer from the fear of 'knowing' and the fear of the abuse and everything. In high school I could know things before they happened. For instance, I would fall down the stairs coming down to the locker room in gym class and immediately, as if it was uploaded from a computer, I would then remember the dream from the night before when I had fallen and split my knee open. Of course, I would start crying and everyone thought I was in pain from falling but the crying was because I knew it (what was going to happen).

As a young mother, my kids would be in school and I would be shopping maybe at Macy's and I would know to leave early. I'd think to myself, I need to get moving and allow extra time to get home. So I would drive home, see the accident, see the backup of cars, and then I would know (remember) there was going to be an accident and that's why I needed extra time to get home. Some things were just out in out knowing and I didn't know what to do with that. I didn't have anybody around me that was gifted, nobody in the family, nothing like that, so I would just reap the benefit of the knowing and simply got very good at blocking my mind as to where that came from. I didn't want to know; I knew I was different but couldn't fathom just to understand what was happening to me all the time since I was little.

Fears were huge; I was always afraid, I hated myself and didn't understand why my parents didn't love me. But on the other hand, there were times; I remember walking down to church that was a block away where I would sit during the service by myself. I felt accepted there. I remember once in a while having the thought that

I had an angel walking with me and I would smile, but it would only last a little while, then fear would set in again. I didn't know what to think; I didn't know what to do; all I knew was that I was sad and bad things would always happen to me.

Did you ever tell anybody about this when you were young, like confiding in a friend? No. The first time that I inkled (gave an inkling) to someone was my husband. I was 24 years old and walking in the kitchen, we lived in Rockford, Illinois, at the time, and I looked at him and said, 'we're going to get a really bad phone call. I just wanted you to know it's going to be a really bad phone call.' He said yeah, okay (in a disbelieving tone). Three days later his father called and said he had lung and brain cancer. After we hung up the phone from my father-in-law, my husband, from the other room said, 'I hate when you can do that!' I hadn't even noticed that he knew I could do that.

The first time I admitted to someone (about being psychic), really came out and admitted, was when I got divorced in my early 30s. I had a friend who was a counselor and I decided that I didn't want to be like all those other divorced couples that fought over children; I wanted to do it right, so I sought out this counselor, Rose. She happened to be a former Catholic nun. I told her (about the gift) and she just laughed and laughed at me and I asked why. She said, 'don't you know how much I would like to have that gift?' I said, 'gift?' because I always called it a curse. She said, 'Laurie, don't you know that all gifts are from God?' It was then that I was more accepting of it. I still didn't know what to do with it but I started to see the times when I needed money and a check would show up in the mail. I remember one time I got my IRS check in the mail a week and a half after I filed it on paper. How did that happen? And I knew when I got it that there was something special about getting it that soon, or (there was) something magical about it.

I was in my 49th year when I heard a voice I knew wasn't mine. He asked me a very simple question. I wasn't scared; I was more curious because I knew I heard that and knew I wasn't crazy and knew it wasn't me, so I decided to get to the bottom of this! I was driven; I just had to find out.

What did the voice say to you? Well, I was at work booting up my computer. I had a picture of this orangutan and this dog that had befriended each other in this animal conservatory out east and the picture always made me smile and that was my desktop picture. He (the voice) said to me, 'what's behind that picture?' I looked at my monitor and knew I wouldn't have thought to ask that question because I wouldn't have thought to ask that question. I thought that if I reached over and tore the picture off, there would just be a blank space, a black space where the picture was. That was my rationale. Over the next three days I knew to keep looking at that picture. It was like when you look at those picture posters and you start to see an image.

For three days I concentrated on the picture and I would hear things like, don't focus, relax your eyes, and I knew not to blink very much. By the third day, the picture lifted off my desktop and what I saw was grass and trees just like in the picture. I was shocked and so excited! I did it and was so proud of myself that I had trained my eyes to do that. I said okay, what is next? I knew that something was going on that I had to find out about, then for a couple days after that, I started looking at everything from a calculator to a door in 3D. I was like, okay, and I knew how to do that. I was ecstatic that something had happened to me and I knew it.

I was standing in my bathroom blow drying my hair before going to work, whistling a happy tune, when I heard, 'there's someone I want you to meet'. I thought 'who was here' and heard, "her name is Catherine." I freaked out. I knew this voice! I trusted this initial voice, but who was this Catherine? My mind started to scramble. This townhouse could be full of spirits. Are they good or are they bad, who are they? Because all I knew about spirits was what I saw in spooky movies. I was afraid! I got to work and hear a woman's voice, 'sit up straight, then you walk and lead with your chest, not with your forehead'. It was obviously ergonomically correct ways to stand and walk and I felt like a robot. I knew that nobody else in the office had a clue as to what was going on.

That's how it (all) started. Shortly after that I was prompted to look online to find a psychic on e-bay. I thought, there are no psychics on e-bay! I went on e-bay, put in 'psychic medium', and there were like 200! I didn't know they sold readings on e-bay, so I just scrolled through until I saw this really sweet looking woman with blonde hair. No more innocence for me; I was on the path! (The psychic was the lady, Sam, who ran the Wonewoc Spiritualist Camp in Wonewoc, Wisconsin, http://www.campwonewoc.org/, and who did either face to face readings or readings on the phone.)

Now that you found her (the camp director), what were you going to do? I hit the 'Buy It Now' button and purchased a reading, giving my phone number and email address and she wrote me back asking for a time and date. I had gone to 36 hours a week at work so knew I'd have Thursday afternoon off. 'What about Thursday afternoon (I asked)? Great! I'll call you at noon.' Coincidently, I had been asked on a blind date by a man I had been talking to a little bit who was a south-sider from Chicago and loved the White Sox and of course, I worshiped the Minnesota Twins and they have a huge rivalry. He said he had season tickets and asked me to go. It was a Thursday afternoon when the White Sox and Twins were in town so I'm all in a tizzy (thinking) oh, no, I don't want to cancel this reading but I want to go to the Twins game.

So, I'm in the car with this guy and we're driving to the ball park and he has to stop for cash. When he does, Sam called and just started in (asking), is your mother's mother alive? I said yes. (Sam continues:) I've got her mother here and she says you come from a long line of strong women. Laurie: That was the opening line that my daughter said at my mom's funeral, I come from a line of strong women, and it blew me away! Oh my God, all of this (psychic business) is real! Why didn't someone tell me? Why didn't I know it? But I knew from the very first sentence that it was all real.

Then soon after, Nancy (Laurie's close friend) and I went to camp (Wonewoc, WI) and it was the last weekend of the season for camp, just like when I was there for the last weekend of camp this year (when I met Laurie for the first time), my three year anniversary! I've only been doing this (psychic work) for three and a half years so I'm kind of a baby; still wide-eyed about it all, not like somebody that's been doing it for years and who don't think twice about what happens. You're getting me on the way up! Nancy and I stayed the whole weekend (at camp) and I was so overwhelmed I just cried because I couldn't believe that my life would have a purpose.

How about an example? About two months ago, I was talking to a medium and she said Spirit is telling you to look at the places you've lived. They are like spiritual markers. I thought what does that mean? Two months before that I had been looking for houses since I moved to Colorado. I had made the big leap, the big plunge, don't know a soul, don't have a job but I'm here so I'm going to settle in and buy a house and wait for the cowboy. (The Cowboy was a man Laurie was shown in a vision. He had a cowboy hat and mustache and Laurie knew she would meet him someday). She didn't know where or when it would happen; only that it would happen.) But, this medium says they are advising not to buy a house because you are not going to be staying in Colorado.

The hell, what do you mean I'm not going to be staying; I moved here, this is my home now. So I've been questioning and asking Spirit why I'm moving, where am I moving, what the heck is going on here? So when the other medium had said to me to look at the places you've lived; they are spiritual markers, I'm sitting at work, downloaded a map of the US and started putting in little points of all the places I've lived. Then I took a ruler and connected the dots. I'm looking at it and thinking it doesn't mean anything to me; it doesn't spell out anything. Well, maybe it looks like a constellation or something cool like that, so I emailed it to (my friend) DK Brainard*, who

---

* see Chapter XIV on DK Brainard

is an astrologer. He took a look at it and said no, it doesn't look like anything to me.

So I was sitting at my other job with not much to do and I was looking at the newsfeed on Facebook. I saw this cartoon that someone had put on there; someone that I didn't know who had friended me awhile back but I didn't know who she really was. I wrote a comment and BING, here was an instant message on Facebook. Hi Laurie, how are you? I don't know much about you. What do you do, blah blah blah. I checked out her Facebook page and she said she is a Kabbalah Astrologer. (This just happened to be Ayala Chen in Chapter XII.) I said, hey, would you mind looking at something for me? Sure!

I got her email address and emailed her the scanned copy of this map of the places I've lived in the US. She wrote back and said, you know, I feel like something is going on here and I don't know what, so just let me sit for a minute and look at this map, but something is definitely going on. I said okay. She wrote, I feel the need to tell you that in church in my Bible study, we're studying the Exodus. Maybe we should look at maps of the Exodus when Moses led the Israelites out of Egypt and in the desert and ultimately to Jericho. I said okay.

She emailed me and said, turn the map around! If you take the map of Exodus and flip it, it is like all the places I've lived in the US in all my life in a backwards Exodus. I was overwhelmed and for the next two days I couldn't think about it; I had to put it in that place to the side until I emailed Sam (from Wonewoc Camp). I explained everything to her and said I don't understand; it looks like a map of a reverse Exodus and it's scaring me. She said why are you scared? I don't know. I'm no Moses! She said, but you are leading people out of the bondage in their minds of child abuse and into a new way of thinking about it, aren't you? It's a metaphor. You are leading people out of the desert of a lot of their left brain abuse like you had because you understand it now. I thought oh my gosh, it's a little too overwhelming!

A couple days later Sam emailed me and said, Laurie, you are not going to believe this, but I had a dream about you but I'm really busy at camp right now so I can't talk. (I was so ticked at her!) I had to know what was happening in this dream! Finally she emailed me and said, we were in Chicago (forgetting I used to live there), and from Chicago we went to Montana, from Montana we went to New Mexico to a place called Ship Rock, but I don't know if Ship Rock is in New Mexico or Arizona. I have known that when I leave here (Colorado), I'm going southwest and then northwest but I didn't know why or how. I realized from reading her email that she had the direction! You see, I was starting to doubt the map of the Exodus; I didn't want that responsibility; it seemed like a huge thing.

I told Sam (from Wonewoc Spiritualist Camp), you had a dream of the places in reverse! Do you see what I mean? She had Montana, then Albuquerque, then Ship Rock. I know that to be the reverse of the way I'm going and that was confirmation (from Spirit) of the reverse Exodus. And she said, oh my God, Laurie, I didn't even think of that. So, she had had a dream of the places I was going to move in reverse and then I could no longer deny the reverse Exodus map. I cried and cried and cried. Things like that, revelations like that are no different than me telling you that you need to take this book more seriously. Sam just confirmed that I need to take what I'm doing for the rest of my life seriously.

What she said was that she and I were in each of these places, which made me feel good that she's going to come visit me. But she said that everywhere we went, and I'm sure this is metaphorically, everywhere we went people gave us flowers and there were marching parades and bands and everybody loved us. She said, 'I don't know the significance. All I know is that I was in those three places.' And so it was Spirit telling me where I was going to be moving but they did it with her in reverse so that I couldn't deny the reverse Exodus math that I was trying to shove aside and not pay attention to. It was a jolt for me.

Does the map continue? The map continues in that I knew that from Boulder I go southwest then northwest and Sam just filled in the blanks. The southwest means the place called Ship Rock, it means Albuquerque and it means, perhaps Montana. Take your finger on Boulder and run it southwest and you end up in New Mexico and if you go northwest, you run into Idaho or Montana. Spirit is telling me where I'm going because I've been asking but they also did it because I believe. Who would know! I go on Facebook and find this Kabbalah astrologer who studies Exodus in her Bible studies. They (Spirit) are working awfully hard on the other side to help me see what reality is. Take it for what it's worth; it really happened and it took me a little while to get over it.

I've had experiences with entities that absolutely (made me) sob for days. You can believe in Jesus, but until you see him, you realize that it as just a belief, not your reality. When it becomes your reality it's a whole different ballgame and is incredibly humbling; it blows your mind. Rosemary Altea said in one of her books that she had seen Jesus. He was the mystic of mystics.

You mentioned that you are a shaman. Tell me about that. A shaman is one who can perform soul retrievals, healings, and receive messages for people through something called a journey. They can access many dimensions and go through an initiation period. I moved to Colorado, I'm looking for a home, I call (a realtor) on a house and this guy, John calls me back and I find out a week later he is a shaman. (Laurie laughs.) Who but me would have that happen? I wrote in my book that something happened to me in a spiritual tornado or vortex; it happened in a meditation like this:

I hear Ian (Laurie's guide) and he says you have to ask. I said, ask what? He said to be whole again. So I step out into my dark mind and say I want to be whole again. I had an experience that I can't explain but now, of course, I understand that it was a soul retrieval; a retrieval of aspects and parts of that four year old child who was traumatized by abuse. I didn't understand it, I didn't want to understand it; I knew it happened. After it was over I got up and went to bed and slept for three hours. I found out later what it was and I understood it.

So, I come to Colorado and meet this shaman (this is John Wayne, Chapter X). He reads my book and he was intrigued about the part about what he calls the soul retrieval. I said what are you talking about? He said the soul retrieval you have in the vortex; I have never known anyone who was able to consciously do that for themselves. (I thought) whatever that means; I knew very little about being a shaman. To make a long story short, a Lakota Indian elder spirit came to me in a vision, painted my face in a specific way, gave me a feather, they call me the brave one. That was my initiation into becoming a shaman.

Before that happened, John, the shaman, got prompted (by Spirit) and called me up one night and said, 'I think I'm supposed to do a soul retrieval on you.' He actually did two for me. The very first time it was the retrieval of an entire life, which I guess is rare because usually it's just aspects or little pieces of emotional break offs that we have. It was a life that I lived, and I forget the date, and I was Henry, a black slave in Mississippi. Immediately it clicked because the first time I came to camp (Camp Wonewoc), that first year on a Saturday night, Sam led a past life regression and I had this experience of meeting this black man. I didn't really believe at that time that it was a past life regression; it just wasn't real to me.

John started telling me that as he journeyed in this life that I lived, Henry had had horrific abusive experiences and he couldn't come in to do this life (with Laurie as a past regression) until now. He needed through all the abuse and the writing of the book (Laurie's book: The Blessing of Abuse) to be over before he could come back into my energy. As John journeyed and listened to Henry, he cried. Because I can access the Akashic records, I asked my household of elders if I could see the life of Henry. Before I even got the thought out of my head they said no. All I was able to see was a black baby. Then, it was as if I was standing on the shores of an ocean and they (elders) said it was "an ocean of pain."

That threw me into an emotional crisis; I didn't know how to act; I didn't know where I was again. So I started acting like a mother to this supposed life of Henry. I didn't quite know how; it was like I'm me and here's the life I lived, but there was this distance like Henry was this different person. It was the only way I could deal with it. It took Metatron, an angel, to come and help my mind understand it, but that is a whole different thing.

Soon after that, John was prompted again that I was supposed to come and a soul retrieval to be done and these (to deal with now) were just fragments; some were fragments of my life as a four year old but there were also fragments of two lives I lived as an American Indian woman, and in one I was a medicine woman. I was a medicine woman at a time when the cavalry was putting us on a reservation; I rode a buffalo and was with the Lakota Tribe. To circle back around, there are Lakota Indian spirits who are helping me to be a shaman. My guide when I journey is a buffalo. That's how I became a shaman.

I guess I thought it was weird when John said that 'I've never heard of anyone consciously doing their own soul retrieval', which I didn't know I was doing at the time; I was just doing what Ian told me to do. I must have been able to do that because of this life as a medicine woman; she must have been able to do that. You can't have gifts now that you haven't worked up to in other lives.

For instance: let's say that a farm in Iowa is haunted and a shaman goes out and journeys and meets a man who lived there in the 1800s who, as he passed, he couldn't see or hear or feel Spirit. He didn't even have much religion. So when you cross over it doesn't mean you can see all your angels and family members and go to the other side; there's no foundation for that. He still is living this life in the 1800s. He doesn't know that he's crossed over; he doesn't see all the angels around him asking him to come. It just doesn't work that way. So, I feel the reason I had that done (being able to do her own soul retrieval) was because I had that life.

Does somebody have to come to you for help, or do you naturally see someone and understand they need the help of a shaman or medium? Not necessarily. One thing I love about the other side is they hold your privacy. Sam may give me a reading and she may use specific words that I get (understand) from my own personal life but she has no understanding of. One time she told me early on that my great grandmother told me I am supposed to be more creative. I took it as meaning am I supposed to paint t-shirts and knit; I took creativity that way. Sam didn't know what she was talking about, saying your great grandma wants you to be more creative. I didn't realize that great grandma was saying (creative) with the gift! There are real privacy issues. When you pray to God, no one else on the other side can hear; that's a private conversation. So, no, I don't always know.

But people that I work with now, it's obvious to me and I'll 'see'. This one particular girl, the office manager, her whole departed family lines up on the wall and I'm counting eight people crossed over. I'll say to her, Mary, do you know a lot of people that have passed? Of course. But I definitely know when I'm supposed to say something. There are mediums that know so and so is cheating on her husband, or they will know about people. I don't do that. Number one, I don't want to know. Number two, I just have a specific purpose; I'm here to help those stuck in the lower dimensions and those with the experience of abuse.

2012 is about the start of the 5th dimension. What I have learned and realized is that I came in, Isis, the Egyptian mother of the gods asked me to do this life. I always thought was Isis was just folklore, I didn't know that it was real, asked me to do this life and what I'm here to do is to help people who are stuck, let's say, in the 3rd dimension in their minds; they are still churning over the abuse, going over and over; they haven't been enlightened. I am here to help them get to the 4th dimension so that when the 5th dimension comes, they can make the leap with the rest of us. So I came in to go to the depths and experience this abuse again to write this book that helps people leap from the 3rd to the 4th dimension and they can make the leap with us into the 5th dimension. It's an awesome responsibility but I do know that it's one of the reasons I'm here.

Can you tell a little about your book and what inspired you to even start on it? Enter Sam again. I had been told many times, Laurie, you love stories, write your own story. I don't like writing; I think it is boring and tedious. I try to write in a journal and it's like whatever. But I've been told that many times by many different people. So I was talking to Sam and she said Laurie, I feel prompted to tell you a story about my girlfriend who was told for three years to write. She had all these reasons why she couldn't. We'd see her and ask have you started writing yet? She'd say I've got this going on and this and I'm just too busy. She was in a car accident and broke both her ankles and with no place to go, she started writing. I knew that was all about me and I knew that my spirit would get me to write somehow, so I started writing.

About that same time I knew that was a wakeup call for me but I didn't know how to write. I'd say I'm not a writer! My ex husband is a writer, my children are writers but I'm not a writer. I was in a bookstore in Minnesota where they have half price books and had to go to the bathroom, so wanted to get out of there. I went to the cashier because I had to go to Target to use their bathroom but on the way I saw this self-help section and thought there was a book on spiritual stories so I just grabbed it and kept going. Two days later when I looked at the books I bought, I saw it was a book on how to write your own spiritual autobiography.

I read the first four or five chapters and understood how I was supposed to put it together and started to write. The thing about writing a book about abuse and it being a spirit led project is that you can't witness that; you can't stand back and be objective. You have to be in it, so I had to go back there in my mind and write from the place of abuse. I can't tell you how many times I would get up from my computer after writing and feel crippled and I would walk down the hallway and get into the shower. It was like I could feel those welts and wounds all over my body again. It was like the water was stinging on my hips and thighs and back. That's how far I had to go into it in order to write that book; it was very,

very demanding that way. Later on it was emotionally demanding and as the truth came out as to the reason for the abuse, I would be emotionally a wreck again; oh my God, oh my God, I can't believe this, what do I do?

It took a year to write it; I needed to take month long pauses. But Spirit helped me write it and even told me what the name of the book was. When they told me it was going to be called, "The Blessing of Abuse," I said, are you kidding? I can't write that! People who are abused are going to hate me! Then when they (Spirit) told me the dedication to my mother and father, the keepers of the contract, (I said) are you out of your mind; my work is dedicated to them? (This was) because I hadn't done the work yet on the book; I hadn't gone through it, I hadn't had the visions, I hadn't had the understanding, but it all happened all together and at the end of the book I understood the choice of title, I understood the dedication, I was no longer a victim. The abuse and the gift went hand in hand to review who I really was.

I imagine there were a lot of tears shed while you were writing. Yes, and do you know what? When I had the most important vision of my life, I can verbatim say out loud the paragraph I wrote about that. I don't remember memorizing it, but I know it and can say it at will whenever I want, and I don't cry anymore. And so, terrific!

Are you teasing me; tempting me to ask what that paragraph is? No, but I can tell it to you. That was the day when all the pieces came together; metaphysically, my family, the abuse, my siblings. That was the day the light bulb went off for the big picture of who I was. I'll always be grateful to Ian and my great grandma because I didn't want to do it. People give mediums and healers the stink eye (saying) oh yeah, right. Mediums don't necessarily want the gift. There's no essay you write that says 'when I grow up I want to be a medium'. Most of us resist it and when people give us crap about it or give us looks and you just want to say hey, I didn't ask for this!

I would love to be one. I feel like you are on your way. For you it's about the foundation; you can't go from the mail room to the presidency without a foundation. How do you get from thinking that being a clairvoyant is something you want, to being clairvoyant? It's different for everyone, but there are sets (certain rules) in between like anything, like getting whatever you want that you had to take to get there. So if you think being a clairvoyant is cool, so maybe you talk to clairvoyants or read books about clairvoyants and you practice meditation and you pretend you have a third eye. You do all these things in the middle until one day when you're meditating, you see this wispy cloud-like thing float in your mind and wonder 'was that something?' You have to have the intellectual foundation in order to get there.

For instance, Spirit can come through, and if I had never seen a giraffe before, not on TV, not in books, did not know it even existed, (Spirit) cannot come through to me and show me a giraffe if it's not something I've experienced before; if there is not even an awareness that I have that one exists. They (Spirit) can tell me about an animal I know nothing about, but they can't show it to me because I have no frame of reference. It's the same with the gift. If you don't have a foundation or frame of reference you can't move on with the gift. Let's say that you think being clairvoyant is really cool but you have this huge fear of what would happen to you if you were clairvoyant. Guess what, you're not getting off the starting blocks until you deal with the fear first.

You can't fool Spirit because you can't fool yourself and so if any blocks or issues are there, it's for your mind to go find them; emotional blocks, whatever, it's up to you to get yourself unstuck towards your goal to be clairvoyant. I believe that if a child is clairvoyant early on, they were clairvoyant in a life before and just came in with the gift already there. I did not choose to be so obvious (having clairvoyance) because my life was supposed to be about here with abuse and in order to go help those still stuck in their minds about the abuse. I taught a class at a college when I got here (Colorado) that was called "Healing from Writing." It was amazing to me (because) Spirit was always there and I would just simply listen to the people and look into their soul because I knew what was coming from the depths of them. They would say what I needed to hear in order to respond, and it was just the coolest thing. There was a particular one at the last class who, when she left, said I didn't believe you when you said I would never look at my life of abuse in the same way again but I want to tell you I (do) look at my life of abuse in a different way and I finally feel like I'm free and can write it down.

She was older than I was. We carry that identity of the hurt victim child with us throughout life. It affects our choices; it affects who we are and until we deal with that, we cannot move on. We're still back there in that 3rd dimension or whatever you want to call it, in that prison; we're still fighting the war.

I don't know what all this means for you but I know that you are gifted already. I know you're going to be finding out more about your gift and it's exciting to hear that you are excited about it. So just as your father said that he wanted you to look at that part of you, that insecure part of you, he wants you to deal with that and let it go. That's the kind of work that is necessary to go higher.

I posted a picture on my Facebook page and it says something like, when you walk in silence without carrying any baggage, that is when you get to the heart of the wilderness, meaning, when you've dealt with everything emotionally and when you're not carrying any of that emotional baggage, then you enter the heart of the wilderness and the wilderness is what is called, the other side or spirituality. You cannot get there if you are not ready and you can't fool God and you can't fool yourself; you have to do the work. I did the work by writing that book and I still do some residual work of things that come up. But for you, those things that you keep quiet in your heart that you know that are there, you need to deal with and to let that go. I don't know how you are going to do it but perhaps you are mirroring me in that maybe as you write your book, some of that will be revealed to you.

Whether that's what they (Spirit) meant, that will help heal you so that you can move into this, I don't know. But you seem to be mirroring me in little ways here and there and that's what Spirit does. They put people together that need to look at each other face to face and understand and hear the commonality and hear why they're linked together. There's a joke in a metaphysical book that if you want to understand what you need to do and what you need to work on, all you have to do is have your archenemy over for dinner because that person knows how to push every button you have and you just sit there and write those things down!

Other dimensions; does that mean astral travel? Here's the joke; very early on I used to love and look forward to going to bed each night even though I was scared because I could go flying! What that meant was: I could go to bed laying on my back and start drifting, drifting to sleep, and when it was time for me to sleep I would flip over on my stomach and all of a sudden I could see the universe and the stars and shooting stars and galaxies and I went flying! Oh my God, how much fun that was! I never really got anywhere. The first time that Ian took me somewhere we started out flying a little bit but we were just 'there'. Ian helped me go to the other side maybe three or four times before I started going myself.

Did you see him at that time? No, but I know he was there. I was such a goofball I didn't understand it. What I came to realize was when Ian showed me a picture of an arcade like an arcade machine when the spaceship is flying through space but it's not really going anywhere, it's just a picture of the rocket going into space on this video arcade game. I began to understand that I'm not really going anywhere when I go flying; I'm not traveling (any) distance, so I just stopped doing that altogether. I missed that feeling but realized I wasn't going anywhere; it was something that helped the mind to understand.

Heaven is not above the clouds and over the rainbow. Heaven is right here inside us. So, after that I understood that when I go to the other side I do the same thing and wait until that moment because I always want to go with my mind. I knew I went to the other side and I could never remember anything and would beg Ian, I want to go to the other side with my mind; meaning I want to be able to remember it and know that I'm there. Once I realized that I wasn't going anywhere when I go to the other side, all I do is get into that state; almost going to sleep and with my mind, picture myself walking into it (the other side).

You know when you're on the other side. You've see movies of the astronauts in space and it's totally silent except the only thing you hear is your heartbeat and you kind of jet along like you have a jetpack. That's how it feels! I see shadow people and things like that but it doesn't seem to be a big deal. You know you're in another dimension and it's not a dimension with oxygen and stuff like that; you are someplace else and it's the coolest feeling ever! I don't know how many dimensions there are; all I know is that I go to a different dimension. I go to a place where I am in spirit. I don't have legs and you have to navigate with your mind which is so hard for me. I just want to lean like on water skis or like a snowmobile where you lean and you turn. You can't do that, so I'm definitely out of my element. I'll tell you a quick story about the second time I went to the other side.

Ian and I traveled to the other side and found ourselves near the ceiling of a gymnasium. I look down and we're just making this circle up above everybody. I'm looking down and all the people look like shadows. Some are standing and some are sitting and they look like they are getting ready for a seminar to start. I'm wondering what they're doing down there, but they are waiting for the meeting to start just like here we have seminars and there's more learning to be done. So you go to these sessions to learn but it reminded me of a gymnasium.

I'm going around in a circle but trying to figure how to get down there with them and land. I don't know how to land, just going round and round and round like I'm in this never ending parking ramp where you can't get out of the parking garage. I see them all below and finally in my mind I say, does anybody know

Inga Nielson? That's great grandma; I'm thinking great grandma! Well, when I had the thought, they all noticed me from down below and they all looked up. When they looked up, they all had a light on their chest and they all beamed that light at me. Then I crashed and burned and I was back in my body. (Laurie said the next in a pensive way.) They all had a light on their chest and they all beamed their light at me at the same time and it was a very profound moment when I realized that there was something larger going on here very early in my awakening. I was beside myself; I couldn't believe. I knew it happened and knew I went there but just couldn't believe it really happened; it was another level of awareness of what is reality and what isn't.

Do you think that everybody perceives the spirit world the same? No! That's obvious! I just want to know the truth, what the truth really is. I understand we all can attract and create our futures and all that, blah, blah, blah. You can't really! I have a big problem with books that say, The Law of Attraction, create whatever you want. Well, you can't create whatever you want; if you're here to learn about poverty, you're not going to win the lottery! And so there is a myth or lie there and I don't like that; it's not real. I just want to know the truth; there has to be an ultimate truth. I know everybody has their own reality, but what is the ultimate truth? I'm learning and it's pretty damned shocking but I'm getting less and less shocked!

I want to tell you about an experience I had when I came back from camp (Wonewoc). I have a friend, who you met (at camp), who knows all things metaphysical. She isn't necessarily clairvoyant or clairaudient, but it's (all about) what she understands; she's going to be a professor of metaphysics. I am her eyes a lot of the time; I'm always prompted to tell her what I see; to give her a visual of them (Spirit). When I saw her in Minnesota, we talked about things on a higher level that I struggle with. You know how people say in books that you have everything you need inside of you and who is it, I think Donald Walsh (author of Conversations with God), who says you can go ahead and call yourself God; it's not blasphemy. God is inside of us, we are God; we are our own creators.

That kind of seems a little abstract for me. I'm more of a visual gal; I have to see it, I have to hear it, I have to understand it and then okay, I'll put it in the bank vault for me. I wake up at 5:00 in the morning and am barely awake, and see in my third eye this outline of a person. I see Spirit with me, or I see Spirit with you, but very rarely do I see shadow people and he was like a shadow. It's like if you took a black piece of paper and then took a white crayon and drew a person. The only way I could know a person was there was because of the outline. There's the universe and here's the guy standing there. Struggling to stay awake, I see him move and he looks like oil in water. He's from another dimension or he's in another dimension so when he moves, if you were to put a couple drops of oil on water and shake it, that's what it would look like; he jiggled. When he moved, that moved me in some way and helped me wake up because I always think that Spirit taps me on the shoulder and that's how I wake up. It must move my aura or energy field but it feels like someone is tapping me on the shoulder and waking me up.

So I'm a little more awake and all of a sudden I see the universe start up like when I go flying; where you see stars, you see the movement of the galaxy, you're moving past stars, past the moon. In my mind I think that Spirit wants me to go flying but then I hear 'no'. I refocus and realize that the only movement is not in the background; the movement of all that is, is right inside this shadow person. You see, in the background there is no movement; the only movement is within this spirit, this person, this entity that's standing in front of me. And I had the thought that that's what they mean when they say that everything we need is already inside of us. I was given this visual of the person and the universe is in this person. As soon as I had the thought and made the connection, I fell back asleep. That helped me understand on another level of consciousness, another level of awareness.

Can I back up just a bit? I went to a past life regression for the first time this summer with Sam (from camp). I did not feel it was real, and yet, I moved through one whole life. It was in 1877 and I could describe everything all the way up to my death. I wondered if I had made it up, being a creative person. But do you or other mediums ever latch onto someone else's past life and be able to describe it to them, or is it only the person who can discover their own past life? If somebody comes to you and asks you to do that, then they are giving their permission. So you can access it through the Akashic Records, you can access it by journeying, or you can access it just through Spirit because you gave your permission. Like a shaman; a shaman lies down and basically goes to sleep with drum beating music. But the person who wants the shaman to journey for them lay next to them (next to the shaman). That is giving consent; yes, I am here and I want (the shaman) to do that. You state your objectives and what you hope to accomplish and then you do the journey. So people that come to camp (Wonewoc) are giving their consent by being there and they are asking for information.

I would love to hire you to do this with (my) past lives, but seeing you are in Colorado I guess it wouldn't work. One of the things a shaman does is hold a crystal in his hand. If there are soul fragments from other lives that could come back in, the first part of a soul goes into the crystal as the shaman journeys, and when it's done, the person who wanted the journey will sit up and you (the shaman) (will) blow through the stone into a person's back, the receiving part of the heart, and you blow those aspects back in that way. You can still do it (without being side by side), as John (see Chapter X on John Wayne) found out with someone who lived in another state. He asked Spirit, how am I supposed to do this if there is soul retrieval to be done? Then he dropped his crystal and a little piece fell off so he mailed the little piece to someone who just blew the aspects into that person in the other place (where they lived). So, just as he had been asking Spirit how to do a retrieval long distance, he dropped his favorite stone and a little piece broke off and at first he was pissed, but then thought, oh, I get it! So you can journey for people that way.

I have to tell you I'm a beginning shaman, but would love the opportunity because there aren't many people practicing this, just like accessing the Akashic Records. There you go straight to your Council of Elders and they will come through with information for you and you can ask questions. Your Council of Elders had to have approved your plan before you came in. And they are allowed to look old on the other side where everyone else looks like they are 30 because of their wisdom and all of that, but they check your plan to make sure it is not too hard, that you are focused and on task, and they approve it before you come in to do a life. That is very, very cool. I had one done early on and again was blown away by the information I received.

Now I can talk to them, my Council of Elders, directly like when I asked about my life as Henry. They wouldn't show me anything, but what I thought was it was my imagination. Here was this black man who lives in this town all by himself; all his family was dead and blah, blah, blah. The only reason I hung onto the memory of that, was at the very end, as he's dying, because Sam always asks how you died, he looked at me and I looked at him and he had my eyes, meaning the eyes that I have now. I recognized all the little inflections as I recognized they were my eyes and he said to me, you don't need family to be happy. I was shocked because of course, as I was in the midst of this abusive family and the turmoil and all of that. That was the only thing I hung onto that (I thought) maybe could be real.

Finding out in his coming back that he chose to stay away until a certain time in this life, it's like the past life regression that I had; he was in this tunnel by himself and nobody was there except him. So something so insignificant that I thought was not something real turned out to be a huge part of who I am.

If you ever want to practice, I'm here. Definitely we can do an Akashic reading, but you know, journeying as a shaman is fine (but) usually the shaman or you will get information or be prompted about something that needs to be done. What I mean is, you have this feeling that, I don't know how to describe it, but you know something is going to happen; you're anticipating something but you don't have anything on your calendar. Or you feel; why do I have this certain aspect about my personality. It's kind of on your mind and bothering you a little bit. Why do I always do such and such and then it could be time for something to happen.

For instance, my son thinks he's going to have to come someday and put me in a hospital because I hallucinate. (He) does not believe in anything I do and he worries about me that I'm sick (psychologically).

Have you ever said to yourself, I don't know why I said that, or what made me do that because look what that created? Well, that's you; that's your higher self pulling yourself into the experience and then you'll get yourself out. I can't tell you how many times it has happened to me. Your higher self will say things or do things that in scary moments you have to deal with. It happened when I moved here and they (Spirit) kept telling me it's for your higher good, it was you who asked this to happen; four months of fear where I didn't have a job, I had just moved here and my landlord started having what I thought was a nervous breakdown. I don't know the laws of Colorado, I don't know where to go, I don't have any money; how am I going to get myself out of this and it was only Spirit, step by step for four months and I came up on solid footing and get that now, but at the time I thought what the hell is going on! Why are you doing this to me? Well, they weren't doing anything. It was my higher self that I needed to toughen up. So your soul takes over and it will say things, and do things, and pull you into situations and you're just like holy shit.

Where is your metaphysical outlet? Is there a place where you live where you can talk about these things? Pretty much just reading, though at camp we decided to start a spiritualist church in the fall. Are there mediums who live in the area that are helping? (I explained about the alternate week meetings that would take place in one of the camp hotel rooms during the fall and winter and until Wonewoc Camp started up again in late spring. We would have the service much like the camp services where people would receive a brief message, that is, a short version of a psychic reading, and could also receive healing if a healer was available.) I'm talking about a physical outlet; you have books, you have the internet, you have spiritual friends, but you have something physical that you participate in and that's great! There's an energy, a peace at camp, that I don't get other places sort of like going off into a different world.

It's a different dimension. We use the word 'dimension' for different parts of our lives and things we do. But it's much the same on the other side. Different dimensions just means a different way of looking at something or a different experience. It's the same. It is a different dimension for you because you feel good, there's so much energy around you; it is a different dimension of your life and is also a different dimension.

The day I realized that when Spirit is holding your hand; let's say I put my hands out like this and I'm praying or whatever (Laurie held her hands outstretched), and I could feel my hands tingle, Penny (see Chapter XIII on Penny) was the first to point out that your hands are on the other side. When I understood that, I realized that the other side, heaven or whatever you want to call it, is just right here; you just have to go through to a different dimension. It made a big impact on me. Penny is a wonderful person and I wish you could go to one of her circles in Minnesota.

Things happen to you in that circle. That's where I had this; I was meditating and this American Indian guy shows up and I had my third eye ceremony (see Laurie's book, The Blessing of Abuse). I actually saw this purple stone, which I was corrected later because it was an amulet. But I saw a purple stone in my forehead and then saw what looked like putty going around it. It was like they were implanting it spiritually in my forehead; I watched it happen. Things happen with her (Penny); she's a very strong spirit just like Sam is.

Here's something I have wondered for a long time. Why do so many mediums seem to have trouble reading into me? So many just look at me and they are unable to connect or get anything from me. I would say that many mediums are just beginners so don't think that mediums cannot read you based on that (having a beginner). I was able very easily to understand and read you and see your father and your grandmother; there was no problem there. I don't want that to be a block; don't let that stay in your mind that people can't read you because, guess what, people won't be able to read you. So, no, it's not hard to get into your energy; it's not hard to read you.

Why do you get readings when you don't really have to anymore? Because it's fun! I love supporting women owned businesses but I also love supporting mediums. And perhaps I learn things here or there that help me pull everything together. You know, Spirit is very good at labeling a situation or making it clear; it just speeds things up. You could go to counseling for five years or you can go to a medium for a half hour and sometimes when you understand about yourself and your life, it would have taken you (those) five years to get to what you would have from regular counseling.

For me, if I go to a medium, it's like oh, I understand now, that all comes together, boom, I'm done. It saves me maybe a couple of months of things rattling around in my brain where I was trying to make something clear. You know, mediums don't always get more information just because we are mediums; sometimes it's exactly the opposite because we have our own lessons to learn and our own emotional baggage to get through; we're not given a free ride! Sometimes we need a little clarity too.

Is there anything you would say to people that don't believe in spiritual matters; do you have something that might convince them or does just giving them a message convince them? I never try to convince anyone. If I hear someone saying, 'oh look, there's the medium booth woo woo', I might give them a little bit of a look but for the most part, I smile, because they are in for the biggest shock of their life. I was there also! (Laurie was like that in her past.) I guess what I would say to people who don't believe is that the day is coming when you will have an experience that you don't understand, and when that happens you can go to science, you can go to your pastor, or you can go to a medium. The day is coming. So just know that it's okay not to believe or disbelieve; either way there is no judgment. You are here for a reason, many reasons, and you will find that out one day. No pressure.

That's a great conclusion! Let me know if you ever want to know about Spirit and entity on the other side, like Jesus and why he came and what he said. I have talked to God once; it was quite an experience. I have seen the archangel Michael. So, there are entities that are going to be in my book (Laurie's second book: My Soul's Journey: Wildflower) as well as experiences, you know, places that I've been and what I've come to understand.

— CHAPTER 16 —

CINDY KAZA

Bio: Going Beyond: Medium Cindy Kaza is an evidential medium. Evidential mediumship is a style of mediumship practiced around the world that puts heavy weight on the medium's ability to bring through extremely specific evidence to the sitter. This evidence can include, but is certainly not limited to, names, personality traits, physical ailments, favorite past times, and phrases often used by loved ones in spirit.

Cindy has been extremely intuitive since her childhood. At the age of 10 she had her first memorable experience with a spirit. During this "awakening" Cindy began searching for answers for her experiences and became aware of her multi-faceted abilities as a psychic medium. As an adult, she began training not only in the U.S., but also at the renowned Arthur Findlay School of Intuitive Sciences in Stansted, England, where she is once again studying as this book is completed.

Cindy is sharing her gift with the world through the power of television, film and live performance. For more information, or to book Cindy Kaza, visit her official website at www.mediumcindykaza.com.

Cindy drew my interest when she was working on starting a psychic TV show going in Texas. As she was doing a lot of traveling, she was not available for a live interview so I asked her to write down some thoughts for me.

When did you find you had this gift? How did it affect your life growing up? Has it developed into other gifts and/or become stronger, or even changed from what it was? I had my first, memorable experience with the other side when I was 10 years old. A girl in my elementary school died in a tragic car accident and there after she appeared to me in the middle of the night. It was horrifying at the time, and I believe it scared me so much that I shut that part of my abilities off for many years because of that experience.

Although I didn't "see" spirits for many years after my first experience, I was VERY intuitive growing up. I never felt as though I was alone. I always had an understanding of there being a great presence of something around me, even though I couldn't describe it then. I knew things about people that I shouldn't have known and I was very, very sensitive as a child. I felt very misunderstood growing up and always very out of place and different. It was difficult being so intuitive at such a young age because I didn't understand that many of the emotions I was having or experiencing were, in fact, not mine at all. I was picking up on the emotions of all of the people around me without realizing it.

My abilities are constantly shifting and growing. I started working with automatic writing. That shifted into psychic art. I then decided to really, really develop all of the "clair's" and that's when I realized clairaudience and clairvoyance as being two of the strongest faculties I have. I learn something new every day about how I work. I try new things all of the time and have spent the past 5 years studying mediumship extensively with different teachers from different parts of the world including the Arthur Findlay School of Intuitive Sciences in Stansted, England. I will never consider myself to be finished learning or growing. I love this work so much that it's not even work for me.

Does your gift affect how you view religion? What does enlightenment mean to you? My ability to communicate with the other side has, actually, made me more interested in different religions. I have a deep respect for all religions. I, personally, feel very drawn to the Gnostic Gospels and Christian mysticism. Before I began working as a medium, I harbored resentment towards organized religion but now I find myself seeing the beauty in it, rather than the "human" in it.

Do you use any tools like Astral travel, Pendulums, Tarot cards, or? Currently, I do not use any tools to work as a medium. When doing psychic readings, I sometimes use automatic writing as a tool, but not as often as I used to and mostly just when I'm doing email readings. Tools are helpful and fun, but not necessary.

How are you using your gifts now? Currently, I am working primarily as a psychic medium doing live events. I do private readings as well, but I really enjoy doing platform work. I really, really love talking to people on the other side and giving people on this plane of existence messages that bring happiness and closure. I work for people in this realm just as much as I work for people on the other side. Closure is made in both realms when healing takes place. I work primarily using clairvoyance, clairaudience, and clairsentience.

Would you like people to know some of your true feelings about being a medium? Having the ability to work as a psychic medium is one of the most rewarding gifts I've ever been given in this lifetime. I spent many years searching for who I was and never feeling a sense of peace. Now, I KNOW who I am, what I'm here to do and how to do it. I feel closer to the God of my understanding more now than I ever have. I get so frustrated when mediums say, "This gift is so overwhelming and I'm so burdened by it." If that's how a medium feels about the work, he/she is in the wrong field. Just because somebody has the ability to talk to the other side does not make him/her a good medium. Being a good medium requires empathy, patience, open- mindedness and the ability to deliver messages WITH discernment. It's not about having to be right all of the time or forcing a message onto somebody that they don't understand or aren't ready to hear.

— CHAPTER 17 —

ON THE OTHER HAND

This chapter is completely from my perspective, and I am not trying to persuade anyone in one direction or another. It is just to pique your curiosity and make you think a bit more about how we look at spiritual matters. If you agree, that is fine! If you disagree, that is fine too! We judge from what we know, and we sometimes need new experiences—good and bad—to help us shape new perspectives. I believe in questioning all things!

It seems like many of the psychics on Facebook are competing with each other to make the cleverest statements and get the most likes. I think much of this is drivel that is made to look cute or intelligent to satisfy the ego.

Many posts are truly inspiring and reflect the path I am now taking. Many of those quotes are from long ago. If they happen to encourage you on your path, then they are good.

Quite a few of my psychic friends talk about manifesting things for themselves, including prosperity, cars, relationships, and situations. They are certain that if they hold hard to their belief of those things manifesting (being created), the items will happen. Some do this by mentally thinking about what they want constantly. Others repeat mantras that contain the words of what they want. Some feel they have to say what they want out loud—possibly a certain number of times per day. Would this work for everyone?

What if it is part of your life path—the path you chose before coming into your human existence—to not have money? To not have certain relationships? To not have that car? What if our life lessons can only be learned by not having those things—no matter how much we want them? Perhaps we should be praying for the ability to learn life lessons so we can move up in our spirituality.

What if our life paths are meant to manifest what we need or want? How do we know which path we are on? How do we manifest our wants—or not being able to have what we want—so we can learn lessons? Perhaps we need to always hope and try to attain the things we think are important and be willing to accept failure as a lesson.

Even if we don't try to get the things we want by attempting to manifest them, can we get them anyhow because they are part of our life paths? What if we are naively unaware of our needs (though our higher selves know what we need and want)? What if our spirits and guides are helping them become a reality for us by turning us in the right direction?

There is a lot of ego in what most people think karma is. Many people think ego causes judgment. I think the main feeling we need to foster is love. When we veer from loving (selfless love or whatever), we get a gut (intuitive) feeling of doing something bad or wrong. This may be right, but karma should not be used in the context of sin or judgment or punishment. To judge with ego (veering from love) causes us to think of punishment, which is not right either.

When we don't love, we feel a separation from universal love. We push our feelings and thoughts into karma, which many people consider a type of punishment/reward system. I believe we are here to learn love and the facets of that are infinite. That is why we all have so many different experiences. When we send out good vibes, the universe amplifies them because they are *loving*. When we send out bad vibes, they are amplified. We fall short of universal love.

The ego mind says, "This is good and bad."

I think it goes beyond that. As long as our journeys (paths) follow universal love, we continue to learn—even if we occasionally send out bad vibes. Even the perception of evil can turn toward universal love, if we so choose, making us all part of the same light.

Osho, an Indian mystic, says, "If you suffer, it is because of you. If you feel blissful, it is because of you. Nobody else is responsible—only you and you alone. You are your hell and your heaven too."

We make our own happiness and unhappiness. We decide how we want to feel up to a point. What if learning in this lifetime means a life full of excruciating pain? What if it means a life of unbearable mental anguish that is caused by others who are out of our control? It is impossible to consider that a disabled child in a life of pain is bringing that on himself or herself. Is a starving person in the deserts of Africa bringing the starvation on himself or herself?

We can cause some of our dilemmas or illnesses by keeping our thoughts in the wrong vibrations. Much of what happens is not the fault of thinking "wrong" or attracting trials and pain. We may have planned these things before we came to the earth plane, but we are not responsible for all the things that are caused by our thoughts.

Some people can will themselves to get better or create miracles, but if something is meant to be, it will find a way to be—no matter what we try to do. Saying that we manifest *all* our calamities shows the ego heaping on punishment for sins instead of those things being our life lessons that we are here to learn.

Some people say dysfunctional chakras cause diseases on physical and/or emotional levels. To take it a step further, disease is caused by broken chakras. A broken second chakra causes physical problems with the bowels, uterus, kidney, or bladder. Emotional problems include being embarrassed or guilty, placing blame on others, and denying pleasure. For each broken chakra, people advise clearing out the chakras to become whole again.

I do not get a positive feeling or vibe from that interpretation. That is like religion making people feel guilty about being sinners and causing their own problems with sin. People mistakenly have brought their present and former religious upbringings and shoved them into taking the place of chakras.

Becoming judge and jury is not a good thing. If we are enlightened, we do not judge or force our belief systems on others. A broken chakra might cause problems like that, but no one can say for sure.

Could healing your broken chakra also heal your affliction? Certainly! What if we decided to go through a certain affliction before we even came to the earth plane in order to learn? Perhaps that illness is the result of an agreement in order to make a life lesson more meaningful.

Those who try to make us feel guilty about having an illness by telling us it is our own fault are merely heaping their own judgments and their own guilt upon us. They carry a belief in sin and punishment rather than learning and becoming more enlightened. Instead of judging, those people need to work on helping us heal. It can include healing our chakras—but only with the attitude of healing us out of love and not ridding us of a punishment caused by our own selves.

— CHAPTER 18 —

THE ELEPHANT IN THE ROOM

Being spiritual is like the proverbial group of people with an elephant in the room. They are all blind, and they all touch the elephant in a different spot. Who is really telling the truth about what the elephant is? They are all wrong, but they are all right!

Taken from Wikipedia*: Elephant in the room

The Buddha twice uses the simile of blind men led astray. In the *Canki Sutta*, he describes a row of blind men holding on to each other as an example of those who follow an old text that has passed down from generation to generation. In the Udana (68–69), he uses the elephant parable to describe sectarian quarrels. A king has the blind men of the capital brought to the palace, where an elephant is brought in and they are asked to describe it.

When the blind men had each felt a part of the elephant, the king went to each of them and said to each: "Well, blind man, have you seen the elephant? Tell me, what sort of thing is an elephant?"

---

* https://en.wikipedia.org/wiki/Elephant_in_the_room

The men assert the elephant is either like a pot (the blind man who felt the elephant's head), a winnowing basket (ear), a plowshare (tusk), a plow (trunk), a granary (body), a pillar (foot), a mortar (back), a pestle (tail), or a brush (tip of the tail).

The men cannot agree with one another and come to blows over the question of what it is like, and their dispute delights the king. The Buddha ends the story by comparing the blind men to preachers and scholars who are blind and ignorant and hold to their own views: "Just so are these preachers and scholars holding various views blind and unseeing ... In their ignorance they are by nature quarrelsome, wrangling, and disputatious, each maintaining reality is thus and thus." The Buddha then speaks the following verse:

O how they cling and wrangle, some who claim
For preacher and monk the honored name!
For, quarreling, each to his view they cling.
Such folk see only one side of a thing.
This I truly believe.

— CHAPTER 19 —

FINAL EXAM

In the summer of 2014, I finally decided to get some blood work done at the clinic. Thyroid, celiac, and diabetic problems run in my family. The lab took some vials of blood, and I was good to go home. By the time I got home, the doctor called and told me to get right to the hospital, which was more than an hour away. The calcium levels in my blood were off the chart, and I could have had a seizure at any time.

Having had kidney problems in the past, I didn't worry too much. I figured the problem was probably another big stone that was refusing to pass. In no time, I was being poked and pricked by needles that pulled out vials of blood. An IV pumped me full of saline.

A short time later, a young doctoral resident came into the room. Tom was concerned enough that I couldn't brush off the situation with my usual joking. It appeared that calcium as high as mine could indicate cancer.

Time stopped while my mind tried to believe the bombshell that had just been dropped on me. Cancer only happened to other people—not me—and he had only said it *could* be cancer. I told myself I felt healthy and vibrant as ever, but I had to admit I had slowed down in the past couple years. I figured it was only from putting on belly weight.

I talked to Tom about my potential diagnosis, hoping above hope that he was wrong. After he left, I checked online for the symptoms of each malady he had named. I figured I might easily find a solution for any disease.

When he came back to check on me, I was able to talk about the possibilities. With great relief to me, he said that signs pointed to parathyroid shutdown, which was not a big problem compared to everything else out there. However, after more tests, his diagnosis came back potentially as multiple myeloma, a type of plasma cancer.

My kidney began shutting down, and the creatinine levels were problematic. After more pokes and more tests, they decided I needed an ultrasound of my kidney area to try to narrow down what was happening. The hum of the ultrasound machine made me sleepy, and the tech person applied what looked like a big anti-perspirant roller to my skin to peer inside my abdomen.

It was late when I got back to my room, and I went to sleep, figuring everything would work itself out the next day. I dozed throughout the night, and the nurses came in to check my blood pressure. They left my door wide open and allowed all the hallway noises to keep me awake. They did not seem to understand that I did not want my room door opening constantly! The hallway was too noisy, and I would have to get up after each visit to shut the door. I didn't know it yet, but that was the least of my problems.

In the morning, I was greeted by a cart full of needles and was poked multiple times. My arm was already full of big blue blotches from the previous day's attacks.

That afternoon, Tom looked more serious than ever when he came into my room. He sat down, took a breath, and said, "There is a huge mass in your abdomen, and it is already full of blood connections to your body, veins and arteries, creating its own organ that we cannot remove."

The situation was surreal. I didn't know how to handle it. I sat in denial and disbelief and didn't say anything. I was scheduled for a CT scan, and I had to wait until the following morning for the results. There was nothing encouraging in the images.

My cancer doctor explained the CT scan pictures and spent more than an hour educating me about various types of cancers. At the time, he could only suspect lymphoma, but there were six-ty-three kinds of lymphomas to choose from. He would need biop-sies over the next two days. The mass in my abdomen was at least the size of a football, and there was cancer in my lymph nodes. They were swollen. One biopsy would delve into one of the large masses, and one would take out bone marrow from my hip bone to see if the cancer had entered my bones.

I had a visit from a dear friend, earth angel, and psychic. Tatiana painted me a picture that reminded me of the eye I sometimes see staring at me when I meditate. She sat me down and said, "You need to name the tumor."

I started to chuckle, but I realized she was giving me some of her wisdom. By naming the tumor, I could know it personally and deal with it on a personal level.

"Sure," I answered. I thought back to *The Producers*, which is one of my favorite comedies. "The tumor's name will be Fat, Fat, Fatty!"

"Talk to it!" Tatiana announced. "You need to think of some creative ways to tell the tumor to go away. You are a creative person. Think of imaginative ways to get rid of it. Maybe think of releasing Pacmans into your body that will devour the tumors up. You can think of other ways yourself!"

"Ask it why it's there and ask what it has to say to you. This is why you would name it, not just to tell it, 'Fat, Fat, Fatty, get the hell out of me! This is a key part of hypnotherapy, having a dis-cussion before serving the eviction notice. It (the tumor) is there for a reason and often illnesses seem to think they are helping us somehow. It's like the fat cells that we hate are actually protecting us from toxins and can also be protecting us from our fear of being raped or from intimacy. In the case of cancer, there is something else there and a discussion can give clues about that."

She did some healing by putting her hand over the tumor and telling it to go away. Before she left, Tatiana saw some of my favorite candy snacks on my tray, which my thoughtful children had brought. "No sugar!" she asserted.

I recalled the doctor telling me that cancer feeds directly on sugar.

When Tatiana left, I put away my candy and have not looked at it since.

Later that day, I was ushered to a downstairs storage room, or at least a room that looked like one. The four doctors cleaned me up and started injecting numbing solution into my abdomen. I couldn't watch the rest, but I could certainly feel it as they made a slit and inserted a stainless tube down to the tumor. They brought out a machine that had to have been eighteen inches long; it looked like a tubular mousetrap. When it sprung, it would instantly drive a needle into the tumor to take a sample and retract at nearly the same time. This went on four times, and I was done.

The next morning was another biopsy. Having heard about drilling into my bone and sucking out the marrow with a little vacuum cleaner, I opted for being sedated. Since they were going that far, I assumed they were pretty sure the cancer was already in my bones.

The last test was a PET scan so the doctors would have a comparison while they treated my cancer. As part of the poverty class in Wisconsin, I was represented by conservatives who cared more about making money for themselves and cared little for the "poor and elderly" (see Charles Dickens's Christmas Carol: Are there no workhouses? No prisons? "If they would rather die," said Scrooge, "they had better do it, and decrease the surplus population.")

So my test was refused by the state as being unnecessary. It was refused the following day and the next, and I returned home a day later to receive a personal notice from the state saying the same. I can't help but compare it with the years I worked for group homes. The insurance companies determined how sick the individual was instead of that decision being up to the doctors. If a mentally hand-icapped resident had a cavity, the state had the tooth pulled instead of fixing it.

A week went by with nothing being done to attack my cancer. I was frustrated beyond belief. On Friday, I would get the results of my biopsies, the name of the cancer, and how it might be attacked. Two of my daughters, a son, and a son-in-law came to sit with me for a long afternoon of mostly anxious waiting.

I think my kids were anxious, but I was somehow removed from it all. Was it my belief in things spiritual that calmed me? Did the spirits and angels surrounding me and who take care of me offer me comfort? Was it an outpouring of love and healing from my family? Was it spiritual and psychic friends who said it was not my time to go? Was it denial on my part and just not believing what was happening?

When the doctor finally got to my room, we were ready to listen.

"You have follicular lymphoma, stage 4," he said. It was in my bones too. He went over the history of the disease and treatments, and he told us what we had most wanted to know: my chances for survival.

As he talked, my body relaxed. I felt hope building one block at a time. Most people with that cancer can go into remission for a while. It does come back like a chronic disease, and it is harder to get rid of each time, but living past the short-term was now a possibility. I thought back to my life-changing psychic reading with Rosemary Altea. My dad had told me there would be some trouble with health down the road, but they would have medicine to fix it.

One of my daughters is into healthy lifestyles, and she put me on a strict diet. As Hippocrates said, "Let food be thy medicine and medicine be thy food."

Laurie said, "Physician (healer), heal thyself!"

On a daily basis, I was loaded with bales of vegetables, seeds, and fruit. The limited carbs and sugars I consumed had to be ones that were locked up tightly in the food and did not release heavily—and all at once—into the blood.

Kale rules the day, though it still is like eating soaked leather to me. Quinoa, beans, and vegetables make quite a tasty dish. I got a wok and consider myself the Wok King. My meals are only limited to my imagination and creativity. Olive or coconut oil starts each dish. I have discovered that onions and lots of fresh garlic in the hot oil make the house smell like a restaurant. I add chopped kale, vegetables, and fruit, and the result is close to heavenly—compared to not having anything that has any taste. I miss sugar. I miss it a lot! The idea of having a nice cappuccino with sweet rolls or homemade bread with butter spurs me on to get rid of the cancer.

Over a year has gone by—a time full of monthly chemo, feeling sick, feeling better, and feeling sick again. Does that mean I have sat idle? No. I have used the time to meditate and focus on the cancer. I tell it that it is time to go where it can be more useful—maybe into another dimension. Fat Fat Fatty has my permission to leave. I own my cancer. It started in my body, and it can end in my body.

I take walks down my country road with my college daughters and dog. Sometimes I go alone, taking deep drafts of the clean air, grasses, wildflowers, freshly mown hay, trees, and dust from passing tractors. I talk to my loving family on the other side of the veil as I walk. When they are with me, a chill runs from my head down my back to my feet. I do not doubt they are supporting me with their love and suggestions.

Each day, multiple times, I give myself healing thoughts. Most important, I am happy to spend another day on the earth plane. No matter what the future brings, I'll try to let my light shine with a smile and laughter and loving feelings.

I am a lightworker. Before I came to earth I volunteered to direct my energy at aiding the earth in healing from the distress of all things negative. We all have mountains to climb and my trials are my teachers helping me grow one moment at a time. I have healing in my hands whether you believe or not, for what you believe is your issue alone, not mine. I live by example, ever learning from the mistakes of myself and others, growing in the ways of Spirit and mindful that no matter what we believe, religion or no religion, we have an unlimited power; a power to love, a power to heal, a power to manifest great things through our spirit. I trust my intuition to guide all that I do as I listen to that still, small voice within my heart.

Whether you believe anything in this book or not doesn't matter. If it helped open your mind and be aware that not all things are black and white, I have succeeded. Life is a spiritual adventure we are on. It is a voyage to learn from. It helps our souls grow while we have use of our human bodies. Make the most of your life.

Printed in the United States
By Bookmasters